T0301621

Multinational Firms, Innovation and Productivity

Multinational Firms, Innovation and Productivity

Davide Castellani,

Professor of Applied Economics, University of Urbino, Italy

Antonello Zanfei,

Professor of Industrial Economics, University of Urbino, Italy

Edward Elgar
Cheltenham, UK • Northampton, MA, USA

Published by
Edward Elgar Publishing Limited
Glensanda House
Montpellier Parade
Cheltenham
Glos GL50 1UA
UK

Edward Elgar Publishing, Inc.
136 West Street
Suite 202
Northampton
Massachusetts 01060
USA

A catalogue record for this book
is available from the British Library

Library of Congress Cataloging in Publication Data

Castellani, Davide.
   Multinational firms, innovation and productivity / Davide Castellani,
   Antonello Zanfei.
      p. cm.
   Includes bibliographical references and index.
   1. International business enterprises–Management. 2. International business
enterprises. I. Zanfei, Antonello.   II. Title.

HD62.4.C385 2006
658′.049–dc22   2006002679

ISBN–13: 978 1 84542 198 4 (cased)
ISBN–10: 1 84542 198 1 (cased)

Printed and bound in Great Britain by MPG Books Ltd, Bodmin, Cornwall

Contents

Figures

Tables

Acknowledgements

This book is the result of a research programme we have shared over the past decade, merging complementary interests, learning paths and academic experiences. Several colleagues and friends have contributed to making this possible. Without implying them in any of our errors and flaws, we wish to give credit to these people.

Many of the ideas developed in this book, as well as much of the empirical material it is based upon, stem from a number of EU-funded research projects we had the opportunity to participate in, which include: *Dynamic Capabilities, Growth and Long-Term Competitiveness of European Firms* (Dynacom), *Assessing the Impact of Technology and Globalisation* (Aiteg), and *The Structure of Innovation and Economic Performance Indicators* (Siepi). Funding from the Italian Ministry of Research is also gratefully acknowledged, with specific reference to Prin-Cofin 2001 and 2003, and Firb 2003. Some of the debates we have attended within the framework of the *Network on Innovation Studies*, financed by the Norwegian Research Council in 1999–2004, were also very helpful in bringing our research hypotheses closer to maturity. During this period we have also benefited from the stimulating research environment at Iefe-Università L. Bocconi in Milan, at the Departments of Economics of the Universitat Pompeu Fabra, and of the University of Ancona, at the Centre of International Business Studies of the London South Bank University, at the Institute of International Integration Studies of the Trinity College in Dublin, at the Instituto Complutense de Estudios Internacionales in Madrid, and at the Science Policy Research Unit (SPRU), University of Sussex. The Faculty of Economics at the University of Urbino has been the home to most of our restless discussions from which many of our ideas have emerged.

We owe a debt of gratitude to the scholars who gave us the possibility of joining a rich and extensive 'invisible college' on the themes of innovation and international production. In particular, at various stages of this research programme, we benefited from discussions, exchanges of ideas and useful conversations on topics relevant to this book with: Carlo Altomonte, Bernadette Andreosso, Cristiano Antonelli, Gianni Balcet, Giorgio Barba Navaretti, Martin Bell, Christian Bellack, Stefano Breschi, Claudio Cozza, Paola Criscuolo, Giovanni Dosi, Nigel Driffield, Dieter Ernst, Rinaldo Evangelista, Jan Fagerberg, Alfonso Gambardella, Ove Granstrand,

Riccardo 'Jack' Lucchetti, Franco Malerba, Josè Molero, David Mowery, Ram Mudambi, Alessandro Pagano, Giulio Perani, Mario Pianta, Francesco Pigliaru, Lucia Piscitello, Frances Ruane, Enzo Rullani, Francesca Sanna Randaccio, Roberto Schiattarella, Salvo Torrisi, Marco Vivarelli, Sergio Vaccà, Bart Verspagen and Nick Von Tunzelmann.

Special thanks go to John Cantwell, Simona Iammarino, Rajneesh Narula, Grazia Santangelo and Ed Steinmueller, colleagues and friends who provided precious suggestions and valuable comments on the original planning of this book and on draft chapters. Grazia Ietto Gillies followed the whole project of this book very closely, encouraged us in its design, read the whole draft volume and generously offered a number of fine comments and suggestions. We owe her our warmest gratitude.

Several people provided us with valuable technical and organisational support. These include the very kind and efficient people of the editorial team at Edward Elgar, Peter Cullen, who proofread the first draft of this book, and Mary Cruz Braga, who indefatigably carried most of the burden of the paperwork and administrative issues relating to the research projects in which we have been involved.

Hanna and Rosalba bore the consequences of our working on this book, with all the time we subtracted from our family lives. Their closeness and encouragement played a vital role in leading us to the end of this project.

Last but not least, we like to think that this book would not have been possible without the very immaterial support given by Gaia, whose love goes beyond all seasons. It is to her that we dedicate this book.

Introduction

Multinationals play a fundamental role in innovation and productivity growth. Indeed, 98 per cent of the top 700 R&D spenders are multinational firms (MNFs) and account for more than two-thirds (69 per cent) of the world's business R&D (DTI 2004). A few of these companies (such as Ford Motor, Daimler Chrysler and Siemens) individually invest in R&D more than the overall expenditure of some developed countries, such as Spain, Switzerland or Israel. Moreover, a growing share of innovative activities is no longer concentrated in the home country, but is carried out by MNFs on a global scale. This can be illustrated by the fact that the share of national R&D held by foreign firms in a sample of 30 (developed and developing) countries rose from 10.3 per cent in 1993 to 15.9 per cent in 2002, reaching values well above 50 per cent in Ireland, Hungary and Singapore (UNCTAD 2005).

These data highlight a specific, albeit crucial, aspect of the more general process of globalisation, which implies a growing interdependence of firms, industries, and economic systems. As part of this process, MNFs can play a key role as vehicles for the international transfer and creation of technology or, more generally, as institutions bridging different innovation systems. However, MNFs also have relevant degrees of market power, can crowd out domestic activities in host countries and appropriate rents, often at the expenses of local firms. Until the early 1980s, a large part of the literature has viewed the MNFs as 'quasi-colonial' institutions, exploiting their technological advantages abroad. This perspective has led to scepticism over the activities of MNFs and has, for a long time, provided a rationale for policies aimed at discouraging inward foreign direct investments (FDIs). Over the last two decades this view has gradually changed and the literature has stressed the potential benefits of MNFs. The attitude of policy makers has also evolved towards a more benign approach to incoming multinationals, whose activities in host countries are now seen as directly beneficial and as a potential source of externalities. To illustrate this changing attitude, one might simply consider that 94 per cent of 2,156 cases in which host governments modified their policy of FDI selection and control in 1991–2004 resulted in being more favourable to foreign investors, including subsidies and more liberal admission rules (UNCTAD 2005). It remains that empirical evidence on the actual impact of multinationals on host economies is still mixed and there seems to be a growing consensus among scholars that substantial diversities exist in the extent to which different MNFs contribute to the global generation and transfer of innovation. This volume adopts this latter perspective. It focuses on how and why firms differ in internationalisation, innovation and productivity, and examines the implications of this diversity within industries. In particular, it shows that the economic impact of multinationals depends largely on intra-industry heterogeneity.

Our line of argument is organised into three analytical steps. The first step will be to focus on the way in which MNFs organise their innovative activities across national borders. We first challenge the view of MNFs as 'quasi-colonial' institutions exploiting foreign markets by way of technological advantages accumulated in their home bases. We shall highlight that there are important technological and institutional factors that induce multinationals to combine the exploitation of their proprietary advantages with an increasing access to local sources of knowledge. We shall argue that the increasing importance of asset seeking activities is leading firms to organise their innovative activities according to what we identify as a *double network* structure. Multinationals develop both internal webs interconnecting the innovative activities of a growing number of affiliates located in different countries; and external networks through which these affiliates set up linkages with foreign firms and institutions to further exploit their knowledge assets and gain access to local resources. To the extent that multinationals increase their embeddedness in different local contexts by means of both internal and external networks, they accentuate their natural role as *bridging institutions*: MNFs increasingly connect geographically dispersed innovation systems, being conditioned by, and contributing to, their characteristics and evolution. Overall, this evolution of firms' innovative activities on a global scale has the important implication that multinationals will increasingly differ in terms of the intensity and variety of their technological advantages.

This leads us to the second step of our study, that is heterogeneity in internationalisation, innovation and productivity. We build on the emerging literature on heterogeneity, international trade and FDIs to show, first, that firms do differ in terms of both innovation and productivity according to their degree of involvement in international activities. This reflects a combination of self-selection mechanisms, implying that more efficient and innovative firms will be more capable of competing in foreign markets; and of knowledge accumulation processes due to the fact that international involvement allows firms to access local sources of competitive advantages. Second, we highlight that heterogeneity can also be observed *across multinationals*, according to the number, strength and variety of economic and innovative systems they connect, and to the way these links are organised. As a consequence, MNFs differ from one another in terms of their productivity and innovative performances. Third, there will be heterogeneity *within multinationals*, reflecting the uneven distribution of advantages among units belonging to MNFs. Tension exists between international dispersion and concentration of innovative activities, which *inter alia* determine a variety of technological profiles according to the position of units in multinational organisations.

The study of intra-industry heterogeneity paves the way to the third step of our analysis, namely the economic impact of multinationals. Here the idea is that it is not enough that multinationals enter or increase their presence in a given economy to generate spillovers. It is not even only a matter of how they are 'motivated' towards asset-seeking activities as revealed, for instance, by the nature and distribution of their advantages relative to local firms. We submit that heterogeneity of both foreign and domestic firms needs to be examined in detail in order to capture the economic impact of multinationals. In other words, the key issue is that *not every* foreign firm is a good source of externality and *not every* domestic firm is equally well placed to benefit from MNFs. From this perspective we explore the slippery area of horizontal spillovers which have attracted considerable empirical work, but where recent studies have found weak and often contradictory evidence. First, we submit that foreign firms are likely to have a different impact according to their own technological profiles and to their degree of embeddedness in local contexts. Second, their impact also depends on the characteristics of domestic firms, in terms of absorptive capacity and ability to challenge foreign firms in national and foreign markets. Exploiting the results from the previous analytical step, we argue that the degree of international involvement can be a good proxy for such conditions to hold. Third, we compare spillovers due to the expansion of foreign firms in host countries, to spillovers from the expansion of domestic owned multinationals in their home countries. By so doing we are able to explore the implications of heterogeneity across MNFs, given that foreign firms and domestic owned multinationals belong to different groups. By the same token, the implications of heterogeneity within MNFs can also be captured, given that foreign firms are by definition affiliates of a multinational based elsewhere, while firms belonging to a domestic owned multinational group may either be parent companies or national affiliates.

The book is organised into three parts according to the three steps briefly described above. Part I (Chapters 1 and 2) develops a general framework for the analysis of the links between innovation and international production. Chapter 1 discusses the widely accepted distinction between asset exploiting and asset seeking FDIs, and introduces the view of MNFs as a double network. This allows us to draw implications for the international organisation of innovative activities and for the analysis of intra-industry heterogeneity. Chapter 2 reviews the empirical literature on the evolution of MNFs towards a double network structure. In particular, using a sample of the world's largest MNFs in the chemical and electronics industries, we find that the characteristics of the internal network of multinationals are associated with the propensity to engage in external linkages, such as mergers and acquisitions, joint ventures and strategic alliances.

Part II (Chapters 3 and 4) goes deep into the analysis of how firms differ in innovation, productivity and internationalisation. Chapter 3 focuses on different approaches to the analysis of the relationship between international involvement and intra-industry heterogeneity in terms of innovation and productivity. Chapter 4 discusses the less explored issues of heterogeneity across and within multinationals. Both chapters provide sound empirical evidence drawn from a large sample of Italian manufacturing firms that supports the idea that differences in international activities are related to significant heterogeneity in innovation and productivity. In Chapter 3 we find that firms with a high involvement in foreign activities also exhibit better economic and innovative performances. In particular, the companies with the highest international involvement, namely firms with production activities abroad, are characterised by both the highest productivity premiums and the highest R&D efforts and innovative performances. By contrast, Italian multinationals with a lower commitment to foreign markets, i.e. with only non-production activities abroad (such as subsidiaries involved in distribution activities), do show levels of productivity that stand between those of multinationals with production activities abroad and those of mere exporters, but they do not innovate more than the latter. In Chapter 4 we show that while foreign firms perform better than domestic firms as a whole, this is not the case if domestic-owned multinationals are distinguished from uninational firms. In particular, we find that parent companies of domestically owned multinationals exhibit higher R&D, innovation and productivity, as well as a higher propensity to set up technological alliances with local counterparts than affiliates of foreign multinationals. However, systems of origin seem to play a role. In particular, US-owned firms outperform affiliates of multinationals from other countries and reach productivity levels similar to those of Italian multinationals.

Part III (Chapters 5 and 6) develops a thorough analysis of the impact of MNFs on host economies in the presence of heterogeneous (foreign and domestic) firms. Chapter 5 reviews the literature on MNFs and productivity spillovers, discusses some methodological issues, and highlights useful insights from several empirical studies on this topic. The chapter also recalls the main results of our comparative analysis of productivity spillovers from foreign presence in three EU countries (France, Italy and Spain). We show that the effects of foreign presence on the productivity of domestic firms differ across countries and highlight that technology gaps between foreign and domestic firms do help explain these differences. These results are used as a first move in analysing the role of heterogeneity of foreign and domestic firms as an important predictor of spillover effects. Chapter 6 draws together the ideas developed in previous chapters and discusses the implications of heterogeneity of foreign and domestic firms for the analysis of spillovers. Original evidence is provided in this chapter, too. In particular, we find that on average foreign multinationals do not determine any significant external effect on domestic-owned firms in Italy. However, positive spillovers are associated with the activity of foreign affiliates investing more intensively in R&D, and with those which have been established in the country for a longer period of time. Furthermore, exporters seem to benefit more from foreign multinationals than non-internationalised firms and domestic multinationals, while non-internationalised firms appear to benefit from the expansion of domestic multinationals. This result is consistent with the idea that policies aimed at attracting foreign multinationals can be complemented with measures supporting the growth of domestic multinationals.

Besides the analytical contributions to the ongoing literature on the role of MNFs in innovation and productivity growth, we believe that this volume offers at least three further motives of interests, related to some of the methodological choices that we have made. First, we try to bridge different theoretical approaches and streams of research, drawing from international trade, international business, industrial organisation and economics of innovation literature. While boundaries between disciplines matter, we also believe in the virtues of cross-fertilisation. Moreover, there are clear advantages from a more comprehensive analysis of the multi-faceted relationship between innovation and international production.

Second, we integrate the survey of empirical evidence and illustrative case studies from previous research, with systematic econometric analysis based on large datasets. In particular, we use a sample of the largest European, US and Japanese multinationals in electronics and chemical industries, which enables us to focus on the role of MNFs internal network in explaining their pattern of technological collaborations and other forms of external linkages. Furthermore, we exploit an extensive dataset on ownership structure, multinational activities and performances of European firms. The dataset, named Elios (European Linkages, Internationalisation and Ownership Structure), is obtained at the intersection of two commercial databases, Dun and Bradstreet's *Who Owns Whom*, and Bureau Van Dijck's *Amadeus*, and collects firm level data for selected EU countries over the 1990s (see

Appendix). This data source has been further integrated with firm-level information obtained from Eurostat's Community Innovation Survey on the innovatory activities of firms in Italy, which allows us to evaluate the links between international production and technological change in a more direct and comprehensive way. This gives us the possibility of exploring different aspects of the relation between internationalisation, innovation and productivity.

Finally, while our work is mainly directed to an audience of researchers, graduate students and academics, individual chapters will be of interest for undergraduate students who could utilise it as further reading, in combination with traditional textbooks of international business, international economics, industrial economics and economics and management of innovation. The 'modular use' of this volume is also facilitated by the fact that each chapter, while strongly interconnected to the others and justified as a part of a wider analytical framework, is self-contained. This means that the topic being treated will be framed in the literature, methodological issues will be addressed and recalled when needed, and results discussed in clear terms, avoiding excessively technical jargon. These characteristics make the book useful also for practitioners, who might be particularly interested in the strategic and organisational implications of the analysis, especially in Chapters 1, 4 and 6. Policy makers will be particularly interested in the analysis of firm heterogeneity and of the effects of multinational activities (Parts II and III).

PART I

The changing role of multinational firms in innovation

An extensive literature has long highlighted the strong interconnections between innovation and the multinational activities of firms. Seminal contributions by Hymer (1960) and Dunning (1970) have emphasised that the possession of a superior technology is one of the fundamental factors generating their distinctive business advantages. Vernon (1966) placed innovation at centre stage as the most important dynamic force underlying multinational expansion. More recently, Caves (1996) argued that 'the affinities between R&D and the multinational enterprise are numerous', and observed that the extent of R&D spending constitutes an excellent predictor of multinational activity in an industry. A number of studies have also called attention to the fundamental role of MNFs as producers and disseminators of knowledge and technological innovations across national borders (Teece 1977; Cantwell 1989; Narula 2003). A shift has emerged in this literature from early emphasis on the 'transfer of MNFs' technology' to the host countries towards a more comprehensive view of the links between internationalisation and innovation, wherein attention is given to the process of 'global knowledge creation and exchange'. This changing perspective implies consideration of different aspects, including the nature of FDI decisions, the international dispersion of innovative activities, international learning and technology sourcing strategies, and intra-firm knowledge transmission across national borders.

Part I of this volume will adopt this broad perspective and analyse the changing role of MNFs in the generation, adoption and diffusion of technological innovation. We shall argue that this changing role is only partially captured by existing evidence on the growing share of R&D carried out abroad. There are a number of reasons to support this view. First, it is well known that not all relevant innovation occurs as a result of R&D investment. The immediate implication is that it is the overall internal network of multinationals, and not only the international network of R&D labs, that

7

matters for innovative performances of MNFs. Second, the motivation of FDIs affects the actual innovative outcome of MNF activities. Attention should be given to whether and how firms' international activities (including those that are different from offshore R&D) contribute to knowledge creation and circulation on a global scale. Third, the organisation of innovative activities also matters. We shall submit that MNFs increasingly need to combine internal networks of innovative subsidiaries with external networks of collaboration with foreign firms and institutions endowed with complementary competencies and assets.

Chapter 1 will develop this analytical framework, drawing together different streams of literature on the theory of the MNF. Chapter 2 will review some of the evidence consistent with this framework with specific reference to the changing organisation of innovative activities across national borders. An important implication of the analysis in this part of the volume is that innovative behaviour and performance will significantly differ according to the characteristics of MNFs' internal and external networks. We particularly emphasise that, by means of these networks, MNFs end up connecting a variety of innovation systems, and in turn are affected by their characteristics and evolution. This contributes to differentiating MNFs from one another, hence increasing intra-industry heterogeneity. Examining MNFs' diversity has important implications for the analysis of their impact on the economies in which they are active. The relations between intra-industry heterogeneity and internationalisation, and the analysis of spillovers from multinational activities in the presence of heterogeneous firms will be the subject matter of Parts II and III.

1. Views on multinational firms and innovation

1.1 INTRODUCTION

This chapter introduces our analysis of the two-way link between innovation and internationalisation. On the one hand innovation is a key engine of internationalisation as it largely contributes to make it profitable to compete in foreign markets. On the other hand, internationalisation creates important innovation opportunities. In this context, multinationals play a key role in the international exploitation and generation of innovative advantages. A crucial distinction in this respect is between international operations aimed at utilising pre-existing advantages of MNFs (asset exploiting FDIs) and those aimed at gaining access to local sources of knowledge and competitiveness (asset seeking FDIs). We argue that: (a) technological and institutional factors have contributed to increasing the importance of asset seeking strategies, and (b) the latter largely overlap and co-exist with asset exploiting in most circumstances. This evolution has important implications for the organisation of innovative activities of MNFs. In particular, the combination of traditional asset exploiting objectives with increasing asset seeking activities entails a transition of multinationals towards a *double network structure*. On the one hand MNFs are more and more characterised by the interconnection of a large number of internal units that are deeply involved in the company's use, generation and absorption of knowledge. On the other hand, units belonging to the internal network tend to develop external networks with other firms and institutions that are located outside the boundaries of the MNF, in order to increase the potential for use, generation and absorption of knowledge. The development of external networks is thus largely complementary to the growth of multinationals through internal networks. Extending the analysis to a more general level, one can observe that each of the external actors with which MNFs are interconnected across countries are themselves involved in extensive webs of relationships with other firms and institutions. In other words, by becoming embedded in different local contexts, MNFs act as *bridging institutions* connecting a number of geographically dispersed economic and innovation systems. As a result, they

9

are conditioned by, and contribute to, the evolution of different contexts in which they operate.

Section 1.2 provides a general view of the links between international production and innovation. Section 1.3 addresses the distinction between asset exploiting and asset seeking FDIs as key strategies for the global generation, diffusion and utilisation of knowledge, while in section 1.4 we provide some evidence consistent with the idea that such activities play a relevant role in the recent evolution of MNFs activities. Section 1.5 highlights some evolutionary forces underlying this increasing importance of asset seeking FDIs. In section 1.6 we examine the tendency of MNFs to adopt a double network structure as a means to combine asset exploiting and asset seeking strategies and in section 1.7 we discuss some of the organisational issues which are raised by this evolution of the MNF. Section 1.8 extends the analysis to a more general level and examines the role played by the MNF as a bridging institution, connecting geographically dispersed economic and innovation systems. Section 1.9 concludes and draws implications for the analysis which will be carried out in the other parts of this book.

1.2   TECHNOLOGY AND INTERNATIONALISATION

How do innovation and technology relate to internationalisation processes? One way to look at this link is to focus on the so-called globalisation of technology and innovation. Archibugi and Michie (1995) have proposed a useful taxonomy identifying three different aspects of this ongoing process. The first aspect involves national and multinational firms as well as individuals engaged in the *international commercialisation of technology*. Key indicators of these activities are international trade flows, especially of high technology products, and cross-border patenting, both of which reflect the global utilisation of knowledge. The second aspect refers to *international technical and scientific collaborations*. These involve national and multinational firms, universities, research centres, as well as individual researchers active in these institutions. The third aspect is the *global generation of innovation*, i.e. R&D, product and process innovation taking place in labs and plants located abroad. This involves exclusively multinationals, which are by definition the only institutions setting up value added activities in more than one country. The most important indicator of this aspect of the globalisation of technology is R&D expenditure abroad as a share of total R&D of MNFs. There is rather clear evidence that all three aspects of the globalisation of innovation have been increasing over the past decades (Archibugi and Iammarino 2002; Narula and Zanfei 2005).[1]

However, by focusing on the globalisation of technology and innovation, one can capture only part of the links between technology and internationalisation. In fact, it is not merely a matter of how dispersed technological activities are across national borders. The issue we want to raise here is that technology and innovation co-evolve with international production as a whole. In other words, all cross-border activities of firms, no matter how innovative they are (hence including those with no innovative content at all), will have some direct or indirect connection with R&D and innovation either at home, or abroad or in both locations. In a nutshell, we shall recall here three key features of this co-evolution. First, innovative activities are among the most important determinants of advantages which make international operations profitable. Firms with high R&D spending are likely to open up new paths of profitable innovation to be exploited in different markets, and not only in the home market. They will be able to reduce costs below those of their rivals or to rapidly introduce new products, thus expanding their international market shares (Cantwell 1989; Cantwell and Sanna Randaccio 1993). By the same token, international expansion allows the spread of fixed costs of innovation over larger volumes of sales. Each firm expanding in foreign markets thus takes advantage not only from economies of scales in production, but also in R&D and knowledge creation (Mansfield, Romeo and Wagner 1979; Petit and Sanna Randaccio 2000). Moreover, by extending the market for new products and processes, internationalisation creates the conditions for a more extensive division of labour among firm-units involved in the generation and use of knowledge. From this perspective, innovation is a fundamental engine for internationalisation which, in turn, creates the incentives for more intense and efficient innovative efforts (Caves 1996).

Second, the two-way link between internationalisation and innovation is not only a matter of incentives, but also of learning from foreign contexts. International operations may also be a means to interact with, and gain access to, foreign sources of knowledge which (together with other advantages obtained through internationalisation, for example a higher bargaining power vis-à-vis labour force and other stake holders) help increase firms' competitiveness (Dunning and Narula 1995; Zanfei 2000; Frost 2001). Access to foreign sources of knowledge is guided by, and filtered through, knowledge assets which are already available within the firm. Hence, firms need some distinctive advantages (competencies) not only to gain access to, and compete in, foreign markets, but also as a means to absorb local knowledge (Cantwell 2000). The more they invest to accumulate advantages, the greater their absorptive capacity, and the more likely they will further expand their knowledge basis.

Third, to the extent that firms undertake FDI strategies oriented to gain access to local assets there may be important implications for the analysis of spillovers accruing to local firms as well. Different forces are at work here. On the one hand, asset seeking FDIs are attracted by the existence of domestic firms endowed with some valuable and complementary skills and competencies. When this is the case, local firms are also likely to have the absorptive capacity which enables them to gain access to foreign firms' assets, if these are valuable and complementary. In other words, asset seeking strategies and the generation of spillovers to local economies can be mutually interdependent on one another.[2] Moreover, this interdependence is likely to be self-reinforcing: the more foreign firms set up asset seeking activities in local markets, the more they will be available to transfer knowledge to indigenous firms and institutions. And vice versa: the more local firms are willing to access knowledge from foreign sources, the more they will be ready to transfer knowledge back on a reciprocity basis. On the other hand, multinationals may well be in a position of relative weakness in the specific technological field in which the investment takes place, and use asset seeking strategies to overcome this fragility. If this is the case, local firms may not have access to valuable complementary competencies of the MNF. The latter may behave as a free rider and 'run away with the technology' as soon as it gains access to it (Coombs et al. forthcoming). In sum, asset seeking FDIs will not necessarily generate (mutual) spillovers. It is the interaction between the motivation of FDIs and the structural characteristics of both foreign and domestic firms that determines the direction and intensity of spillovers. Foreign firms must have something to 'learn' and something to 'teach', and the same applies to domestic firms. Furthermore, knowledge flows from MNFs towards local firms (and vice versa) need to be organised, and this requires a serious commitment of the parties involved and a favourable environment, particularly for the creation of durable and effective linkages between MNFs and local firms and institutions. This opens, *inter alia*, a wide area of possible interventions for public policy in the crucial areas of intellectual property rights, competition, FDI promotion, selection and 'after care'. The issue of spillovers, with specific reference to externalities created by MNFs to the benefit of local firms, will be tackled in Part III of this book.

1.3   A KEY DISTINCTION: ASSET EXPLOITING AND ASSET SEEKING

A consolidated view in the literature is that firms need to be endowed with some distinctive advantage to be able to compete in foreign markets. As we shall see in Chapter 3, this view is based on some insights put forth by

Hymer (1960), which have been thereafter elaborated and subsumed in a number of contributions in the literature on FDIs and multinational firms. Among other important developments, several authors have insisted on the idea that ownership advantages are at least partially endogenous to international production. In other words, while some foreign investment decisions are aimed at exploiting some prior advantages, other multinational strategies may well pursue the objective of gaining access to further assets that are complementary to firms' already existing advantages. Consistently with this view, Dunning (1993) distinguishes four different FDI strategies: resource seeking, market seeking, efficiency seeking and asset seeking. The first three can be grouped into the broader category of 'asset exploiting' FDIs, as they represent different modes of extracting economic value from advantages firms are already endowed with. When firms pursue resource seeking or efficiency seeking objectives, their specific assets are combined with low cost production factors available locally. In the case of market seeking FDIs, multinationals are attracted by the perspective of exploiting their ownership advantages on a larger scale. By contrast, 'asset seeking' investments are aimed at gaining access to specific competencies which reinforce firms' ability to compete in foreign markets.

Although the asset exploiting versus asset seeking juxtaposition applies to all kind of FDIs, it has been used particularly with reference to the internationalisation of R&D.[3] Asset exploiting R&D investment abroad occurs when firms wish to improve the way in which existing assets are utilised (Dunning and Narula 1995). That is, firms may seek to promote the use of their technological assets in conjunction with, or in response to, specific foreign locational conditions. This has been dubbed also as home-base exploiting (HBE) activity (Kuemmerle 1999). Locational conditions may require some modifications to the product or processes in order to make them more appropriate to local conditions. In such activities, the technological advantages of the firm primarily reflect those of the home country. Such FDIs lead to a duplication of the MNF's home base activities. In fact, under these circumstances, operations carried out in the host location *substitute* for the ones the firm may have wished, *ceteris paribus*, to undertake at home (Zander 1999), but can be undertaken more efficiently elsewhere. Asset exploiting strategies thus correspond by and large to the traditional view of the organisation of innovative activities. Referring mainly to the US-based multinationals, Vernon (1966), Kindleberger (1969), Stopford and Wells (1972) theorised a quasi-colonial relationship between the parent company and foreign subsidiaries, wherein the latter replicated the former's activities abroad, with strategic decisions – including R&D and innovation strategies – being rigidly centralised in the home country. In particular, Vernon emphasised that co-ordinating international innovative activities would be too costly, due to the difficulties of collecting and controlling relevant information across national borders. Host countries and foreign subsidiaries would then play a role almost exclusively in the adoption and diffusion of centrally created technology (more on this view in Chapters 3 and 4).

In the case of asset seeking FDIs (Dunning and Narula 1995) or home-base augmenting (HBA) investments (Kuemmerle 1999), firms aim to improve their existing assets, or to acquire (and internalise) or create completely new assets through foreign-located activities.[4] Once again, this may be particularly, albeit not only, the case of investments for the creation of R&D facilities. In fact, access to complementary technology assets available locally may well occur through learning at the plant level which might either be embodied into improved goods and processes, into blueprints such as user manuals or codified practices, or into routines and tacit competencies (Zanfei, 2000). The assumption in such cases is that the foreign site provides access to *complementary* location-specific advantages that are not as easily available in the firm's primary or 'home' base. In many cases the location advantages are associated with the presence of other firms endowed with high quality technological skills and competencies (Cantwell and Iammarino 2003). The investing firm may seek to acquire access to the technological assets of other firms, through different channels. These include spillovers that derive from agglomeration economies, direct acquisition (by means of M&As), R&D alliances, or, less frequently, arms-length transactions.

There are several reasons why such asset augmenting activities would be hard to achieve through arms-length transactions. Some of these reasons are associated with the nature of technology. When the knowledge relevant for innovative activities is located in a certain geographical area and it is 'sticky', foreign affiliates engage in asset augmenting activities in these areas in order to benefit from the external economies and knowledge spillovers generated by the concentration of production and innovation activities in specific regional or national clusters. The tacit nature of technology implies that even where knowledge is available through markets (as technology markets generally tend to be under-developed), it still needs to be modified to be efficiently integrated within the acquiring firm's portfolio of competencies. In addition, the tacit nature of knowledge associated with production and innovation activity in these sectors implies that 'physical' or geographical proximity is important for transmitting it (Blanc and Sierra 1999). While the marginal cost of transmitting codified knowledge across geographic space does not depend on distance, the marginal cost of transmitting tacit knowledge increases with distance. This leads to the clustering of innovation activities, in particular at the early stage of an industry life cycle where tacit knowledge plays an important role (Audretsch and Feldman 1996).

The discussion on asset exploiting vs. asset seeking activities thus bears important similarities to the debate on the local nature of technological spillovers in the economics literature (e.g. Jaffe et al. 1993). If knowledge spillovers are indeed localised, one may expect that local knowledge bases tend to differ with regard to focus and quality. The only efficient way for a firm to tap into a local knowledge base would then be to be physically present in such a local environment, which is indeed what we have defined as asset augmenting activities.[5]

In sum, asset exploiting activities are primarily associated with demand-driven innovative activities, with the internalisation of technological spillovers as a secondary issue, while asset augmenting activities are primarily undertaken with the intention to acquire and internalise technological spillovers that are host location-specific. Broadly speaking, the former represent an extension of R&D work undertaken at home, whereas the latter represent a diversification into new scientific and technological problems, issues or areas.

1.4 HOW IMPORTANT ARE ASSET SEEKING ACTIVITIES OF MULTINATIONALS?

Empirical studies have traditionally focused on asset exploiting activities of multinationals. This is the case of pioneering studies by Safarian (1966), Mansfield et al. (1979), Lall (1979) and Warrant (1991) which (more or less) implicitly assumed that the internationalisation of R&D is mainly aimed at adapting technologies for selling in host markets. Hence, international R&D activities was by and large considered as demand driven.

More recent works have focused their attention on asset augmenting motives for FDIs in general, and for international R&D activities in particular. It is worth distinguishing two basic approaches in the literature. On the one hand several works have called scholars' attention to the circumstances under which alternative FDI strategies are likely to take place. On the other hand, a number of studies have attempted to highlight to what extent asset seeking actually occurs.

Examples of studies focusing on the circumstances which would favour asset seeking (rather than directly measuring their actual importance) are several works on Japanese FDIs in the EU (Neven and Siotis 1996) and in the US (Kogut and Chang 1991). These contributions found that investment flows were higher in industries where Japan exhibited a lower R&D intensity than the host countries. Based on this evidence, these studies concluded that

Japanese firms were willing to access foreign sources of knowledge to compensate their technological weaknesses in those industries. More recently, a number of empirical works have addressed the issue of FDI motivations by looking at the patterns of patenting activites of MNFs. Among others, Patel and Vega (1999) analysed US patenting activities of 220 firms (over half of which are European and one-third are US based) with the highest inventive activities abroad. They compared the Revealed Technology Advantages (RTA) of MNFs at home (in terms of patents obtained at the headquarters level) and of host economies.[6] Based on this comparison, Patel and Vega found that multinationals most frequently carried out inventive activities in technological fields where they were already strong at home. By contrast, they obtained little evidence to suggest that MNFs go abroad to compensate their weaknesses. They interpreted these findings as consistent with the view that international innovative activities are mostly aimed at providing technical support to offshore manufacturing plants, and at adapting products, processes and materials to suit foreign markets.[7]

Le Bas and Sierra (2002) applied Patel and Vega's methodology to a sample of 345 MNFs with the greatest patenting activity in Europe between 1988 and 1996, which accounted for about half of total patenting through the European Patent Office. They emphasised that MNFs with high RTAs in a given field may pursue different motivations in their technological activities abroad. On the one hand, they are likely to exploit advantages created at home, when the host economy has no RTA in the same field (asset exploiting). On the other hand, they may aim at accessing complementary knowledge assets, if the host location has some revealed advantage in the same technological field in which MNFs are specialised at home (asset augmenting). Le Bas and Sierra (2002) confirmed the finding by Patel and Vega, that MNFs seldom internationalised their activities to compensate for a technological weakness at home (13 per cent of all observed cases) – hence pure technology sourcing turned out to be rare. Much more frequent was what they dubbed as asset exploiting (30 per cent of cases). However, what is even more interesting is that the most frequent circumstance was asset augmenting, when the MNF had an RTA at home in the presence of an RTA of the host economy in the same technology (47 per cent of all cases).[8] This may indicate the formation of 'centres of excellence' in which strong domestic research environments function as attractors of asset augmenting multinational activities. Moreover, the authors showed that this circumstance had become more frequent over the examined period.

Other works have utilised case studies and interviews with managers of foreign R&D units to identify the orientation of their activity. Detailed analyses have highlighted that asset seeking strategies play an important role in a number of manufacturing industries in North America, Europe and Asia. Miller (1994, p. 37) studied the factors affecting the location of R&D facilities of 20 automobile firms in North America, Europe and Asia, and found that an important motivation is to establish 'surveillance out-posts' to follow competitors' engineering and styling activities. In their study of 254 Japanese manufacturing firms, Odagiri and Yasuda (1996, p. 1074) noted that R&D units are often set up in Europe and in the US to be kept informed of the latest technological developments. Similar results are obtained by Florida (1997, p. 90) who analysed 186 foreign affiliated labo-ratories in the US. In some cases market oriented R&D units are found to evolve into technology oriented ones, as shown by Rondstadt (1978) in his seminal investigation of R&D investment abroad. In other circumstances, foreign R&D units experienced no major shift in their characters, as observed by Kuemmerle (1999).

The contributions we have just reviewed, although based on different methodologies, do provide some evidence of the fact that MNFs' invest-ment decisions are frequently aimed at accessing foreign sources of know-ledge. However, they do not investigate whether and to what extent MNFs are actually sourcing knowledge from abroad.

Path-breaking empirical work in this field was carried out by Almeida (1996) who used patent citation data to evaluate the extent to which foreign based firms relied on local knowledge. He found that patents cited by foreign affiliates in the semiconductor industry in the US were more likely to originate in the US, but he also supported the view that patents granted to foreign firms are cited more often than one would expect by other patents originated in the same region. Frost (2001) used the same methodology and showed that only the more innovative affiliates tended to draw upon local sources of knowledge. Similarly, using patent citations of Japanese firms in the US, Branstetter (forthcoming) found that knowledge sourcing actually occurred through R&D and product development facilities.

Patent citation analyses focusing on MNF activity in the US thus found consistent evidence that foreign firms source technology from the host country. This is no surprise, given that in most high-tech sectors US firms are world leaders, and it is very likely that foreign firms have more to learn in these cases. Studies referring to other countries of destination of FDIs, provide a more blurred picture on the importance of asset seeking. Using a methodology similar to the one proposed by Almeida (1996), Cantwell and Noonan (2002) showed that MNE subsidiaries located in Germany between 1975 and 1995 sourced a relatively high proportion of knowledge (especially new, cutting-edge technology) from this host country. Altogether these data lend support to the idea that foreign owned techno-logical activities undertaken in Germany are often asset augmenting.

Applying an augmented production function framework, Driffield and Love (2004) found that the productivity of foreign firms in the UK benefited both from investment in the domestic R&D intensive sectors and from the activities of other multinationals. Criscuolo et al. (2005) focus on a large number of recipient countries and obtained less straightforward evidence. Using both USPTO and EPO citations the authors found that US affiliates in the EU relied mainly on home-region knowledge sources, while EU affiliates in the US, especially when they had an R&D mandate, had a relatively higher propensity to cite patents granted in the host country.

In sum, the evidence on asset seeking activities of multinationals is not conclusive. However, the examined studies provide some empirical support to two important statements. First, multinationals are often, and increasingly so, attracted into areas where they have something to learn from local sources of knowledge. This might be interpreted as a signal that MNFs pursue asset augmenting objectives, although the actual implementation of such objectives is a different matter. Second, there is evidence of the fact that MNFs do source relevant knowledge from host economies, at least when they are located in some technologically advanced geographical areas (particularly the US and several EU regions) and in some industries (especially science-based ones).

1.5 FACTORS UNDERLYING THE EVOLUTION OF STRATEGIES AND STRUCTURE OF MNFs

In the previous section we discussed some empirical evidence supporting the idea that asset augmenting internationalisation is relevant and has gained momentum over the past two decades. In this section we focus on a more general discussion on the dynamic factors underlying this trend (Zanfei 2000). There seems to be a wide agreement on the very general statement that changes in the 'competitive environment' are the main determinants of the alleged evolution of international activities. More specifically, reference is made to the quickening pace and widening scope of technical change and to the globalisation of markets.

1.5.1 Technical Change, Global Markets and Asset Seeking FDIs

To discuss the role of these dynamic factors in the evolution of multinational firms, one may refer back to Dunning (1995). He focused on some general trends in the fields of technology and of demand. With reference to technological factors, he highlighted at least five sets of evolutionary pressures affecting the strategy and structure of MNFs (Dunning 1995,

p. 468). First, technical change has raised the fixed costs of a wide range of manufacturing and service activities; second, it has increased the interdependencies between distinctive technologies that may need to be used jointly to supply a particular product; third, it has enhanced the importance of multipurpose, flexible technologies, such as microelectronics, information processing and transmission, and biotechnology; fourth, it has often determined a reduction of product life cycles; and fifth, partially as a result of the previous changes, it has forced firms to upgrade their core competencies and improve their competitive advantages.

As far as trends on the 'demand side' are concerned, Dunning (1995, p. 468) emphasised the increasing variety of markets MNFs are forced to deal with, as a factor that is further spurring firms to increase their ability to compete dynamically. However, his interpretation of the so called 'globalisation of markets' is not shared by all scholars. Discussing this aspect is at least partially beyond the scope of this work. Suffice here to notice that a number of contributions have emphasised an opposite view. According to this interpretation, a process of homogenisation of markets would be actually taking place, as a result of imitation, cultural cross-fertilisation and contamination, favoured *inter alia* by progress in communication technologies. This view, submitted in the late 1970s and early 1980s by Vernon (1979) and by Levitt (1983), has received attention in part of the business literature (Porter 1986 and Martinez and Jarrillo 1989), and has been more recently resumed in the less academic debate on the social consequences of globalisation (see Kaldor et al. 2003 for a review).

Neither position appears to be supported by convincing and conclusive evidence. However, for the purpose of the present analysis, it is important to observe that the more local contexts are different, the higher the likelihood that there are valuable complementary assets to be accessed and utilised locally. In other words, asset seeking FDIs can be a response to high and increasing diversity of local contexts.

Considering local contexts as sources of competencies and of technological opportunities, and less as constraints to the action of multinational enterprises, marks a fundamental departure from the conventional approach to international business. Hedlund (1986, pp. 20–21) caught the essence of this new way of theorising the role of local contexts: 'The main idea is that the foundations of competitive advantage no longer reside in any one country, but in many. New ideas and products may come up in many different countries and later be exploited on a global scale.' Kogut (1989a, p. 388) expressed a complementary view: 'What is distinctive in the international context, besides larger market size, is the variance in country environments and the ability to profit through the system-wide management of this variance'.[9]

From this perspective, Dunning's position can be fully appreciated and enriched if we take the 'value of diversity' into the appropriate account. He submitted that the *combination* of the technical determinants recalled above, with the differentiation of demand induced by globalisation, would increasingly force firms to be more dynamically competitive, and cause firms – and particularly large hierarchies – to reconsider both the scope and the organisation of their value added activities (Dunning 1995, p. 468–470). In the light of the previous discussion, we should add that demand diversity is only part of the variety MNFs have to deal with. Local contexts can be considered as differentiated and evolving sets of cultural values, institutions and norms that influence the behaviour of economic agents and their ultimate performances.[10] It is this ever increasing variety, and not only demand diversity, that – combining and interacting with technical change – pressures for MNFs to adopt asset seeking strategies.

1.5.2   The Changing Nature of Technology and the Role of Local Contexts

Our understanding of MNF evolution could be significantly improved if we examined in greater details the interactions between technical change, on the one hand, and the variety and evolution of local contexts, on the other. One way to proceed is to briefly consider, first, some of the emerging changes in the nature of scientific and technological progress that are affecting a wide number of industries, and then the impact of these changes on the role of local contexts. We shall thereafter draw some implications for international business in general. The more specific implications on the internal and external organisation of MNFs are discussed in sections 1.6 and 1.7.

Let us start with scientific and technological factors. Arora and Gambardella (1994) have emphasised that a number of scientific advances over the past 30 years together with the remarkable evolution occurred in the field of instrumentation, particularly computers and communication devices, induced a significant increase in the availability and use of what they call 'general and abstract knowledge'. Following their definition, we can identify 'abstract' knowledge with the ability to represent phenomena in terms of a limited number of 'essential elements', making abstraction from the specific context in which such phenomena were originally observed; and 'general' knowledge with the ability to relate the outcome of a particular experiment to the outcomes of other experiments that may be distant from a historical, geographical or even logical point of view. New (computer based) experimentation technologies enable researchers to test theories more rapidly and effectively, and even to prove theories that could not be tested with old instruments. Scientific advances improving the theoretical understanding of problems make it possible to formalise concepts and ideas, so that relevant information can be processed with new instrumentation.[11] The wider pool of generic knowledge that is becoming available within and across firm boundaries increasingly requires that firms gain timely access to 'contextual' knowledge, that is information on specific applications environments and user needs. Moreover, as the costs of knowledge codification fall, and the potential for applications of knowledge expands, the division of innovative labour in the generation and in the utilisation of technologies also increases (Arora et al. 2001).

This line of argument brings us to the second step of our analysis: the changing nature of scientific and technological progress enhances the role of local contexts as a source of economic value for the innovating firms. In other words, it is context-specific knowledge that makes the difference and determines the competitive advantage of firms. Context-specific knowledge is highly complementary to the development of general and abstract knowledge. Two reasons can be proposed here. First, general and abstract knowledge is 'sterile' from an economic point of view, if considered in isolation from contextual knowledge. In fact, companies with a high general and abstract knowledge endowment, but with no contact with contextual knowledge, are not able to evaluate actual user needs and expectations, and will then encounter very limited commercialisation opportunities. This will undermine the very possibility of funding R&D efforts and the generation of knowledge itself. Second, generic knowledge basis can be further expanded through the contact with context-specific information. Application experience may highlight puzzles and problems to be solved, thus stimulating research at all levels, and eventually generating new generic knowledge (Rosenberg 1969). Furthermore, localised, context-specific experience conducted at the level of both manufacturers and users can eventually be decontextualised and enrich generic knowledge as well.[12]

The described trends have fundamental implications for international business. First, advances in information processing and communication technologies increase the incentives for firms to codify knowledge and lower the cost of exchanging information between different and distant nodes of a MNF's internal network (Santangelo 2001). This is the most commonly considered aspect in economics and business literature. Second, developments in the theoretical understanding of phenomena together with computational progress increase the rapidity and effectiveness of the process through which knowledge can be decontextualised, codified and transferred to different sites where it has to be employed.[13] As a result of this process, local knowledge can be decontextualised to enter the cycle of generation of new economic value (Becattini and Rullani 1993). In the case of transnational companies, this implies that subsidiaries can specialise in specific knowledge creation activities, contribute their own bits of knowledge to the network, and gain access to other specialised inputs at a lower cost and with greater potential advantages than in the past. Research and development phases can be separated and assigned to distinct and geographically distant units within the MNF or to foreign external units with complementary competencies (Criscuolo 2004). Third, the growing possibilities offered by science and technology to generalise, codify and transfer knowledge, make it more and more necessary for firms to gain access to local resources and competencies, wherever these may be available, and to absorb the stimuli deriving from local applications experiences (Tunisini and Zanfei 1998). Examples illustrating these aspects of international division of innovative labour, occurring across different phases of R&D or between R&D and commercialisation activities, will be discussed in Chapter 2.

The dynamic factors we have considered thus appear to increase the importance of asset seeking FDIs. However, this does not imply that these substitute the more traditional asset exploiting activities. There are at least two basic reasons why asset seeking and asset exploiting activities can be expected to co-exist. On the one hand, to the extent that asset seeking investments are undertaken, new technological opportunities are opened and explored. The exploitation of these opportunities will require complementary assets which are not necessarily available locally. This will call for further FDIs which are asset exploiting in nature. On the other hand, whenever products are multi-technology-based, one firm may be marginally ahead in one technology, and its competitor in another. This will imply that the same firm might be oriented to exploit superior technology in one area, while undergoing exploratory strategies to augment competencies in another (Criscuolo et al. 2005). This is another reason why firms often engage in both asset augmenting and asset exploiting activities simultaneously.

1.6   MULTINATIONALS, INNOVATION AND THE DOUBLE NETWORK STRUCTURE

We have argued that there are important dynamic forces leading to an increase of asset seeking activities. The combination of these strategies with more traditional asset exploiting FDIs entails a transition of MNFs towards a *double network structure*. This view of the evolution of MNFs emphasises a fundamental change in the internal networks of knowledge creation and transfer within the MNF, combined with a growing recourse to external networks of inter-firm alliances (Zanfei 2000). On the one hand, MNFs are more and more characterised by the interaction among different internal units (affiliates and business centres) that are deeply involved in the creation and use of knowledge. The traditional organisational model, based on the vertical, unidirectional transfer of knowledge from the centre to the periphery, is being gradually replaced. Enterprises and business units belonging to the multinational group and located in different countries are not only able to passively adapt knowledge generated elsewhere. They are also able to generate and circulate new information, and are more and more tied to one another by means of cultural (values and languages), rather than hierarchical linkages. On the other hand, enterprises and units belonging to the internal network tend to develop external networks, with other firms and institutions that are located outside the boundaries of the MNF, in order to increase the potential for use and generation of knowledge. These cooperative relations do not only involve the central units of the MNF, but they more and more concern the decentralised units as well, which increasingly use such networks to gain access to local sources of knowledge and applications abilities.

This view brings together the results of studies which are often kept separated, spanning from the analysis of international technological alliances (Dunning 1995; Mowery 1988; Hagedoorn 2002; Castellani and Zanfei 2004), to contributions on the international dispersion of firms' innovative activities (Granstrand et al. 1993; Cantwell 1995; Zander 1999; Patel and Pavitt 2000; Cantwell and Iammarino 2003); and from works on the organisation of R&D and innovation within multinationals (Hedlund 1986; Bartlett and Ghoshal 1989; Fors 1997; Cantwell and Mudambi forthcoming) to the literature on MNFs' embeddedness in local contexts (Nohria and Ghoshal 1997; Andersson and Forsgren 2000; Foss and Pedersen 2002; Andersson et al. 2005). See Zanfei (2000) and Narula and Zanfei (2005) for a comprehensive review of these different streams of literature. We shall focus below on a key aspect of the evolution of MNFs towards a double network structure, namely the complementarities and interactions between internal and external networks.

1.6.1 Complementarities Between Internal and External Networks

The expansion of an MNFs' internal network of foreign subsidiaries may well be a substitute for external networking in a number of circumstances. For instance, the commercialisation of products, especially in their post-paradigmatic phases of development, can be effectively carried out either by creating new sales affiliates or by setting up contractual agreements with external sales agents. By the same token, when the appropriability regime is strong enough to guarantee firms from free riding problems, some asset seeking may well be accomplished either by means of local subsidiaries used as 'listening posts' or 'technological windows' to absorb and develop new ideas (Patel and Pavitt 1991); or through alliances with local partners used as vehicles to learn from the local technological environment (Bureth et al. 1997). In other circumstances, internal and external networks may co-exist, reflecting a dynamic interdependence between the two processes. The creation of internal networks of subsidiaries pursuing asset exploiting objectives may generate new technological opportunities and induce firms to set up external networks as a means to carry out asset seeking activities. The causality could also run the other way around: external networking may create opportunities to be exploited by means of internal networks.[14] Exploring the relationship between internal and external networking requires a better understanding of the mechanisms through which one affects the other. How does the development of internal networks favour (or prevent) the setting up of external networks? More specifically, how do internal networking strategies affect the likelihood that external networks are used to enhance asset seeking activities, and vice-versa?

Some useful insights can be derived from the literature on multinational experience (see Castellani and Zanfei 2004 for a review). Since *multinational experience* is, by and large, a function of the extension, geographic spread and duration of firms' presence in different countries, we shall simply use this term as a synonym of *internal networking*. The purpose of the present analysis is to highlight how multinational experience/international networking affects external network development. Different streams of literature have shown that this impact is an indirect one, as internal networks can be expected to influence external networks either by reducing uncertainty (section 1.6.2) or by creating economic opportunities (section 1.6.3).

1.6.2 Internal Networks, Uncertainty and Cooperation

Drawing from transaction cost literature, several works have argued that an extensive internal network of foreign subsidiaries, as a proxy of firms' multinational experience, is a fundamental means to reduce *external uncertainty*. This uncertainty stems from the unpredictability of factors that are largely (albeit not entirely) exogenous to the behaviour of individual firms, such as the variety and volatility of international markets, of technological opportunities and of institutional conditions. Geographic and cultural distance will negatively affect the ability of firms to predict foreign demand, technology and institutional conditions. The idea is that by expanding their internal networks, firms will be able to better evaluate foreign contexts, to assess the costs and risks of further international operations, to adapt to environmental diversity, and to perceive local opportunities. Under these circumstances, firms become more willing to commit resources and to adopt higher control modes of governance in international activities.

By contrast, to the extent that the development of a wide network of subsidiaries yields greater knowledge on foreign environments (reduces external uncertainty), diminishing returns are associated with flexible and less commitment intensive modes of information gathering (Gomes-Casseres 1989). This will increase the likelihood that advantages from cooperation (e.g. lower sunk costs, shorter set-up and shut-down time) are outbalanced by transaction costs and organisational problems (shirking and conflicts).

Other contributions emphasise the impact of internal networking on another type of uncertainty, namely *behavioural (internal) uncertainty*, having an opposite effect on external networking. As suggested by Robertson and Gatignon (1998, p. 520), behavioural uncertainty concerns the difficulty of observing and measuring the adherence of contracting parties to the contractual arrangements and the difficulty of measuring the performance of these parties. This kind of uncertainty is critical for opportunism to arise in the absence of control mechanisms. The inexperienced firm might not be in a position to accurately assess the performance (outputs) of economic agents active in foreign markets, thus it might resort to monitor their efforts (inputs) by extending hierarchical control (Erramilli 1991; Anderson and Gatignon 1986). Experience created by an extensive web of foreign subsidiaries may reduce internal uncertainty and lower the desirability of hierarchical control mechanisms by two means. First, by increasing mutual trust between MNFs and local counterparts.[15] Experienced firms are likely to have a history of relations with local firms and institutions, through which they get acquainted with one another, share goals and competencies, and become less inclined to adopt opportunistic behaviour (Zucker 1986; Lyons and Mehta 1997). This can be envisaged as a learning by cooperating process: mutual trust is an immaterial asset which is generated through interaction, and creates a business environment which is conducive to further collaboration with the same partner(s) (Bureth et al. 1997; Andersson et al. 2005).

Second, multinational experience reduces the risk of opportunistic behaviour of foreign counterparts (hence diminishing internal uncertainty) by increasing outside options and the credibility of retaliation strategies. In a different analytical context, Kogut (1989b) points out that having other ties increases the stability of collaborative ventures because it allows one party to retaliate in case a partner behaves opportunistically, either by punishing the same partner in different transactions; or by resorting to different partners to accomplish the same tasks. In a similar vein, we shall suggest that MNFs with extensive internal networks in foreign markets will have greater opportunities to retaliate in case a local party deviates from a contractual agreement, therefore reducing the risk that such opportunistic behaviour occurs.[16]

1.6.3 Internal Networks, Technological Opportunities and Collaborative Networks

Other streams of literature pay a closer attention to the role of multi-national experience/internal networking in favouring asset seeking strategies and dynamic efficiency.[17] In particular, several contributions focusing on the evolution of high technology industries, highlight the need to explore and rapidly exploit new opportunities, either new businesses or new technological developments. From this point of view, strategic alliances appear to be appropriate means to search for and utilise new ideas, stimuli and bits of knowledge. In other words they represent 'an attractive organisational form for an environment characterised by rapid innovation and geographical organisational dispersion in the sources of know how' (Teece 1992, p. 20). The need for a timely and effective knowledge access may spur firms to choose strategic alliances even when short term, static (transaction and organisational) cost minimisation would point to different forms of linkages. Consistently with a more general view of complementarity between internal and external competence accumulation (Cohen and Levinthal 1989; Rosenberg 1990; Arora and Gambardella 1994), multinational experience – which is associated to the expansion of firms' internal network of foreign subsidiaries over time – can be identified as a fundamental asset that helps increase a firm's *exploration potential*, i.e. its possibility to search for and absorb external knowledge (Cantwell 1995; Castellani and Zanfei 2002, 2004). This view appears to be consistent with a number of studies which highlight the mutually reinforcing nature of intra-firm and inter-firm networks, through which generic as well as applications and market oriented knowledge assets can be searched for and accessed.[18] The relevant implication for our purposes is that multinational experience/internal networking can be expected to expand the exploration potential and hence lead to a greater recourse to international collaborative ventures.

To summarise, part of the existing literature suggests that multinational experience/internal networking will reduce external uncertainty and will thus have a *negative impact* on collaborative linkages (as opposed to hierarchical control modes). By contrast, other contributions highlight that internal networking can have a *positive* effect on external networks, when internal uncertainty (and opportunism) is reduced. As we have shown, this can occur if multinationals, by expanding their presence in foreign markets, either reinforce their relationships with local partners based on (mutual) trust; or use their internal networks as a means to credibly retaliate against partners which deviate from contractual agreements. Finally, works stressing dynamic efficiency considerations lead to the conclusion that internal networking will increase firms' exploration potential and hence favour the recourse to external networks of international collaborations rather than hierarchical linkages.

In the light of the previous discussion, it thus appears that the actual impact of internal networking on external networks is at least partially an empirical issue. The interpretive ambivalence we have highlighted calls for a more detailed analysis of the characteristics of MNFs' internal networks of subsidiaries and of their impact on external networks. The idea is that multinational experience – identified by firms' internal web of foreign subsidiaries – should be considered a multifaceted concept. As we shall further discuss in Chapter 2, different characteristics of internal networks can be expected to have a distinct effect on the key determinants of linkage creation we have focused on above: uncertainty and exploration potential. These characteristics include the number, geographic spread and length of establishment of foreign affiliates in local economies. Some of these characteristics will also be considered when analysing heterogeneity across multinationals in Chapter 4, and the difference in the impact of MNFs on host economies in Chapter 6.

The point to be stressed here is a more general one. Our arguments for the growing recourse of MNFs to asset seeking FDIs, as reported in section 1.5, suggests that dynamic complementarities between internal and external networks are likely to become more and more important too. In other words, assets seeking activities proceed hand in hand with the evolution of MNFs towards a double network structure. In fact, the expansion of firms' internal network of foreign subsidiaries may create the conditions for a more effective exploratory activity in foreign locations and increase the possibility to search for, and absorb, external knowledge. This augments the expected payoff from the development of external networks, and increases the likelihood that asset seeking objectives are pursued.

1.7 ORGANISING THE INTERNATIONAL GENERATION AND USE OF KNOWLEDGE

In the previous sections, we have argued that, especially in industries characterised by a high dynamic competition, MNFs should be moving towards a *double network structure*, by expanding both their internal networks of subsidiaries and their external networks of collaborations with local partners. This raises a number of organisational issues. In fact, the creation, transfer and exploitation of technological assets within the MNF requires a division of labour among semi-autonomous units located in different countries. These units should in turn be able to engage in external networking and have the incentive to circulate knowledge and assets acquired locally at the global corporate level (Zanfei 2000; Criscuolo et al. 2005). In other words, foreign affiliates need to be endowed with sufficient degrees of autonomy, in order to be in a position to absorb external knowledge; but these autonomous units may lack the incentives to make such knowledge available to the rest of the MNF and to adopt technologies produced elsewhere in the MNF (Blanc and Sierra 1999). This calls for an organisational structure which allows autonomy, through maintaining internal cohesion. In the following, we shall address the three issues separately. First, why should the degree of decentralised units' autonomy increase within MNFs organised as a *double network*? Second, what are the consequences of such autonomy for the degree of knowledge transfer within the MNF? Third, how can the MNF ensure internal cohesion among autonomous units?

1.7.1 The Autonomy of Units Within the MNF

To the extent that local contexts are a fundamental source of opportunities and competitive assets for MNFs, centralising information and strategic decisions is more and more likely to be *ineffective* for several reasons. First, the increasing variety and variability of challenges stemming from local context augments information asymmetries between headquarters and subsidiaries. This will reduce the possibility for headquarters to effectively control the subsidiaries' on-going operations. Such a view is consistent with agency theory, in which the headquarters (principal) are expected to try and secure that the subsidiary (agent) behaves in accordance to the former's goals. Within this framework an increase in information asymmetry will entail a shift from direct control to output control: the principal (parent company) will more effectively evaluate the final performances of the agents (subsidiaries), allowing them a greater discretionary power in the process leading to a given output (O'Donnell 2000)

Second, the more subsidiaries extend their ability to use and generate relevant information through interaction with local contexts, the more they will be constrained in their action by local requirements. This will reduce the possibility for the headquarters to effectively control decisions of foreign subsidiaries. Some authors have emphasised that centralisation of decisions within multinationals may be undermined by the growing need subsidiaries have to enter partnerships with other firms and institutions that are active in their host countries. As Forsgren and Johanson (1992, p. 27) have put it: 'The wish for freedom in the subsidiaries cannot be explained solely by a general desire for autonomy; it probably also stems from the demand of actors in the industrial network, e.g. local authorities and trade unions.' From this perspective, the higher the MNF's involvement into external networks with local counterparts, the greater the autonomy of units belonging to the internal network.

Third, centralising decision making is also highly ineffective in markets characterised by intense dynamic competition because it would negatively impact on the number and variety of learning patterns. Florida (1997, p. 87) submits that that when foreign R&D plants are subject to complex reporting and central control, there may be negative consequences both on the affiliates' innovative performances and on their ability to recruit and attract high quality scientific and technical human capital. Moreover, centralising decision making will reduce the firm's ability to understand local business environment and hence to develop close relationships with local counterparts, hence further diminishing its innovation potential (Andersson et al. 2005).

Allowing greater autonomy to subsidiaries would instead create greater incentives for the subsidiary to take profitable initiatives at the local and global levels (Birkinshaw 1997). It would also create an incentive structure that is more conducive to creativity and innovation among local workers and managers (Bartlett and Ghoshal 1989), and would be more attractive for qualified researchers (Criscuolo 2004). Moreover, it will increase the possibility for local firms to establish enduring and tight relationships with local counterparts, and ultimately to enhance knowledge absorption and creation (Andersson et al. 2005). *Inter alia*, a higher autonomy of units belonging to the internal network will favour the firm's ability to explore a wider range of collaborative patterns with local partners. In other words, there is a two way link between the autonomy of subsidiaries and external linkage development: on the one hand external networks reduce the headquarters' possibility to control some decisions, increasing the discretionary power of subsidiaries; on the other hand, subsidiaries' autonomy enables them to explore a wider number of collaborative patterns.

To summarise, the affiliates' autonomy is by and large shaped by the characteristics of the environment in which the MNF is active: the larger the variety of challenges and opportunities offered by local contexts, and the higher the intensity of competition based on innovation, the greater will be the need for autonomy within the MNF's organisation. Autonomy will also be higher the larger and the more binding are external networks with local counterparts. As autonomy will in turn favour collaboration, the increase of autonomy can be expected to be, *coeteris paribus*, a cumulative process.

1.7.2 Centrifugal Forces and Constraints to Knowledge Circulation

As we have just highlighted, autonomy guarantees that affiliates are fully integrated into local contexts and are enabled to maximise learning and accumulation of application-specific knowledge. However, autonomy can constrain the circulation of knowledge within MNFs, thus dramatically reducing the advantages of specialisation and undermining the process of knowledge accumulation as well. There are two such constraints to knowledge circulation:

1. *Constraints on the adoption of new technology by foreign affiliates.* Subsidiaries with a large autonomy may not be willing to utilise knowledge that is available within the multinational group. This reluctance to adopt knowledge may be due to a number of reasons. New technology originating elsewhere within the MNF may turn out to be incompatible with technological choices autonomously made by the decentralised unit, deriving from previous adoption of different standards, or of research programmes implying a pre-determined sequence of innovative steps (Arthur 1988). Cultural resistance can also play a role, as a result of a limited ability to evaluate technological alternatives, or of other institutional factors (nationalistic orientation of local decision makers, lack of trust, 'Not Invented Here' syndrome). Furthermore, foreign affiliates are often forced by host country governments to source at least part of their inputs and technology locally, thus reducing the rate of adoption of knowledge from parent companies. Finally, not all foreign affiliates possess the 'absorptive capacity' – most often associated with firm size and human capital endowment – needed to adopt technology from parent companies, and from other parts of the MNF (Teece 1977; Cantwell 1995; Gupta and Govidarajan 2000). The non-adoption of knowledge can be a problem for the MNF for at least two reasons. First, it may put a brake on rationalisation efforts – for example, by inducing subsidiaries to 're-invent the wheel', or impeding the diffusion within the multinational network of a new, more efficient standard – and worsen compatibility problems within the network. Second, by refusing to adopt technology available within the MNF, the reluctant subsidiary does not contribute to the exploitation of knowledge economies of scale at the network level, thus reducing the incentives of other parties to invest in the generation and codification of specialised knowledge.

2. *Obstacles to the transfer of knowledge from affiliates to other units of the firm.* Autonomy of subsidiaries may also put a brake on their willingness and capability to contribute their own knowledge to the network. We have already observed that some of the subsidiaries' strategic moves may be constrained by the need to obey to local rules, or to decisions that are jointly taken with external parties. For example, some of the results of these co-operative ventures may be subject to contractual

constraints which do not allow subsidiaries to freely circulate knowledge within the MNF. Furthermore, to the extent that foreign affiliates access external knowledge they can bargain with the headquarters the transfer of such assets, in order to maintain their autonomy and strategic mandates. This process is likely to produce a suboptimal disclosure or degree of knowledge transfer within the MNF. In other words, the process of reverse technology transfer may not be working properly (Criscuolo 2004). Among other consequences, autonomy may thus end up increasing, rather than reducing, the cultural and organisational distance between the headquarters and affiliates, which is considered a fundamental source of communication problems (Buckley and Carter 2004). Besides, subsidiaries will be less willing to transfer knowledge if their local markets are large, implying that their incentive to pursue knowledge economies of scales through the network will not be so compelling. Autonomy may also generate problems with the actual access to knowledge available in the network. If a subsidiary is reluctant to contribute knowledge to the network, other parties belonging to the MNF may retaliate against it by either reducing its possibility of access to available knowledge or refusing to adopt its knowledge when and if circulated in the network.

1.7.3 The Internal Cohesion of MNFs

The arguments developed in the previous section suggest that decentralisation of decision making needs to be complemented with a close attention to the factors favouring internal cohesion of MNFs and balancing out centrifugal forces. The risks attached to autonomy without integration have been effectively summarised by Ghoshal and Bartlett (1995, p. 148): 'In the absence of . . . an integration process, decentralised entrepreneurship may lead to some temporary performance improvement as existing slack is harnessed, but long term development of new capabilities or businesses is seriously impeded.' Hakanson and Nobel (2001) argue that the degree of integration between a subsidiary and the rest of the company is the primary predictor of knowledge transfer from the subsidiary to the headquarters or to another subsidiary. Moreover, they submit that the highest reverse technology transfer (from periphery to the centre of the MNF) should be found when subsidiaries are both highly embedded in the local environment and highly integrated within the MNF.

While there is a wide agreement on the need to ensure integration to favour internal cohesion, there is much lower convergence on whether it should be attained by means of hierarchical control or via more informal means, such as the rotation of personnel and the sharing of cultural values and of 'strategic visions'. On the one hand, Gupta and Govindarajan (2000) posit that centralisation encourages flows from headquarters to subsidiary. On the other hand, Egelhoff et al. (2003) point out that centralisation might well favour knowledge transfers from headquarters towards subsidiaries, but it would not imply as strong flows from subsidiaries towards headquarters, nor between subsidiaries. This calls for innovative co-ordination modes that ensure an acceptable degree of cohesion, while safeguarding the autonomy and creativity of MNF units (see Martinez and Jarrillo 1989 and Zanfei 2000 for a review of the literature on this issue). From this perspective there seems to be some convergence on two ideas. First, decentralisation processes within MNFs are likely to be associated with the adoption of 'subtle' and informal coordination mechanisms (Hedlund 1986; Egelhoff 1984; Hedlund and Rolander 1990). Second, the role of headquarters is subject to fundamental changes: central offices are gradually abandoning their traditional function as centres of control and are more and more involved in setting the rules of the game, monitoring competencies and organising resources for the joint exploration and exploitation of technological opportunities by MNF units (Dunning 1993; Cantwell 2001).

There are, however, some centripetal forces at work, independent of administrative mechanisms adopted. A wide literature on MNF internal organisation has shown that affiliate autonomy is severely constrained by a system of interdependencies in terms of knowledge, technology, products, markets (cf. Dunning 1993, Ch.8 for an extensive review of these cohesion mechanisms). We here suggest that, as a result of the evolutionary process examined in section 1.5, additional incentives come into action, stimulating affiliates to co-operate with one another and to transfer knowledge within the MNF.

Increasing centripetal effects are partly the result of growing competitive pressures. Coping with globalising markets and evolving technology implies that each unit will be induced to collaborate with the headquarters and other units to solve problems that neither the headquarters nor subsidiaries can individually solve (Evans 1992, p. 92). Furthermore, a powerful incentive to co-operate within the network is the expectation to take advantage from potential *economies of scale in the generation of knowledge*, due to the large variety of alternative uses of knowledge itself that are accessible through the transnational network (Grandinetti and Rullani 1996). It is worth noting that units active in small sized markets can enjoy greater advantages from belonging to the network, than subsidiaries with large markets. In fact, subsidiaries with small markets would never attain economies of scale in the accumulation of context-specific capabilities, if they could not generalise it and transfer at least part of their knowledge through the network (whereas subsidiaries with larger markets could attain greater returns on their investments thanks to their local sales).

1.8 MULTINATIONALS AS BRIDGING INSTITUTIONS

The evolution of MNFs towards a *double network structure* entails that they increasingly act as *bridging institutions* connecting a number of geographically dispersed economic and innovation systems. In fact, each of the external actors with which MNFs are interconnected across countries are themselves involved in extensive webs of relationships with other firms and institutions. Therefore, MNFs are embedded in sectoral, regional and national contexts whose characteristics and evolution affects, and are influenced by, their behaviour and performances. From this perspective, multinationals are not the quasi-colonial institutions exporting technological and organisational standards from the home to the host country, as described by Vernon (1966, 1971) and Stopford and Wells (1972). Instead, they can play a role in levering upon each system's peculiarities, through a process of search, recombination and exploitation of assets. Admittedly, MNFs are likely to impact on the economic environment where they operate, but not in the unidirectional way that was described in the classic contributions of the 1960s and early 1970s. To the extent that MNFs increasingly act as bridging institutions, they are more and more exposed to the inertial constraints and to the pressures for change characterising each of the economic and innovative systems which they connect.

On the one hand, there are some system-wide inertial forces which may put a brake on the MNF's deployment of global asset exploiting and asset seeking strategies. Differences in natural factor endowments, in the organisation and specialisation of industries, in the national stocks of knowledge, and in national economic and political institutions seem to create important impediments to the cross-border integration of innovation systems (Foray 1995; Niosi and Bellon 1996; Gregersen and Johnson 1997). Developing linkages with external networks of local counterparts may be expensive and time consuming, as compared with the low costs of maintaining the integration with the innovation system in the home location (Narula 2003; Carlsson 2003). Linkages with firms and institutions are both formal and informal, and may take years to create and sustain. Government funding institutions, suppliers, university professors, private research teams, informal networks of like-minded researchers take considerable effort to create, and once developed, have a low marginal cost of maintaining. Even where the host location is potentially superior to the home location – and where previous experience exists in terms of other value adding activities – the high costs of becoming familiar with, and integrating into a new location may be prohibitive. This cost constraint is particularly binding in the case of R&D FDI decisions (Narula and Zanfei 2005). Firms are constrained by resource limitations, and by the need to reach some minimum threshold size of R&D activities in every distinct location. As such, to maintain more than one facility with a threshold level of researchers means that the new (host) location must offer significantly superior spillover opportunities accruing to the MNF. In other words, the host location must provide access to complementary resources that are simply not available anywhere else, and which cannot be acquired by less risky and more efficient means. The high costs associated with integrating into the host location's systems of innovation – in contrast to the low marginal cost of maintaining its embeddedness in its home location's innovation system – may thus increase the fixed costs firms have to overcome in order to expand internationally.

On the other hand, some of the inertial factors at work at the home system level may also act as key inducing mechanisms for firms to internationalise their own activities, including R&D facilities. Institutional bottlenecks and resource shortages can be expected to stimulate a creative reaction, inducing firms to look for market or technological opportunities abroad. The role of FDIs as a creative response to resource scarcities has been emphasised by Franko (1976) in the case of European firms, and by Ozawa (1979) with reference to Japanese multinationals. The impact of institutional characteristics and constraints as a determinant of the internationalisation of innovative activities has been examined by Zanfei (1993) with reference to the US telecommunications industry, by Mowery (1988) for the US aircraft industry, and by Lam (1997) for the Japanese and UK electronics industry. See Chapter 4 for a more extensive discussion of the role of economic and institutional constraints in internationalisation processes.

Narula (2003) provides a stimulating analysis of the ambivalent role of the inertia of innovation systems and of how firms may be influenced in their internationalisation decisions. He observes that national innovation systems and industrial and technological specialisation of countries change only very gradually, and – especially in newer, rapidly evolving sectors – much slower than the technological needs of firms. In other words, there may be *systemic* inertia. When innovation systems cannot respond to a technological discontinuity, or a radical innovation that has occurred elsewhere, there is a mismatch between what home locations can provide and what firms require, this gives rise to a suboptimal lock-in. Firms are induced to respond to this inertia, but their response is itself conditioned by their own resource endowments and by their degree of embeddedness in the home innovation system. Using Hirschman's terminology, Narula (2003) suggests that firms will choose among three different possible options: exit, voice and loyalty. They may venture abroad and seek to internalise aspects of other countries' innovation systems, thereby utilising an 'exit' strategy. Of course, firms rarely exit completely, preferring often to maintain both domestic and foreign presence simultaneously. There are costs associated with an exit strategy, reflecting the characteristics and constraints of their innovation systems of origin and the costs of integrating into a foreign innovation system, as mentioned earlier. Firms may minimise these costs by importing the technology they need from abroad if a market for it exists, or through a cooperative strategy with a local firm if tacit components of knowledge prevail. Firms could also follow a second alternative. They can use a 'voice' strategy aimed at modifying the home-country innovation system. For instance, establishing a collective R&D facility, or by political lobbying. Firms are inclined towards voice strategies, because it may have lower costs than exit. But voice strategies also have costs, and may not be realistic for SMEs, which have limited resources and political clout. Such firms usually cannot afford an 'exit' strategy either. They will most likely utilise a third alternative, a 'loyalty' strategy, relying instead on institutions to evolve, or seeking to free-ride on the voice strategy of industry collectives, or larger firms.

The discussion above highlights that multinationals will significantly differ according to the characteristics and evolution of their system of origin, to the response they are able to give to constraints and stimuli deriving from it, and to the opportunities they will capture through their contacts with foreign innovations systems. Relative to less internationalised firms, MNFs will be in a position to gain access to a larger variety of stimuli and opportunities generated by the different innovation systems (of origin and destination) in which they are active. They will also have a greater possibility to contribute to the evolution of their own system of origin, and of the foreign systems in which they are active. Their actual impact will depend *inter alia* on the level of economic development of both the home and the host countries, and particularly on the strengths and weaknesses of firms and institutions characterising the national innovation systems of origin and destination.[19] It will also depend on the strengths and weaknesses of other countries in which the MNF is active, whose characteristics can be absorbed and transmitted to each of the systems it connects.

Furthermore, as they increase their degree of internationalisation, multinationals will be able to respond to constraints and stimuli stemming from their own systems of origin and of destination using a wider variety of alternative strategies. Referring back to Hirschman's taxonomy used by Narula, MNFs will have the possibility of spanning from exit, to voice and loyalty in each of the contexts in which they are active. Moreover, they will be able to reinforce voice strategies by using the credible threat of exiting at a lower cost than most local counterparts. The larger the number of innovation systems they are bridging, and the more these systems have technological stimuli and opportunities to offer, the wider the span and quality of assets they can gain access to; and the greater will be the spillovers which will potentially accrue to host economies as well. MNFs will thus differ significantly in terms of the number and quality of economic and innovation systems they connect, and they will deal with heterogeneous firms and institutions in each of the countries in which they do business. From this perspective, the extent to which knowledge advantages will actually accrue to MNFs and to host economies will largely depend on the interactions between heterogeneous agents. Parts II and III of this book will proceed deeper in the analysis of the nature, determinants and effects of this heterogeneity. We shall examine the variety of firms involved in internationalisation processes, diversities in economic and innovative performances across and within multinationals, and the variety of spillover effects they have on host economies.

1.9   CONCLUDING REMARKS

This chapter has provided a general framework for the analysis of the links between innovation and international production. We have suggested that there are a number of ways of looking at these links, the most popular of which is to focus on the globalisation of technology. We have argued that the latter view captures only part of the issue. In fact, innovation has a much more pervasive role in internationalisation processes. On the one hand, it is one of the most important engines of international production. On the other hand, international operations may result into technological opportunities and into the access of new sources of knowledge. Having adopted this broader view of the innovation-internationalisation links, we discussed the increasingly used distinction between asset exploiting and asset seeking international activities. We have provided arguments and evidence to support the increasing importance of the latter, i.e. strategies aiming to augment firms' technological advantages. We have also suggested that the growing recourse to asset seeking strategies, combined with more traditional asset exploiting activities, goes hand in hand with the transition of MNFs towards what we dubbed as a *double network structure*. Focussing on the changing organisation of innovative activities across national borders, we have submitted that multinational firms have growing incentives to expand both their internal networks of subsidiaries and research centres, and their external networks of relationships with local firms and institutions. In fact, the two networks play a crucial and complementary role in the generation and use of knowledge, and hence in determining the evolution of competitive advantages of multinationals. Internal networks are needed to take roots in local contexts, learn about local institutions and knowledge sources, and increase the capacity of firms to explore and use technological opportunities. External networks are the vehicles through which such exploration potentials can be fully utilised to gain access to complementary assets, especially in industries characterised by a high degree of dynamic competition. To the extent that multinationals increase their embeddedness in different local contexts by means of both internal and external networks, they accentuate their natural role as *bridging institutions*: MNFs increasingly connect geographically dispersed innovation systems, being conditioned by, and contributing to, their characteristics and evolution. Using this conceptualisation we are enabled to extend our view to a more general level. In fact, asset seeking strategies can be interpreted as a process through which MNFs, expanding their internal and external networks, are not only able to rely on complementary assets supplied by firms and institutions directly interacting with them. They can also indirectly take advantage of the competencies which their local counterparts are able to draw on by means of their own local and international relationships.

The framework we have developed has two important sets of implications which will be fully discussed in Parts II and III. First, our way of characterising MNFs helps explain the heterogeneity of actors involved in international production. Multinationals will differ according to their recourse to asset seeking activities, and to the extent to which they combine such activities with asset exploiting capacities. Their ability to deploy this combination of strategies will be affected significantly by their internal and external networks. By expanding their internal and external networks differently, and in different locations, they will gain access to largely distinct competitive assets. These sources of diversity account for a large proportion of intra-industry heterogeneity in terms of economic and innovative performances. We shall develop a thorough analysis of the links between intra-industry heterogeneity and internationalisation in Part II of this volume.

Second, the effect of MNFs on the economic systems in which they are active must also take into account intra-industry heterogeneity. To the extent that MNFs are asset seeking, they are interested in gaining access to local sources of knowledge, and will be available to transfer some technology on a reciprocity basis. From this perspective, the actual intensity of spillovers created to the benefit of the host economy, will largely vary according to the characteristics, innovativeness and performances of multinationals. Moreover, the extent to which spillovers materialise will also reflect the characteristics of local firms, some of which may well be themselves multinationals. The analysis of spillovers in the presence of heterogeneous (foreign and domestic) firms will be carried out in Part III of this volume.

2. The double network structure of multinational firms: a review of the evidence

2.1 INTRODUCTION

In Chapter 1 we suggested that traditional asset exploiting strategies increasingly co-exist with asset seeking activities, through which multinationals gain access to knowledge sources in foreign locations. We also argued that this growing importance of knowledge sourcing abroad goes hand in hand with changes in the organisation of innovative activities, towards what we identified as a double network structure. In this chapter we shall review the evidence which can be considered consistent with this evolutionary process. In section 2.2 we draw on the rather scattered evidence concerning the different aspects of the double network structure: the international dispersion of innovative activities, the degree of autonomy of subsidiaries, the extent to which subsidiaries are embedded in host economies and involved in collaborative ventures with local firms, and intra-firm knowledge flows. In section 2.3 we illustrate evidence on the complementarity between internal and external networks. In section 2.4 this complementarity will be examined with reference to the electronics and chemical industries. Section 2.5 concludes.

2.2 EVIDENCE ON THE DOUBLE NETWORK ORGANISATION OF INNOVATIVE ACTIVITIES

As discussed in Chapter 1, to the extent that asset seeking strategies are deployed, MNFs are likely to resort to what we defined as a *double network structure*. Some of the scattered evidence produced in different studies using a variety of methodologies can be considered at least consistent with this idea. First, the extensive literature on international R&D investments can be used to support the view that an increasing number of affiliates are becoming directly involved in innovative activities. Second, a few studies have illustrated the role of autonomy of subsidiaries in knowledge creation and use. This is again a crucial feature in MNFs' double network structure, as autonomy can be expected to enhance creativity and be necessary for interaction with external parties. Third, some evidence also exists concerning affiliates' involvement in external networks of cooperation with local firms and institutions. Fourth and finally, some studies illustrate the extent to which knowledge is being transferred within MNFs, supporting the idea that some degree of internal cohesion of the double network structure is actually achieved.

2.2.1 The International Dispersion of Innovative Activities of MNFs

An important component of the evolution towards the double network structure is the increasing involvement of different units of the MNF in innovative activities. This process implies the international dispersion of knowledge based activities once geographically concentrated at the head-quarter level. It is important to stress that this dispersion of knowledge generation, absorption and use is all the more effective in terms of advantage creation the more it is diffuse and pervasive. In other words, knowledge based competition requires that the largest number of units belonging to the MNF, including those specialised in phases that are distant from research, product and process design and development, participate to this process as a means to expand both asset exploiting and asset seeking potential of the MNF. Hence the evidence concerning the geographic dispersion of MNF R&D and patenting, which is available and will be discussed below, is only the top of a much more massive iceberg, representing the entire volume of MNFs' value added activities which contribute to knowledge creation, absorption and use. Having said this, it remains that offshore R&D and inventive activities are a relevant, quantifiable aspect of this process, which needs to be evaluated. There seems to be a general convergence in the empirical literature on at least three 'stylised facts' concerning the international dispersion of R&D and patenting activity.[20]

1. *R&D is among the least internationalised segments of the MNFs' value chain.* Production, marketing and other functions have moved abroad at a much higher rate. This is generally true for MNFs, even though there are significant differences, across countries, sectors and firms within industries, in the internationalisation of both production and R&D (Pearce 1990; Warrant 1991; Patel and Pavitt 2000; UNCTAD 2005). Even the most internationalised MNFs concentrate at home the largest shares of their more 'strategic' activities, such as R&D and headquarters functions (Benito et al. 2003).

2. *The internationalisation of R&D and patenting activities has grown historically, although patterns vary significantly by area of origin.* One can observe at least four such patterns (Cantwell 1995; Cantwell and Janne 2000; UNCTAD 2005). First, countries such as Switzerland, the UK and the Netherlands, which have historically been home to large MNFs, were long time investors also in R&D and have greatly expanded their offshore innovative activities since World War II. For example, UK multinationals already obtained 27.7 of their patenting from research located abroad in 1920–39, have expanded this share to 41.9 per cent in 1940–68, and maintained much the same share thereafter. A second group of countries (which includes France and Germany) has relatively few large multinationals, and their outward R&D investments and innovative activities abroad have grown more gradually in the last 80 years. Their share of patenting activities has grown from 3–4 per cent in 1920–39 up to 7–8 per cent in 1940–68 reaching 10–13 per cent in the mid-1990s. A third group includes a few major offshore investing countries whose R&D and inventive activities abroad have declined after 1914 and returned to pre-World War I levels only recently. This is the case of Sweden and, most importantly, the US, home of a number of MNFs which have a relatively low proportion of their R&D and patenting activity abroad. US multinationals' share of patenting from foreign research was 7–8 per cent in the decade after World War I, fell below 4 per cent in the two decades before and after World War II, and went back to 7–8 per cent in the mid-1990s (see Cantwell 1995 and Cantwell and Janne 2000 for details). Finally, a fourth group of countries has until very recently played a minor role in the internationalisation of R&D and are now aggressively entering the world scene in this respect. This group includes very different country profiles, most notably Japan and a number of developing countries, especially from Asia. The R&D expenditure of Japanese MNFs abroad rose from 1.9 billion dollars to 3.3 billion in 1995–2002 and its share of total Japanese R&D doubled from 2 per cent to 4 per cent. The internationalisation of R&D by MNFs from developing countries is very recent and the top R&D spenders are still relatively small. However, there is evidence of large R&D investment projects by MNFs originating from China, India and Korea (UNCTAD 2005). Despite these variations across areas and countries of origin of MNFs, the general trend seems to be one of growing internationalisation in R&D and innovative activities. Using SPRU data, Dunning (1994, pp. 73–74) had already noted that the share of US patents of the 727 world's largest firms attributable to research in foreign locations (i.e. outside the home country of the parent company) was on average higher than

10 per cent in the second half of the 1980s. In 7 out of 11 industrialised countries identified as originating foreign direct investments, and most noticeably in the US, there has been an increase in patents attributable to the foreign affiliates of multinational enterprises over the 1969–86 period. Patel (1996) examined patents granted by the US Patent Office to a sample of 569 MNFs over the 1969–90 period, and showed that all firms, except for those originating from Canada and Japan, had expanded the proportion of inventive activities carried out abroad. More recent surveys confirm that MNFs, especially those originating from Europe, are expanding their R&D activities abroad (Edler et al. 2002; von Zedwitz and Gassmann 2002). Firms appear to have increased their R&D spending abroad from 15 per cent of their total R&D budget in 1995 to 22 per cent in 2001 (Roberts 2001). Quite consistently with these findings, UNCTAD (2005) estimated that R&D spending of foreign affiliates in 30 economies, accounted for 99 per cent of global business R&D in 2002. According to these estimates, foreign affiliate R&D expenditures – which largely reflect foreign direct investments in R&D – amounted to 29 billion dollars in 1993 (representing 10 per cent of global business enterprise spending in R&D). By 2002, that spending had more than doubled to 67 billion dollars, or 16 per cent of global business R&D. Surveys undertaken by EIU (2005), based on interviews made to managers of the world's largest R&D spending firms, suggest that the pace of R&D internationalisation may have been accelerating in the most recent years.

3. *There is a high (but evolving) geographic and sectoral concentration of R&D FDIs.* More than half of the 700 world's largest private R&D spenders recorded in the UK DTI scoreboard in 2004, of which at least 98 per cent are MNFs, are concentrated in three industries: electronics hardware, automotive and pharmaceuticals. Based on weighted averages of responses in a questionnaire sent to over 300 of these firms in 2004–05, it is estimated that firms internationalise slightly less than 50 per cent of their R&D in chemical industries, more than 35 per cent in pharmaceuticals, and between 30 and 32 per cent in electronics, information technology and automotive industries (DTI 2004). The geographic concentration of MNF activities in high technology industries is also considerable. As reported by UNCTAD (2001), 71 per cent of all foreign affiliates in biotechnology are concentrated in five countries, as compared with 63 per cent in semiconductors, 50 per cent in consumer electronics, 44 per cent in automotive, and less than 40 per cent in textile and apparel and in food and beverages. Overall, developed countries are by and large the main host locations of foreign R&D activities by US MNFs, as they attract some 84 per cent of total R&D expenditure of

these firms' foreign affiliates (Moris 2005). The largest component of US foreign R&D investments is directed towards the EU, which gathers some 58.8 per cent of total spending. However, the share of R&D expenditure of US foreign affiliates in developing economies has almost doubled since 1994, from 7.6 to 13.5 per cent in 2002. R&D spending located in Asian developing countries as a share of global research expenditures of foreign affiliates of US MNFs has been growing fast, having tripled from 3.4 per cent to 10 per cent in the same period. In a number of (developed and developing) countries, foreign affiliates carry out a remarkable share of the overall R&D expenditure of the host economy in which they are active. In 2003, their share of local R&D exceeded 50 per cent in Ireland, Hungary and Singapore. Overall, according to the survey carried out by UNCTAD (2005) the share of foreign R&D in the business R&D of developed countries has been growing gradually from 11 per cent in 1996 to 16 per cent in 2002. In the developing countries for which data are available, the share of foreign affiliates grew faster than in developed countries, from 2 per cent in 1996 to 18 per cent in 2002.[21] Within developed countries, a few technologically advanced regions, where most R&D tends to concentrate, seem to attract the bulk of offshore innovative activities of MNFs (Mariani 2002; Cantwell and Iammarino 2003; Verspagen and Schoenmakers 2004).

The above evidence cannot be used to support the idea that technology has been fully globalised, as it is still true that most of R&D and patenting activities are concentrated in the MNFs' home countries. As Patel (1996) has shown, only Belgian and Dutch firms appear to have invented new products and processes abroad more than within their home countries, and only 43 out of its 569 sample firms located more than half their technological activities outside their countries of origin. However, we are making a different point here. There appears to be strong evidence, produced *inter alia* by Patel himself, of a significant *increase* of the extent to which innovative activities are being internationalised. Moreover, in spite of the geographic concentration of R&D FDIs, which remains a key feature in the internationalisation of innovation, there seems to be growing involvement of countries and regions which used to play a marginal role in this process. The international dispersion of innovative activities thus involves a greater number of firm units within MNFs and a larger number of countries, but proceeds hand in hand with a selection of regions in which R&D FDIs are attracted. This is the result of both asset exploiting, adaptive activities which follow international production to serve the highest growth markets; and the efforts of firms to increase their competitiveness by gaining access to foreign sources of technological competencies. The latter is in turn guided by a combination of forces. On the one hand, the rising complexity and growing costs of technological development in a number of industries is driving MNFs to search for skills and complementary assets wherever these are available. On the other hand, asset seeking investments flow to centres of excellence in advanced countries, in which access to local knowledge (especially tacit) is facilitated by proximity to centres of technological excellence and related infrastructures; and to newly industrialising countries where abundant low cost talent pools are increasingly available. Overall, the growing geographic dispersion of R&D and innovation is consistent with the view that multinationals are expanding their internal networks of innovative units beyond national boundaries, as a means to exploit prior technological advantages, rationalise value added activities, and gain access to foreign sources of knowledge and skills.

2.2.2   The Interactions of Subsidiaries with Local Contexts

The expansion of MNFs' internal networks of subsidiaries and research labs involved in innovative activities is only part of the story. Multinationals organised as double networks are also characterised by a complementary development of external webs of relationships with other firms and institutions, through which they attempt to gain access to local sources of knowledge. This local networking process is often referred to with the term 'embeddedness'. Even though there is some variety in the conceptualisation of network embeddedness (Dacin et al. 1999), most writings recognise that at least two aspects are involved. The first is the nature and intensity of relationships between MNFs and local counterparts, which may take the form of supply agreements, joint ventures and technical alliances. The second is the degree of mutual adaptation which results of this interdependence (Lane and Lubatkin 1998). It is worth stressing that both patterns of local involvement we have just recalled play a fundamental role in multinational companies' changing organisation of innovative activity. On the one hand, by adapting to local practices, particularly in the field of human resource management, MNFs are able to maintain those norms and rules of conduct that are encoded in the local workers' culture, thus safeguarding their incentive structures and creative environment. This implies that multinational firms can improve the effectiveness of their own innovative activities abroad (Vaccà 1996). On the other hand, through the development of alliances with local firms, subsidiaries can gain access to external innovative abilities, and extract economic value from the application of the knowledge available within the transnational company.

Let us now briefly recall some of the empirical findings along the two research lines we have mentioned.

Adaptation to local practices Rosenzweig and Nohria (1994), using evidence from questionnaires mailed to 1055 firms, have examined human resource management procedures adopted by US affiliates of non-US multinationals. Using this evidence, the authors have found that: (a) human resource management is an area in which work practices tend to resemble those adopted in the host countries, especially regarding timeoff, incentive structure (benefits, bonuses, etc.), gender composition; (b) the higher the incidence of local factors on the history of the subsidiary (pre-existence of a local firm, age of affiliate company, its size and dependence on local input suppliers), the higher the resemblance to local human resource management practices; and (c) resemblance to local practices is also positively influenced by the degree of international experience of the parent company. This reflects a higher capability of the MNF to be flexible and culturally open, thanks to a longer exposure to foreign markets. Rosenzweig and Nohria's results are consistent with the data reported in the study conducted by Warrant (1991, p. 96). In the majority of the cases she examined, managers of decentralised R&D labs abroad are 'regularly' hired locally (53.3 per cent of cases) or are at least 'occasionally' hired on that basis (33.3 per cent). Only in 7.1 per cent of total cases R&D managers were 'never' hired on a local basis. Research findings are less clear-cut with regard to the criteria adopted for training of R&D personnel (it is still rare that training 'never' occurs locally, but in the majority of examined cases training is carried out on a local basis only 'occasionally'). The research carried out by Caligiuri and Stroh (1995) also provides complementary evidence on the potential advantages associated with strategies based on the local adaptation of human resource management practices. Using data from interviews with human resource professionals in 46 MNFs, the authors found that local responsiveness in human resource management generates better performances than strategies based on centralisation and imposition of home country practices (ethnocentric strategies). Andersson et al. (2005) use a broader definition of mutual adaptation, encompassing such aspects as product and process technology, standard operating procedures, and business practice, and address the issue of how control modes affect this aspect of embeddedness. They collected interviews with top managers of 69 Chinese and 89 Finnish subsidiaries of Western owned multinationals (of which 30 per cent originate from Nordic countries, 40 per cent from other EU members, and 20 per cent from the US) in 2000–02. Based on these data, the authors find that the headquarters' use of ex-post evaluation criteria, rather than direct control on ongoing operations, has a positive effect on the subsidiary's propensity to adapt their practices to local contexts. This is consistent with the idea we have discussed in Chapter 1, that co-ordination modes leaving greater decision making power to affiliates (hence greater autonomy) favours the embeddedness of multinationals. In particular, coordination based on knowledge development as a performance evaluation criterion is found to have a higher impact than criteria based on net/operating profit as an indicator of performance. This is not surprising, as the latter criteria emphasise shorter term considerations which cannot easily be made consistent with the effort required in adapting to local business practices.

The recourse to cooperative relationships with local firms   Andersson and Forsgren (1996) have analysed 15 Swedish multinationals and 78 of their affiliates. They found that subsidiaries tend to set up extensive networks of economic relationships (including long term supply contracts) with local suppliers and clients. According to these authors, the frequency and intensity of transactions carried out within such 'external networks' heavily influence the affiliates' behaviour and performances, including innovation. Their study shows that the majority of relationships activated by the examined subsidiaries involves local companies, thus confirming their effort to 'take roots' in the local context. Furthermore, it is rather common (25 per cent of the sample) that the number and relevance of relationships developed with suppliers and clients which are external to the MNF are higher than intra-firm transactions. The most frequent circumstance (45 per cent of the sample) is that in which the number of economic relationships with partners that are external to the MNF is approximately as high as the number of intra-firm transactions. More generic evidence on linkages can be obtained from the Merit-CATI database which recorded some 10,000 Strategic Technology Partnerships (STPs) involving over 3,500 companies in the 1960–98 period (Hagedoorn 2002). Within this context, international STPs have grown considerably in absolute terms, while their share of all STPs oscillated between 60 per cent and 50 per cent over 1960–98 (Hagedoorn 2002). More recently, UNCTAD (2005) reported a doubling of new international technological alliances, from 339 to 602 in 1991–2001, and a growing importance of non-equity forms of cooperation, whose share increased from 78 per cent to over 90 per cent of total agreements. The increasing share of non-equity alliances is consistent with the emerging view that, in an age of rapid technical change and globalisation of markets, MNFs increasingly need to resort to technology partnering as a relatively low cost way of gaining timely and extensive access to knowledge sources across borders (Zanfei 2000; Narula 2003). Given this general trend, one can observe a considerable variation by sector and by geographic area. Technological agreements appear to be most likely in the domain of new materials, pharmaceuticals, biotechnology and information technology, From a geographical perspective, STPs, even more than R&D activities in general, largely involve Triad economies rather than developing economies. Developed country firms participate in 99 per cent of STPs as recorded by the MERIT-CATI dataset (Hagedoorn 2002). The geographical concentration of STP in highly industrialised areas, together with an increasing role of alliances involving US firms might have to do with the fact that the largest investors in R&D are from those areas: firms which are most active in technological collaborations tend to be based in countries where technological accumulation is the highest. Several empirical studies have supported the idea that networks of relationships with local companies, especially suppliers and customers, have a positive effect on performances at the firm level. In particular, a positive correlation has been observed between the intensity of these agreements and subsidiaries' sales growth, market share and profitability as well as competence development (Andersson et al. 2003). There are also indications of a positive relationship between a subsidiary's degree of local embeddedness and its influence on strategic decisions in the MNF, including R&D (Almeida and Kogut 1999; Andersson and Forsgren 2000). The work by Yamin and Otto (2004) is illustrative of this line of research. They use patent citation and co-patenting data to track cross-border knowlege flows for a sample of 20 MNFs in the 'biopharmaceutical' sector. Utilising multiple regression analysis, they find a positive relationship between external knowledge flows (measured by the number of co-assignees as a percentage of all patents) and innovative performances (measured with the number of patents per expenditure in R&D). Their findings confirm the positive impact of external knowledge flow intensity and variety as factors favouring inventive activities in the examined industry.

2.2.3 The Autonomy of Decentralised Innovative Units

As we argued in Chapter 1, a key aspect of the changing organisational pattern of MNFs is the autonomy that decentralised units are actually endowed with. In fact we noticed that some degree of autonomy of subsidiaries can play a crucial role enhancing creativity and innovation within the MNF, as well as facilitating the embeddedness of affiliates in local contexts. Morevover we submitted that as subsidiaries take roots in host economies and develop external networks of relationships with indigenous firms and institutions, they will need further autonomy.

Reviewing the empirical evidence on this important organisational issue implies an incursion into an extensive literature on the management of the multinational subsidiary, which has by now emerged as a distinctive field of investigation (see Young and Tavares 2004). Without pretending to cover all the various streams of this literature, it suffices here to recall: (a) some of the existing evidence on subsidiaries' autonomy in fields that are relevant for technology and innovation; and (b) some of the relevant studies on the actual impact of autonomy on firms' (innovative) performances.

Regarding the former aspect, several studies have long identified R&D and technology choice as one of the areas in which the centralisation of decision making was highest (Young et al. 1985; Van den Bulke and Halsberghe 1984). This was tentatively confirmed by more recent researches which concluded that subsidiaries have greater autonomy in non strategic decisions, and in more operational areas, such as approving finance for minor projects, setting wage rates and domestic marketing (Edwards et al. 2002). However, not all areas of technology management appear to be centralised. Warrant (1991) conducted one of the earliest and most detailed fact-finding studies on the actual degree of decision making in the field of R&D and technology management. Based on questionnaires to managers of some 150 mainly European companies, she showed that a remarkable share of firms in her sample considered autonomy to be either 'high' or 'very high' in a number of circumstances. This is, for instance, the case of decisions on technical alliances (75 per cent of responding firms), but also of decisions concerning the allocation of R&D resources (66 per cent), and research planning (55 per cent). By contrast, autonomy is either 'weak' or 'very weak' when technology transfer decisions are at stake. These data were collected through questionnaires given to headquarter managers. They may thus reflect 'wishful thinking' more than the actual trends in decision taking. However, they signal that managers are making (or willing to make) efforts to reconcile learning and flexibility advantages of autonomy with the need to guarantee a certain degree of knowledge circulation within the MNF.

The study carried out by Florida (1997) on 186 foreign affiliated laboratories of US based manufacturing firms also provides some evidence on these aspects. He highlights that the process of decentralisation of decision making has by now involved firms that were traditionally making recourse to a high centralisation of resources and strategic decisions. In particular, he found that headquarters make relatively few efforts to transfer abroad the management and organisational systems associated with R&D laboratories in the home countries, and that foreign affiliated R&D laboratories possess considerable autonomy in the development and management of their scientific and technical agenda.

There are important sectoral specificities in decision making decentralisation. Criscuolo (2004) examines the organisation of knowledge creation and transfer in 6 of the largest European pharmaceutical corporations. She finds different patterns of centralisation and autonomy even within firms, according to the type of activity carried out by research units. While development activities (from pre-clinical development to registration) are usually centralised and highly geographically concentrated, usually in the home country and in the US, the discovery process is highly decentralised and dispersed on a geographical base. This international division of labour seems to favour access to multiple external knowledge sources, tapping into centres of excellence around the world and/or internal knowledge sources from R&D units within the MNF, as we theorised in Chapter 1. The Glaxo case is particularly illustrative of the high degree of autonomy involved in this process. As recognised by one interviewee, the individual 'centres of excellence of drug discovery' (CEDDs) are conceived 'almost like separate companies, they have their own budget, their own ways of working . . . they are almost in competition, they are evaluated based on the value that the particular CEDD delivers to the business'. While a high autonomy may undermine intra-firm communication and the sharing of knowledge within the organisation, something which requires complex socialisation mechanisms, it is perceived as an effective means of guaranteeing the advantages of specialisation and flexibility in the discovery phase (Criscuolo 2004).

The organisational issues we have just highlighted introduce the second topic we have mentioned earlier, namely the extent to which autonomy affects actual innovation performances. Important insights on this aspect can be drawn from case studies and quantitative analyses conducted on small samples of firms. Ghoshal and Bartlett (1989, p. 370) cited the cases of Unilever, ITT and Philips as MNFs whose subsidiaries are endowed with considerable strategic and operational autonomy. They compared the innovative behaviour of these firms with that of multinationals with highly centralised resources and eventually observed that relatively autonomous subsidiaries created and diffused more innovations but were also comparatively more resistant in adopting innovations created elsewhere.[22] One should incidentally note that this evidence is consistent with our assumption that a trade-off exists between innovation enhancing effects of autonomy, and its likely negative impact on knowledge circulation within MNFs' internal networks (see Chapter 1, section 1.7).

The importance of this trade-off is also reflected in other contributions on the links between autonomy and innovative performance of MNFs. On the one hand, several studies find that subsidiaries in leading-edge industry clusters are more autonomous and have greater international market scope than subsidiaries in other sectors (Pearce 1999; Taggart and Hood 1999; Birkinshaw and Hood 1998). This reflects, *inter alia*, the fact that autonomy would favour relationships with local suppliers and customers, which would in turn generate new knowledge, ideas and opportunities and thereby benefit the entire corporation (Andersson and Forsgren 1996; McEvily and Zaheer 1999; Birkinshaw et al. 2005). Autonomy is further reinforced by local linkages, which influence the behaviour of subsidiaries and partially subtract them from central control (Andersson and Forsgren 1996). Moreover, innovative subsidiaries are found to be more likely to have the necessary bargaining power to negotiate a higher degree of autonomy within the MNF. As we shall see in greater detail in section 2.2.4, this also guarantees that greater knowledge flows accrue to the subsidiary from within the MNF (Mudambi and Navarra 2004). On the other hand, there is evidence of tighter control of subsidiaries in technological areas that are perceived to be too strategically sensitive (Bartlett and Ghoshal 1989; Martinez and Jarillo 1991). Moreover, a number of works suggest that autonomy *per se* is not enough to ensure innovative and cooperative behaviour, and emphasise the importance of other complementary factors, such as: subsidiary's absorptive capacity (Cantwell 1995; Gupta and Govidarajan 2000); externalities and agglomeration economies (Cantwell and Iammarino 2003; Verspagen and Schoenmakers 2004); integration within the MNF (Ghoshal and Bartlett 1995; Hakanson and Nobel 2001).

2.2.4   Intra-firm Communication and Knowledge Transfer

As suggested in Chapter 1, the evolution of MNFs' organisation is strongly influenced by the balance between powerful centripetal and centrifugal forces at work in the process of knowledge generation and use. Coordination mechanisms are designed to govern the balance between these conflicting forces (see Zanfei 2000 for a discussion). As a result of centripetal tensions, reinforced by the use of co-ordination tools, subsidiaries can be expected to participate in the process of transfer and adoption of knowledge within the MNF's internal network. If centrifugal forces prevail, knowledge circulation within the MNF will tend to be inefficient and the cohesion of the internal network will be at risk.

Once again, there is scattered evidence concerning knowledge sharing and on the intensity and effectiveness of knowledge circulation within MNFs. Besides, the perception of the actual functioning of intra-firm circulation of knowledge tends to be biased by the fact that empirical investigations are most often carried out with reference to successful MNFs.

The study conducted by Warrant (1991, pp. 95–96) is one of the first studies providing evidence on the nature and intensity of communication needs within the MNF and of information exchanges that are *actually occurring* (in terms of frequency of messages being exchanged). She showed that knowledge most frequently flowed between decentralised R&D units and central R&D labs, whereas contacts were much less frequent between R&D labs, on the one hand, and marketing and manufacturing departments on the other hand. At the same time, the managers interviewed highlighted that *communication needs* were highest across functional levels.

Particularly, marketing managers and production managers would *need* to communicate with R&D managers, even though they do not actually happen to do so.

A survey carried out by Pearce (1990), based on a sample of 82 firms, examines more closely the 'quality' of knowledge flows within MNFs. He found that in only 25 per cent of considered cases 'promising' knowledge developed by subsidiaries or decentralised R&D labs were actually transferred to the central labs. He recorded a 'slightly higher' tendency to transfer technology the other way around, from central labs towards decentralised centres.

The research carried out by Fors (1997) also sheds some light on the asymmetries of information flows occurring between the centre and the periphery of MNFs, and reaches even stronger conclusions. He uses data of a survey covering a sample of 121 Swedish multinational firms during the 1965–90 period. His findings indicate that firms' R&D undertaken in the home country is actually transferred and used as an input in both the home and foreign plants of the MNF. By contrast, technology stemming from R&D in foreign affiliates does not appear to be a relevant input for home plants. When the analysis is undertaken separately for the two time periods 1965–74 and 1974–90, the share of the gains realised in the foreign plants appears to be increasing, although this trend is not statistically significant.

A recent study by Singh (2004) further highlights the role of intra-firm knowledge flows. Using data on USPTO patent citations of headquarters and foreign affiliates of multinationals from different countries in 1986–95, he runs weighted logit regressions to explain the likelihood that a patent obtained by the Headquarters (H) is cited by a subsidiary (S) and vice versa. He obtains that flows from centre to periphery are, on average, approximately as likely as the other way around. Going into greater details, the likelihood that H transfer more knowledge to subsidiaries is significantly higher in the case of Germany, Japan and France, while the opposite applies in the cases of US, Canada and UK. The picture he provides thus partially contrasts with the one offered by Fors who found that affiliates draw much more knowledge from the headquarters than the other way around. Singh's results are even more consistent than Fors's with our view of the double network structure.

Several works have also focused on factors conducive to increases in knowledge flows within MNFs. A study by Buckley et al. (2003) focuses on the mechanisms enabling the firm to act 'as a social entity', a factor which in their view would facilitate knowledge sharing and transfer within the MNF. They define 'social knowledge' as 'understanding the behaviour of others', as distinguished from the more widely used notions of tacit and explicit knowledge. Examining case studies of technology transfer to and from subsidiaries of four Western multinationals in China, they find that firms which recognise the importance of this notion, and organise co-ordination mechanisms accordingly, achieve a speedier and more effective knowledge transfer than firms that do not.

Papanastassiou and Pearce (1997) pay attention to those characteristics of foreign subsidiaries which appear to contribute to the generation and transmission of knowledge within the firm. These authors have based their analysis on questionnaires mailed to 560 among the world's largest firms classified by Fortune. They identify two 'models' of behaviour which involve more intensive knowledge flows within the MNF. The first is represented by subsidiaries with limited or no local R&D, that specialise in manufacturing activities for the local market, using consolidated technology. Contrary to Vernon's hypothesis, however, this type of subsidiary does not appear to make use only, nor primarily, of technology coming from the home country. In order to effectively carry out this more creative role, technology needs to be conceived as 'a network phenomenon', so that different local sources of knowledge can be utilised according to the host market characteristics and demands. The second model identified by the authors is the most frequent in their analysis. That is subsidiaries that manufacture goods with consolidated technology, but sell them outside the market in which they are based. These firms not only uses technology transferred from the home country labs but also from other countries' R&D facilities. Local R&D, and incremental improvements carried out at the factory level continue to play an important role. The empirical evidence collected by the authors confirms that MNFs' innovative activities are more and more the result of an intensive interchange of technology between different units connected through an internal network of knowledge circulation. It also highlights the key role played by local knowledge inputs, generated both by R&D labs active close to the market, and by improvement activities that are not institutionalised in any research plant. These incremental activities take place within the factory, but also require an effort to acquire relevant information on the nature and characteristics of local demand. Therefore, important learning processes also occur thanks to the abilities and sensitivity of manufacturing and marketing employees, who are in a better position to perceive the challenges and opportunities stemming from the specific context where the firm is active.

In a more recent study of 92 subsidiaries of multinationals active in Greece, Manolopoulos et al. (2005) adopt a similar methodology to highlight that different types of subsidiaries play a distinctive role in the generation and transfer of knowledge. Similarly to previous studies, they show that larger and innovative subsidiaries have granted access to wider sources of internally generated knowledge. This finding is consistent with the results of an extensive research by Mudambi and Navarra (2004). Using data on patent citations of 701 UK subsidiaries of non-UK MNFs active in high technology industries, the authors illustrate knowledge flows within firms and from subsidiaries to and from local firms. They find that multinationals with significant access to local sources of knowledge that are vital to the MNF, increase their bargaining power, are most likely to obtain knowledge creation mandates, and have access to relevant knowledge flows from other units, including the parent company, on a reciprocity basis. There thus seems to exist a continuous feed-back between knowledge mandates, competence accumulation, bargaining power and access to further knowledge from within the firm.

The studies we have briefly reviewed are revealing of the complexity of communication problems with MNFs, especially when new knowledge transfers are at stake. Results are consistent with the widely shared perception that technology transfer and utilisation within MNFs is difficult and subject to a number of constraints. The reviewed analyses do not allow one to draw any conclusive statement on the evolution of intra-MNF knowledge exchanges over time. However they are largely consistent with the idea, submitted in Chapter 1, that knowledge circulation is not automatic, and innovative coordination mechanisms are required to govern centrifugal effects associated with the evolution of MNFs towards a double network structure.

2.3   HOW COMPLEMENTARY ARE INTERNAL AND EXTERNAL NETWORKS?

We argued in Chapter 1 (section 1.6) that the evolution towards a double network structure implies some degree of complementarity between internal and external networks. In fact, by expanding their internal web of subsidiaries involved in specialised innovative activities, multinationals increase their ability to exploit their own assets and to explore technological opportunities available in foreign contexts. The timely utilisation of these opportunities, as well as the access to local complementary assets may require the development of linkages with local firms and institutions. Some of these linkages take the form of mergers and acquisitions, through which specialised assets are fully internalised, thus leading to a further expansion of the internal network. Other links are collaborative in nature, and are aimed to ensure a wider, more timely and reversible access to external capabilities, especially in markets characterised by a high level of dynamic competition and by strong appropriability regimes (Teece 1992). It is the latter type of linkages which we identify with the term external networks.

In Chapter 1 we have suggested that different aspects of internal networks account for distinct linkage creation strategies, ranging from mergers and acquisitions to collaborative ventures. One may identify two broad categories of internal networking strategies each having a distinctive impact on external linkages.[23] On the one hand we stress the role of the presence and experience of multinational firms in specific locations and, on the other hand, we focus on the geographical diversification of the multinational network.

2.3.1   Location-specific Networks and External Linkages

The first way of characterising internal networks consists in emphasising the extent and duration of presence in each of a MNF's foreign locations. We may dub this type of internal network *location specific* as it indicates how a firm is rooted in a given foreign country or region. This type of internal network typically favours the accumulation of knowledge concerning the structural and behavioural characteristics of locations in which firms are active. The more firms are characterised by this type of internal network, the greater their experience of local contexts.[24] On the one hand, MNFs' acquaintance with local user needs increases, and their ability to tap into local sources of application specific knowledge is improved. As a consequence, the effectiveness and likelihood of linkages with local firms will increase (Cantwell 1995; Vaccà and Zanfei 1995). This line of argument is consistent with a more general view of the firm as a knowledge based institution, that constructs capabilities through the interaction between internal and external learning processes (Richardson 1972; Teece 1986; Coriat and Dosi 1998). From this perspective, internal networking can be seen as conducive to the accumulation of absorptive capacity that favours external knowledge sourcing, which could be obtained either by means of M&As or through collaborations.

On the other hand, uncertainty associated to operating in local markets is also reduced. This aspect is emphasised by the market entry literature (Gomes-Casseres 1989; Hennart and Larimo 1998; Nisbet et al. 2003), which adopts a dynamic transaction cost view and focuses on the mode of access to external assets in foreign contexts. The idea here is that an extensive and long term presence in a given region or country will increase a firm's ability to evaluate the challenges and opportunities which may derive from operating in that context. This will reduce the risks associated to commitment intensive linkages (i.e. the creation of Wholly Owned Subsidiaries (WOS) by means of greenfield investments or mergers and acquisitions), and diminish the relative advantages of strategic alliances.

Combining the different streams of literature we have just recalled, it thus turns out that what we called location specific internal network will not only favour asset seeking linkage creation (as suggested in the literature adopting a knowledge based view of the firm); but will also enhance commitment intensive linkages (as argued by dynamic transaction costs literature).

A few empirical studies obtain unambiguous evidence of the positive relationship between this type of internal networking strategies and the creation of WOS (vs. joint venturing). Gomez-Casseres (1989) uses a binomial logit to test the likelihood of setting up WOS (vs. joint venturing) by 187 US MNFs over the 1975–85 period. He draws information on individual subsidiaries and on their MNF parents from Harvard's Multinational Enterprise Project. His proxy of 'familiarity with host country' is an index (from 0 to 16) based on how often the sample MNFs entered one country before another during 1900–76. It turns out to positively (negatively) impact on WOS (joint venturing) as he expects. Davidson and McFetridge (1984) test a binomial logit model for the probability of transferring technology through WOS (vs. licensing) by 32 US based MNFs during the 1945–78 period. Their measure of internal networking is much simpler than Gomez-Casseres': they use a dummy equal to one if there is at least one affiliate in the recipient country in the year prior to new operation, and find that it has a negative impact on licences (vs. WOS). Mutinelli and Piscitello (1998), examining a sample of operations undertaken by Italian firms in mining and manufacturing industries over 1986–93, utilise a similar dummy for country specific experience, together with a further dummy indicating whether the earlier operations by the parent company are in 'culturally similar' countries. For this purpose they adapt a classification of countries proposed *inter alia* by Ronen and Shenkar (1985), and by Gatignon and Anderson (1988). From their binomial logit model both dummies positively affect WOS (vs. joint venturing), although the impact of country experience dummies is not significant for operations directed towards North America.

2.3.2 Geo-dispersed Networks and External Linkages

The second type of internal network we may identify can be dubbed as *geo-dispersed*. The focus in this case is on the geographic diversification of firms' activities. What matters from this viewpoint is how widespread the multinational network is, and not so much how big and/or embedded the nodes of the network are. This concept has been operationalised by either measuring the width of multinational firms' internal networks of affiliates (overall number of affiliates, number of countries reached with some activity); or the relative weight of foreign production, sales and/or R&D and patenting of firms (Dunning 1996; Ietto-Gillies 1998; UNCTAD 1999). Many authors integrate their analysis of the geographic dispersion of firms' activities with the consideration of how significant multinational presence is in given markets, sometimes with considerable analytical details (Cantwell and Iammarino 2003; Ietto-Gillies 2002). However, the geographic dispersion of multinational activities may *per se* be a source of advantages, even when knowledge of specific markets is not so high. The advantages deriving from the extension and geographic spread of activities relate to the possibility of exploring and selecting among a wide range of knowledge sources and of technological opportunities, thus establishing a spatially (and sectorally) diffuse system for the creation of new competencies (Dunning 1998; Cantwell and Piscitello 2000; Zander 1999; Patel and Vega 1999). Collaborative agreements, being less commitment intensive than joint ventures, and even less so as compared with M&As, are by and large a more flexible and reversible means of gaining access to heterogeneous and dispersed external assets and opportunities. See Chapter 4 for a more extensive discussion of advantages related to the geographic spread of multinational activities.

While the impact of multinational presence in specific markets on linkage creation has been often explicitly addressed in empirical analyses (cf. section 2.3.1 above), the effects of what we identified as geo-dispersed internal networking were seldom considered. Most of the empirical literature does not account for the multifaceted nature of internal networks (and of related multinational experience) and treats them as a unified concept. This helps explain some ambiguity in the empirical results when the relationships between some measures of internal networking and linkage creation are explored. For instance, Kogut and Singh (1988), using a multinomial logit model on 228 foreign investments in the US, find that previous entry had a negative impact on subsequent joint venturing, as predicted by market entry literature, but this impact was not significant. Gatignon and Anderson (1988) also use a multinomial logit based on data from the Harvard Project and focus on entry modes in 87 countries between 1960 and 1975. The impact of multinational experience turned out to be positive not only for WOS, but also for lower control modes (minority partnerships, balanced partnerships and dominant partnerships), even though the impact is not statistically significant in the latter group of strategies. Furthermore, one should mention that their measure of international networking is very broad (number of foreign entries the MNC has made to date), and does not capture firms' actual knowledge of specific markets. Hennart and Larimo (1998) use a binomial logit model to examine the determinants of Finnish and Japanese entry in the US. In their model, internal networking is proxied by the number of years of presence of the parent in the host country (the US), without controlling for the extent and geographic dispersion of their overall internal network. They obtained a negative, but non-significant, impact on JV (vs. WOS). While the sign for the Finnish firms of their sample was negative (and significant), as they expected, experience had a positive (albeit non-significant) impact for Japanese parents.

The studies we have just reviewed do not disentangle measures of what we identified as location specific and geo-dispersed networking, and are thus unable to capture their differential impact.

Other empirical contributions explicitly find some positive impact of internal networking strategies and collaborative ventures. This is the case of Dunning (1993 Chapters 4, 6 and 8) for US multinational presence in Europe, Sachwald (1998) for international operations of Japanese firms in the automobile industry in the 1980s, Andersson and Forsgren (1996) for Swedish multinational enterprises in the early 1990s, and McAleese and McDonald (1978) for multinationals in Ireland. These studies do not generally distinguish between cooperative ventures and quasi-market transactions, such as licenses. Moreover, the works we have just mentioned do not test the impact of internal networking using multivariate techniques with reference to large samples of firms. Finally, similar to the studies carried out in the market entry tradition which we cited earlier in this section, they never explicitly control for the extent and geographic spread the examined MNFs' international presence. However, they appear to offer rather systematic evidence that at least some aspects of internal networking may have a positive impact on linkage creation, with reference to a wide variety of sectors and countries of origin and destination of FDIs.

To examine the relationship between internal networking and linkage creation some distinctions thus need to be introduced in order to disentangle the impact of location specific factors from the effects of firms' geographic dispersion.

2.4 INTERNAL AND EXTERNAL NETWORKS IN ELECTRONICS AND CHEMICAL INDUSTRIES

In the previous section we have distinguished between two types of internal networks, we have discussed their likely impact on MNFs' external networking and reviewed some of the existing empirical evidence on this issue. One way to summarise the hypotheses we have discussed is to highlight that *location-specific internal networks*, characterised by an extensive and lengthy presence in a given foreign market, are mainly associated with the ability to utilise knowledge for the solution of context-specific problems. The higher this ability, the greater the opportunities for a firm to enter into linkages with external parties which need to solve such problems. By the same token, this type of internal network, favouring firms' acquaintance with local companies, will reduce the risks associated with commitment intensive linkages. *Geo-dispersed internal networks*, characterised by the number and variety of foreign markets in which MNFs set up their subsidiaries, can be associated with the ability to absorb and select ideas and knowledge assets stemming from heterogeneous sources, and to exploit them on a broader scale.[25] Given the dispersion and variety of opportunities and firms involved in these asset seeking and knowledge augmenting activities, non-equity collaborative ventures tend to be preferred to commitment intensive linkages.

Castellani and Zanfei (2001) have applied a similar framework to analyse the complementarities between different types of internal and external networks in the electronics and chemical industries. See also Castellani and Zanfei (2004) for a more detailed analysis of complementarities between internal and external networks in the specific case in the electronics industry. We here provide a synthetic review of the former study to illustrate how the characteristics of internal networks, in interaction with country and sector-specific factors, may affect firms' decisions to develop different linkage strategies.

2.4.1   Data-Sources and Variable Description

The empirical investigation we refer to utilises a sample composed by all the European, North American, and Japanese manufacturing firms operating in the electronics and chemical sectors listed by *Fortune* 500 (1990 classification). A total of 94 companies were considered.[26] See Table 2.1 for more details on the distribution of the sample firms by sector and area of origin.

Data on international operations of these firms in 1993–97 were drawn from the *ARGO* (Agreements, Restructuring and Growth Operations) database, which uses information from *Predicasts F&S Index* and *IAC-Prompt*.[27] The available information was organised from this source with reference to international ventures by firm, country of origin and destination, type and technological content of operations. We then counted the number of dyadic relationships between each of our sample firms and other firms and institutions from countries other than the home country, over the 1993–97 period. For operations involving more than two partners we counted each single relation between our sample firms and foreign firms.[28]

We complemented these data with the overall number of affiliates, their age, sales and number of employees, as recorded in D&B's *Who Owns Whom*, 1998 edition. All these data were organised by firm and destination country

Table 2.1   Electronics and chemical industries in developed countries: number, size and R&D intensity of sample firms by sector and area of origin

| Sector | No. sample firms | | | | Avg. Sales per firm 1992 (US$ million) | | | | R&D/Sales, 1992 | | | |
| | Area of origin | | | | Area of origin | | | | Area of origin (%) | | | |
	Japan	North America	Europe	Total	Japan	North America	Europe	Total	Japan	North America	Europe	Total
Industrial Chemical	1	2	6	9	9.471	28.090	20.789	21.154	5.2	4.6	5.6	5.3
Petrochemical	3	8	7	18	16.348	38.152	42.400	36.170	0.8	0.6	1.1	0.8
Pharmaceutical		4	5	9		10.611	13.459	12.193		9.1	9.2	9.2
Other Chemical	1	2	1	4	13.787	21.109	12.623	17.157	n.a.	3.0	n.a.	2.3
Total Chemicals	**5**	**16**	**19**	**40**	**14.461**	**27.879**	**26.392**	**25.495**	**1.3**	**2.2**	**3.3**	**2.7**
Computers	5	11	2	18	17.012	12.373	6.121	12.967	7.3	8.3	7.1	7.8
Tlc equipment		4	5	9		24.616	11.246	17.188		5.8	7.6	6.5
Semiconductor	1	3		4	3.546	5.597		5.085	5.1	9.1		8.4
Consumer Electronics	5	1	3	9	28.809	1.271	17.851	22.096	5.5	4.3	5.4	5.5
Other Electronics	5	6	3	14	7.984	17.832	30.702	17.073	7.2	4.1	8.9	6.5
Total Electronics	**16**	**25**	**13**	**54**	**17.036**	**14.385**	**16.471**	**15.673**	**6.3**	**6.4**	**7.6**	**6.7**
Total	**21**	**41**	**32**	**94**	**16.422**	**19.651**	**22.362**	**19.852**	**5.2**	**4.0**	**4.5**	**4.4**

Source: Adapted from Castellani and Zanfei (2001)

to obtain different measures of internal networking strategies. Tables 2.2 and 2.3 illustrate the degree of internationalisation of our sample firms in 55 destination countries, in terms of both internal and external networking.

Negative binomial regressions were run separately for the two macro-sectors of electronics and chemical firms, in order to capture the interactions between internal networking factors and industry specificities, which we expected to be relevant. Different explanatory variables were used to identify *location specific* and *geo-dispersed* internal networking strategies, as factors affecting linkage creation (see Table 2.4).

Measures of location specific internal networks: First, we identified $SUBS92_{ik}$ as the number of subsidiaries of the sample firms (i) in each of the 55 countries (k) at the beginning of the period (1992) This was considered as a proxy of the extension of MNFs' multinational web in a given country. Second, the age of affiliates ($SUBSAGE_{ik}$), measured by the average number of years since the establishment of a firm's subsidiaries in a given country in 1992, was utilised as a measure of experience accumulated by the MNF in the country over time. Third, the relative size of affiliates, measured by the ratio between employees of affiliates in country k and total employees of the MNF abroad (EMP_INT_{ik}), was introduced

Table 2.2   *Internal network of MNFs in the electronics and chemical industries in 1992, by sector and area of origin*

Sector	No. foreign subsidiaries, avg. per firm					
	Japan	North America	Area of origin			Total
			Total	Intra EU	Extra EU	
Industrial Chemical	29	78	152	43	110	122
Petrochemical	14	45	146	33	113	79
Pharmaceutical		72	114	37	77	95
Other Chemical	23	71	95	18	77	65
Total Chemicals	**19**	**59**	**137**	**36**	**101**	**91**
Computers	88	50	52	17	36	60
Tlc equipment		40	85	26	59	65
Semiconductor	39	27				30
Consumer Electronics	83	5	153	55	98	97
Other Electronics	50	60	332	74	258	115
Total Electronics	**71**	**46**	**152**	**42**	**110**	**79**
Total	**59**	**51**	**143**	**39**	**105**	**84**

Source: Adapted from Castellani and Zanfei (2001)

Table 2.3 External networks of MNEs in the electronics and chemical industries, by sector and area of origin, 1993–1997 (total number of operations)

	Joint ventures — Area of origin						Strategic alliances — Area of origin						Acquisitions and mergers — Area of origin					
	Japan	North America	Europe Total	Europe Intra EU	Europe Extra EU	Total	Japan	North America	Europe Total	Europe Intra EU	Europe Extra EU	Total	Japan	North America	Europe Total	Europe Intra EU	Europe Extra EU	Total
Industrial Chemical	21	84	265	38	227	370	10	45	185	44	141	240	1	39	167	79	88	207
Petrochemical	30	219	260	53	207	509	19	250	410	134	276	679	3	68	117	42	75	188
Pharmaceutical		23	125	18	107	148		48	250	57	193	298		28	112	36	76	140
Other Chemical	9	18	19	1	18	46	2	4	3		3	9	17	19	11	2	9	47
Total Chemicals	**60**	**344**	**669**	**110**	**559**	**1073**	**31**	**347**	**848**	**235**	**613**	**1226**	**21**	**154**	**407**	**159**	**248**	**582**
Computers	103	142	34	5	29	279	290	385	57	5	52	732	26	34	4		4	64
Tlc equipment		174	131	38	93	305		295	294	86	208	589		38	33	13	20	71
Semiconductor	2	31				33	5	112				117	1	8				9
Consumer Electronics	152	1	92	42	50	245	280	2	232	47	185	514	29		64	29	35	93
Other Electronics	67	55	237	53	184	359	129	43	287	77	210	459	15	21	84	34	50	120
Total Electronics	**324**	**403**	**494**	**138**	**356**	**1221**	**704**	**837**	**870**	**215**	**655**	**2411**	**71**	**101**	**185**	**76**	**109**	**357**
Total	**384**	**747**	**1163**	**248**	**915**	**2294**	**735**	**1184**	**1718**	**450**	**1268**	**3637**	**92**	**255**	**592**	**235**	**357**	**939**

Source: Adapted from Castellani and Zanfei (2001)

Table 2.4   Internal and external networks in the electronics and chemical industries: variables and data sources

Variable name	Description	Source
DEPENDENT VARIABLES		
JV_{ik}	Number of joint ventures of firm i with partners of country k in 1993–97	ARGO
SA_{ik}	Number of international strategic alliances and cross-licensing operations of firm i in country k in 1993–97	ARGO
AM_{ik}	Number of acquisitions of and merger with firms from country k operated by firm i 1993–97	ARGO
SAT_{ik}	Number of strategic alliances with prevailing technological content of firm i with partners of country k in 1993–97	ARGO
EXPLANATORY VARIABLES		
Measures of MNF experience		
$SUBS92_{ik}$	Number of foreign subsidiaries of firm i in country k in 1992	Dun & Bradstreet
$SUBSAGE_{ik}$	Average age of subsidiaries of firm i in country k in 1992	Dun & Bradstreet
EMP_INT_{ik}	Employment intensity of subsidiaries of firm i in country k, expressed as ratio of local employment on total employees in foreign affiliates	Dun & Bradstreet
$MNFSPREAD_i$	Number of foreign countries where firm i had at least one subsidiary in 1992	Dun & Bradstreet
$MNFINDEX_i$	Average of the ratios: sales of foreign subsidiaries to sales of all subs; employment in foreign subsidiaries to total employment	Dun & Bradstreet
OTHER CONTROL INDEPENDENT VARIABLES		
Company variables		
RD_INT_i	R&D intensity (R&D/Sales) of firm i	Fortune
SAL_i	Sales of firm i, 1992 (US $ billions)	Fortune
Recipient country variables		
$HUMAN85_k$	Average schooling years in 1985 in the total population over 25 (divided by 100)	Barro and Lee (1993)
$PATGDP_k$	US Patent application from country k as a share of GDP	World Development Indicators

Table 2.4 (continued)

Variable name	Description	Source
OTHER CONTROL INDEPENDENT VARIABLES		
SUBSK_I$_k$	Number of subsidiaries in country k of sample firms different from i	ARGO
GDP$_k$	Real GDP per capita in country k, 1992 (US\$ millions)	Penn World Tables Mark 5.6
POP$_k$	Total population of country k, 1992 (millions of inhabitants)	Penn World Tables Mark 5.6
GGDP$_k$	Annual Growth Rate of per capita GDP of country k, 1980–84	Penn World Tables Mark 5.6
VA$_k$	Value Added in Electrical Machinery (ISIC 383) (Chemicals (ISIC 26) in country k as a share of Value Added in Manufacturing (ISIC 300) in the same country, 1992 (current US\$))	UNIDO Industrial Statistics
OWTI$_k$	Own-import weighted tariff rates on intermediate inputs and capital goods	Barro-Lee (1993)
Relation-specific country variables		
WAGELE$_{hk}$	Relative electronics wage differentials: average wages in electronics (chemicals) paid in the host country as a share of average wages in electronics (chemicals) paid in the home country (h) of firm i	UNIDO Industrial Statistics
DISTANCE$_{hk}$	Takes value 1 if the host country k is in the same geographic region of the home country of firm i; 2 if it is in region which is bordering to the home region; 3 if it is not bordering.	Davidson and McFetridge (1984) use the same criteria

Source: Adapted from Castellani and Zanfei (2001)

as a measure of how 'thick' the company's presence is in a given country as compared with its overall international network.[29]

Measures of geo-dispersed internal networking: One measure of companies' exposure to foreign markets is the number of countries in which they had at least one affiliate in 1994 (MNFSPREAD$_j$).[30] Another indicator is the one we named MNFINDEX$_i$, that is the average of international employees and international sales (as a proportion of total employees and total sale).[31] We consider this the global level equivalent of our EMP_INT$_{ik}$. The transnationality index thus identifies how 'thick' multinational presence is all over the world.

These measures of the extent and characteristics of the internal network have been used as explanatory variables of the external linkages established by the sample firms. The dependent variable is a count of the number of linkages created by each firm in each of the 55 destination countries over the 1993–97 period. Given the nature of the dependent variable, separate negative binomial regressions have been run for different modes of organising linkages: Acquisitions & Mergers (AM), Joint ventures (JV), Strategic Alliances (SA). In the case of SAs we were able to separate the aggregate of alliances with prevailing technological content (SAT), and ran regressions using this as a dependent variable.

Company and country level control variables were utilised in all regressions (see Table 2.4).

2.4.2 A Summary of Results

The main findings are summarised in Table 2.5 (see Castellani and Zanfei 2001, for details). The comparison between the two sets of regressions highlights significant differences and a few similarities. The main similarity concerns the positive and significant impact of what we called *location specific* internal networking as a determinant of AMs in both industries. It thus appears that this type of networking is associated with a high degree of

Table 2.5   *Internal and external networks in the electronics and chemical industries: summary of results from econometric tests (negative binomial regressions)*

Dependent variables	Electronics				Chemicals			
	AM	JV	SA	SAT	AM	JV	SA	SAT
Measures of internal network								
SUBS92					++			
SUBSAGE	++							
EMP_INT	++	++			+			
MNFSPREAD			++	++				
MNFINDEX			++					+

Note: Each regression has been run using company and country control, as detailed in Table 2.4

Key:
++ positive and significant at 95 per cent confidence or higher
+ positive and significant at 90 per cent confidence

Source: Adapted from Castellani and Zanfei (2001)

'commitment' to local markets and a high degree of 'control' of MNFs over foreign counterparts. This confirms the interpretation we suggested in section 2.4 combining a competence based view of the firm and a dynamic transaction cost approach. In fact, following the former view, an extensive and lengthy presence in a given country is a factor facilitating mutual acquaintance between multinationals and local firms. As a result, the effectiveness and likelihood of linkages between multinationals and local firms will also increase. Following the latter view, which we have dubbed 'dynamic transaction cost view', we can also explain the choice of organisational modes adopted. The extent and duration of multinational presence, by reducing (external) uncertainty in local markets, favour the adoption of commitment intensive linkages. This will lower the cost and risk of, and increase the expected payoff of, foreign market penetration strategies which require high, irreversible fixed costs, such as mergers and acquisitions.

An additional consideration which helps explain the positive impact of location-specific networking on AMs in the chemical macrosector is related to the particularly large firm size and to the high levels of fixed costs in this industry (Aftalion 1989, Lane 1993). This could be a powerful factor in preventing firms from creating new linkages, unless there is low uncertainty concerning the market and, more generally, about the local context. Besides, the long and painful restructuring that the chemical and petrochemical industries have undergone in the 1980s and 1990s has given a significant impulse for mergers and acquisitions (Arora and Gambardella 1998), and has determined the downsizing of large multinational firms, particularly the ones with excess capacity (e.g. with too many plants in a single country with shrinking demand).

Turning to electronics, it is quite interesting to observe that location-specific networking has a positive and significant impact also on joint ventures, i.e. a strategy associated with intermediate levels of commitment between AMs and SAs. Once again, structural and behavioural characteristics of the examined industry appear to influence our results: an extensive and lengthy presence in a given country can be a fundamental vehicle to the solution of application specific problems emerging in that country, and will generally favour user–producer interactions which play a fundamental role in the electronics industry (Steinmueller 1992; Ernst 1997, 2005). User–producer interactions are becoming more and more relevant in chemical industries (particularly industrial chemicals and in pharmaceuticals) as highlighted in recent studies (Arora and Gambardella 1998; Criscuolo 2004); however, one may presume that this factor is not yet as relevant in this sector as it is in electronics.

A remarkable difference that emerges from our comparative analysis is the quite different role played by geo-dispersed internal networking as a factor favouring linkage creation in the two industries. The results are quite neat in the case of electronics: this kind of internal networking appears to have a positive and significant impact on non-equity, strategic collaborations, and not on hierarchical-control modes of organising linkages (AMs in particular). This is even more apparent when we focus on non-equity technical alliances (SAT). A possible explanation is that an extensive and effective global network of affiliates will provide firms with a wide variety of market and technological opportunities stemming from different countries. In fact, on the one hand, an extensive network of subsidiaries all over the world can enable an MNF to gain access to a variety of technical alliances as a means of searching for, and capturing, new ideas and economically valuable knowledge (Cantwell 1995; Zanfei 2000). On the other hand, by having access to a large number and variety of foreign markets, firms are able to spread the fixed costs associated with technology development over larger volumes of sales (Becattini and Rullani 1993). In other words, the availability of a geo-dispersed network of subsidiaries increases the opportunity to enter 'exploratory operations', and augments the payoff that can be expected from technical alliances in particular.[32]

Quite different from the patterns examined in the electronics industry, geo-dispersed networking appears to have a limited impact on linkages in the chemical industry. In fact, some subsectors of the chemical industries, such as industrial chemicals and petrochemical industries, have been strongly influenced by the development of specialised suppliers of chemical engineering services. Moreover, they have been involved in a number of collaborative ventures for the acquisition of 'standardised' process technology and for the setting up and upgrading of production plants (Lane 1993; Arora and Gambardella 1998). The technologies being transferred are by and large a 'commodity'. This might help explain why the availability of extensive networks of affiliates on a global scale does not appear to be a fundamental asset in linkage creation: supply agreements, which represent an important share of SAs in the examined industry, do not seem to require that the buyer has absorptive capacity nor that it is able to explore technological or market opportunities. In other words, having a geographically dispersed internal network is not so useful under these circumstances, as the importance of worldwide asset seeking is less important in these industries.

2.5   CONCLUDING REMARKS

In this chapter we reviewed the empirical evidence which we found to be consistent with our view of the MNF as a double network of internal and external units involved in the generation, adoption and diffusion of innovation. This has required an incursion into different streams of empirical literature which are most often kept separate. The first stream of empirical literature refers to the international dispersion of innovative activities and to offshore R&D location decisions. While data are not easy to collect in this area, and are hard to compare, there is rather clear evidence that foreign R&D activities of multinationals are growing and represent a remarkable and increasing share of national and regional research in a number of host locations. This is the evidence most commonly considered when talking about the globalisation of technology. However, it is also the least informative, if considered separately from other data concerning how foreign R&D facilities are used, and how they combine with external sources of knowledge.

The second strand of empirical research refers to the role of MNFs in strategic technology partnerships, which complement FDIs in the exploitation and exploration of innovative opportunities. There is rather extensive evidence, collected over a long time span, that illustrates a high and growing number of international technological alliances, with an increasingly dominant role of non-equity agreements. This is consistent with the emerging view of MNFs as institutions whose boundaries are fuzzy: they generally have higher absorptive capacity than non-multinational firms to gain access to external sources of knowledge, and use external linkages to reinforce their asset exploiting and asset seeking strategies.

The third area of empirical research explored in this chapter concerns the role of autonomy of units belonging to the internal network of MNFs. A rather sound result of empirical research in this area is that the most autonomous subsidiaries also tend to be the most embedded in local contexts and the most capable of gaining access to valuable knowledge. However, while autonomy is quite likely to guarantee that subsidiaries get rooted in local contexts (and cumulative effects are at work here: the higher the embeddeness, the greater the autonomy), autonomous units are not necessarily able to effectively use, and transfer, the available knowledge.

The findings on the role of autonomy thus call for an analysis of a fourth field of empirical research, that concerns cohesion mechanisms and the role they play in the creation, adoption and circulation of knowledge within the MNF. Local embeddedness of internal units, as well as their exposure to external knowledge assets, must be combined with investments at the subsidiary level, as a source of absorptive capacity. At the corporate level, costly efforts are also necessary, to set up effective integration based on shared values, objectives and ex-post control mechanisms.

The fifth, and final, stream of empirical research refers to the complementarities and interactions between MNFs' internal networks of subsidiaries and external webs of cooperative alliances. With reference to electronics and chemical industries, we showed that different aspects of internal networks account for distinctive external networking strategies. While location-specific networks of subsidiaries appear to have had a positive and significant impact on mergers and acquisitions in both industries; geo-dispersed internal networks have affected strategic alliances in the electronics industry and not in the chemical industries. Interpretive approaches developed in dynamic transaction cost literature and in contribution emphasising the role of knowledge in firms' evolution help explain these results. However, we have shown that these views need to be corrected and integrated to take sector-specific characteristics into account.

PART II

How firms differ in innovation, productivity and internationalisation

Firms significantly differ (within industries) in terms of behaviour and performances. This has become a major issue in economics. Evolutionary theory places much emphasis on the idea that economic change occurs through interaction among heterogeneous agents in the presence of market selection (Winter 1971; Nelson and Winter 1982). In particular, Nelson (1991) makes a strong case for the economic significance of discretionary firm differences. In his view, firm-level heterogeneity matters because it is an essential aspect of innovation processes, on which dynamic competition is based. The variety of new routines and resource allocations favours technical change and economic progress. By the same token, exploration of new and better ways of doing things help generate further diversity. Significant elements of heterogeneity have also been introduced in equilibrium models of industrial dynamics (Jovanovic 1982, Pakes and Ericson 1998). In a similar vein, an increasing number of macroeconomic models allow for significant violations of the normally accepted hypothesis that any class of individuals is described by a 'representative agent' (Stoker 1993).

Evidence on firms' heterogeneity is now rather extensive. Indeed, intra-industry variance in productivity, wages and profitability exceeds inter-sectoral variance. This has been clearly shown with reference to the US manufacturing industry by Baily et al. (1992) for productivity, Davis and Haltiwanger (1991) for wages, and Mueller and Raunig (1999) for profitability. Bottazzi et al. (2005) have found diversities in labour productivity within machine tool, textile, pharmaceutical and metal products industries in Italy. Several empirical studies have also highlighted persisting differences in the patterns of firm growth (see Dosi et al. 1995; Sutton 1997; Geroski 2000 for reviews).

How does this heterogeneity in performance relate to heterogeneity in internationalisation? One may think of this as a two-way link. On one hand, firm diversity reflects the distinctive advantages which make international operations profitable. That is to say, the more innovative the firm and the higher its level of economic performance, the more it will be able to compete in foreign markets. The use of firms' distinctive competencies in foreign markets requires some retention of knowledge assets within firm boundaries (through internal networks of subsidiaries), as well as some interaction with external parties, including local suppliers and users (via external networks of linkages).

On the other hand, internationalisation can generate new technological advantages and contribute to heterogeneity in innovation and economic performance. Firms expanding their internal and external networks abroad are in a position to better exploit economies of scales, and to move faster and further along their learning curves, thus improving their productivity. However, this is only part of the story. R&D is at least partially (and increasingly) carried out abroad, and this leads firms to accumulate additional advantages through the innovative activities of their own foreign affiliates. Moreover, firms may gain access to foreign sources of knowledge abroad by means of local transactions and through the development of external networks with indigenous partners. Hence, this double network expansion translates into distinctive innovative and economic performances, generating further heterogeneity.

Consistently with this view, we shall analyse different aspects of the issue of heterogeneity and internationalisation. We shall first examine *how performances differ according to firms' degree of international involvement*, from exporting to the establishment of foreign production. This will be the subject matter of Chapter 3, which will discuss the relevant theoretical and empirical literature on this issue, and present fresh evidence on the performance and internationalisation patterns of Italian manufacturing firms. The results of our empirical analysis are consistent with the view that international involvement is affected by firms' technological heterogeneity; but also with the idea that a greater engagement in cross-border activities helps improve innovative and economic performances, hence generating further firm diversity.

We shall then focus on multinational expansion, and analyse *heterogeneity across and within multinationals*. On the one hand, we shall argue that an important determinant of heterogeneity across multinationals resides in the fact that MNFs act as bridging institutions, each distinctively connecting different economic and innovation systems. The performance of a multinational will largely depend on the characteristics of its home system, on the number and variety of foreign contexts in which it is active, and on the specific organisational modes it utilises to connect different systems with one another. On the other hand, diversity within multinationals will be examined. We submit that there are powerful agglomeration forces and tensions for the strategic control of knowledge that tend to favour an uneven distribution of competencies and of technological advantages across units within multinationals. Chapter 4 will examine both these aspects of heterogeneity (across and within multinationals). Again, we shall discuss the relevant theoretical arguments on these issues, review some empirical literature, and present the results of an investigation of multinationals active in Italy. The concepts developed in Chapter 4 can be usefully applied when comparing foreign owned and domestic owned MNFs in a given economy. We shall show that while both foreign and domestic multinationals operating in Italy exhibit greater innovation and productivity than uni-national firms, domestic owned firms with production activities abroad outperform foreign firms in many respects.

The analysis we shall present in this part of the book thus supports the idea that *multinationality* is more relevant than mere *foreignness*, as a criterion differentiating among firms. Our findings highlight that, all else being equal, it may well be that attracting foreign multinational activities raises the overall productivity and innovation of an economic system. However, increasing the share of domestic firms which expand their activities abroad (domestic multinationals) could determine an even stronger effect on productivity and innovation than attracting foreign multinationals. This might help place the role of foreign presence in the proper perspective and help evaluate its desirability in a more informed way. However, we shall argue that it would be misleading to consider policies stimulating inward investments as alternative to measures supporting outward investments. We shall discuss this issue and its policy implications with reference to direct effects of foreign presence in this part of the book; and with reference to spillover effects in Part III.

3. Heterogeneity and international involvement

3.1 INTRODUCTION

This chapter addresses one of the aspects of the issue of heterogeneity and internationalisation, that is the relationship between firm diversity and international involvement. The notion of international (or foreign) involvement has been used by Lall (1980) with reference to the choice between exports and direct investment of US manufacturing industries. Indeed, the same notion can be extended to comprise a wider set of strategies which firms can jointly or separately use to serve foreign markets, and/or to gain access to valuable assets available abroad. Besides exports and FDIs, these strategies include licensing and other agreements with foreign partners, the creation of networks of sales agents, and the setting up of commercialisation affiliates abroad. Bearing this notion in mind, in this chapter we address questions such as 'How do firms differ in their choices of internationalisation strategies?' and 'How do they perform according to their degree of international involvement?'.

Recent developments in trade theory have placed at centre stage the relationship between different modes of internationalisation and intra-industry heterogeneity. The key prediction emerging from this literature is that firms will resort to distinct international activities according to their productivity levels (Helpman et al. 2004). This interpretation has important, albeit not fully acknowledged, connections with a more consolidated view emerged in the theory of international production. Based on the seminal contributions of Hymer (1960), the latter stream of literature has developed a comprehensive analysis of the nature and determinants of ownership advantages, and of their interactions with internationalisation processes.

This chapter places this literature in a wider context, identifies different testable hypotheses on the issue of inter-firm diversity and internationalisation and reviews the empirical literature providing some evidence on this issue. The relationship between intra-industry heterogeneity and international involvement will be explored with specific reference to the Italian manufacturing industry. We shall measure firm diversity in terms of both productivity and innovative behaviour. This marks a departure from most contributions which have either focused on the former or on the latter type of indicators. Although our data do not allow us to make any conclusive statements about the direction of causality between internationalisation and performances, we shall show that greater international involvement is associated with a higher productivity for any given level of innovation of firms. Our findings are consistent with the recently emerged view that cross-border activities may *per se* reinforce firms' competitive edge.

Section 3.2 surveys studies on patterns of internationalisation across countries and industries, which largely neglect inter-firm diversity within national and sectoral boundaries. Section 3.3 reviews the recent trade literature which has conveyed the attention of scholars to the issue of intra-industry heterogeneity and internationalisation. Section 3.4 identifies elements from the theory of international production which have addressed this issue, emphasising the sources of heterogeneity and the dynamic aspects of the heterogeneity – internationalisation relationship. Section 3.5 summarises the views which have emerged on this issue. Section 3.6 reviews the existing empirical literature on intra-industry diversity and international operations. Section 3.7 provides new evidence on the case of Italian manufacturing firms, and examines how their economic and innovative performance aspects relate to their degree of international involvement. Section 3.8 concludes the chapter.

3.2   DIFFERENCES IN INTERNATIONALISATION ACROSS COUNTRIES AND SECTORS

A rather extensive literature has focused on the choice between exporting, foreign direct investments and other internationalisation strategies, such as licensing and joint ventures. However, a large fraction of these contributions have concentrated their attention on how the degree of international involvement differs according to the characteristics of countries and industries, underplaying the role of intra-industry heterogeneity. Let us look briefly at heterogeneity from this perspective before focusing on diversity within industries – which is the main purpose of this chapter.

One can single out three distinct streams of international business and economics literature addressing the issue of heterogeneity across countries and industries.

A first line of research originates from Vernon's seminal contribution on trade, FDIs, and the *product life cycle* (Vernon 1966). Focusing on the US experience in the 1950s and 1960s, he develops a dynamic model wherein firms' export and FDI decisions are ultimately affected by their home country conditions and by the evolution of product technology in the industries in which they are active. Vernon observes that US firms benefit from a wide and dynamic demand expressed by high income consumers at home. This will stimulate innovation in consumer good industries, create a temporary advantage for US firms in these sectors and eventually lead to exports when demand emerges in foreign markets. In his view, firms would choose to shift to foreign direct investment as a result of technological evolution of products. As technology becomes more and more standardised, firms may decide to locate production abroad in order to counter increasing competitive threats and to take advantage of lower costs abroad. Vernon (1974) goes deeper into the analysis of the interactions between market structure and internationalisation processes, distinguishing between 'innovation based', 'mature' and 'senescent' oligopolies. The transition from one stage to the other is characterised by the decreasing role of innovation as a source of entry barriers, the growing importance of economies of scale and, in the last phase, greater recourse to cartels and product differentiation as substitutes for other advantages. In each of these stages one observes different decisions concerning the location of production and how to serve foreign markets.[33] Vernon's insights on the role of market structure are further developed by Knickerbocker (1973). In his study of the geographical patterns of FDIs, this author accepts the product life-cycle explanation of the first multinational move to a given location and suggests that a bandwagon effect will follow as a result of defensive reactions of rivals in oligopolistic markets. His contribution can thus be seen as complementary to Vernon's, as it further highlights how firms' shift from export to FDI is affected by sector specificities, as well as by the oligopolistic structure of industries in particular.

A second strand of research emphasising sector and country specificities in the analysis of international involvement derives from the *transaction cost* literature. Different from the product life-cycle tradition, these contributions are not interested in the (national or sectoral) origin of advantages to be exploited in international markets. They rather emphasise the relative efficiency of alternative modes of organising transactions. The choice of exporting, licensing or FDIs will then depend on how imperfect international markets are for the relevant transactions (Buckley and Casson 1976). Industry, country and regional-specific factors underlie imperfections especially in the markets for intermediate products and for knowledge. The existence of imperfections in these markets largely justifies multinational expansion as an alternative to arm's-length transactions. Firm-specific factors do matter in this framework, as firms may have differential abilities to organise and manage efficiently internal markets

(Buckley and Casson 1976). However, these abilities are relevant to the extent that market imperfections exist, and these will ultimately depend on variables which are exogenous to the firm.[34] A comprehensive application of this approach is given by Buckley and Casson (1981). They propose a transaction-cost type of analysis, wherein the switch from a market (export) solution to a hierarchy (FDI) strategy depends on the relative costs associated to each alternative, for any given foreign demand quantity. However, these costs are specific to the industry one observes. Their model can thus account for inter-industry differences but says very little about intra-industry heterogeneity and its impact on internationalisation.

The third stream of research connects directly to the *international trade* tradition. This literature has long emphasised country and sector specific determinants of internationalisation and has until recently disregarded intra-industry heterogeneity. Partial equilibrium contributions of the early 1970s looked at the export/FDI decision of a monopolist (Horst 1971; Copithorne 1971; Hirsch 1976). Within this framework, firms face a trade-off between proximity to foreign markets obtained by means of FDIs, which saves on transport costs, and concentration of production at home to serve foreign markets via exports, which saves on fixed costs for replicating plants abroad. According to these works, firms can be expected to invest abroad in those industries in which the gains from avoiding transport and tariff costs outbalance the costs of maintaining capacity in multiple markets. More precisely, the prediction is the following: firms are more likely to expand production horizontally rather than exporting, the higher the transport costs and trade barriers and the lower the fixed costs of entry and the size of scale economies at the plant level relative to the corporate level. More recently, these models have been extended to the general equilibrium case with increasing returns and imperfect competition. Within the same tradition, general equilibrium models of trade have been worked out to include international production of the vertical and horizontal types (see Barba Navaretti and Venables 2004 and Markusen 2002 for a review). All of these trade models propose variants of the original proximity-concentration trade-off, which is typically assumed to vary across sectors, across countries of origin and across destination markets.

There are clear differences between the three streams of research we have just outlined. The product life-cycle tradition highlights the interactions between national competitive advantages, technological evolution and oligopolistic strategies in international markets. The internalisation literature emphasises efficiency objectives and focus on transaction cost minimisation. Efficiency considerations are also at centre stage in trade theories. However, the choice of internationalisation modes is the result of production cost (rather than transaction cost) minimisation by monopolistic firms, and strategic considerations have been introduced in general equilibrium trade models with imperfect competition. A common trait of these different streams of literature is represented by a strong emphasis on country and sector-specific determinants of internationalisation. In these models, national and industrial characteristics underlie firms' advantages and market structures, and determine the costs of production and of organising transactions. This emphasis in theoretical modelling has also given rise to a number of empirical studies which have focused on national and sectoral patterns of internationalisation (see Caves 1996, Ch.2 for a review). We shall further discuss these and other approaches when addressing the issue of how performance differs according to country and industries of origin of multinational firms (see Chapter 4, section 2 of this volume). The point to be made here is that these contributions generally disregard diversity within industries in the international involvement of firms.[35] To capture the role of intra-industry heterogeneity one needs to turn to other streams of literature. On one hand, other strands of research in international production should be considered which have further elaborated on some of the insights originally introduced by Hymer (1960). On the other hand, one should refer to recent developments in trade literature which have explicitly incorporated firm diversity. Let us start with the latter.

3.3 INTRA-INDUSTRY HETEROGENEITY: PRODUCTIVITY AND SELF-SELECTION INTO FOREIGN MARKETS

Trade literature has paid increasing attention to the issue of intra-industry heterogeneity and internationalisation under the growing pressure of empirical studies using firm level data. A number of recent works have suggested that more productive firms tend to self-select into the export market.[36] This increasing evidence on the relationship between export and firm performance has stimulated the development of a set of theoretical trade models explicitly allowing for firm heterogeneity (Bernard et al. 2003; Melitz 2004). Although evidence is not as extensive as in the case of exports, there are also several empirical works documenting that multinationals tend to outperform firms with no investment abroad – as in the case of Doms and Jensen (1998) for the US, Barba Navaretti and Castellani (2004) for Italy, Criscuolo and Martin (2003) for the UK, De Backer and Sleuwaegen (2003a) for Belgium, and Pfaffermayer and Bellak (2002) for Austria. Helpman et al. (2004) take some of this empirical literature into account, and extend the original model by Melitz (2004) on firm heterogeneity and exports, to account for a wider set of internationalisation strategies. They assume that servicing a foreign market entails an entry (sunk) cost due to the fact that, for example, firms need to acquire information on the foreign market, establish distribution channels and find the appropriate suppliers of goods and services. Following Horst (1971), Hirsch (1976), Buckley and Casson (1981) and Brainard (1993), whose analysis of market access strategies we have reviewed in section 2, sunk costs are assumed to be lower in the case of exporting than in the case of foreign production (e.g. FDI). By contrast, the former face higher marginal costs, due to such industry and host market factors as transport and tariffs. Given these sector- and country-specific characteristics, Helpman et al. (2004) show that firms choose different internationalisation modes according to their ex-ante productivity. Firms with low levels of productivity can only afford to operate in domestic markets; whereas more productive firms are more profitable in all three activities, i.e. at producing for the domestic market as well as producing at home for exports or producing abroad to serve foreign markets. Rising trade costs will increase the critical productivity required to make exporting profitable; and will lower the critical productivity necessary to make FDI preferable to exports. By the same token, higher fixed costs of operating foreign affiliates increase the level of productivity required to make FDI preferable to exporting. A simple extension of the model makes it possible also to consider other modes of internationalisation (not explicitly considered by the authors) characterised by intermediate levels of sunk costs, such as the creation of affiliates carrying out commercialisation activities only (see Figure 3.1 adapted from Helpman et al. 2004).

In spite of its clear merits, the perspective proposed by Helpman et al. (2004) and related literature does not explore the origins of productivity advantages. Productivity levels are assumed to be drawn randomly from a probability distribution, and – for any given level of trade costs and of fixed costs of operating abroad – determine firms' internationalisation choices.[37] This simplifying assumption has been most frequently adopted in recent trade models, as surveyed by Tybout (2003), and reflects a more consolidated tradition in other fields of (micro)economics, as shown in Gilbert (1989) and in Reinganum (1989). Making specific reference to this latter tradition, Nelson (1991, pp. 64–65) criticises these models wherein firms differ because of the luck of a draw, or an initial condition, which made different choices profitable given certain market circumstances. This would imply that, if the market circumstances were reversed so too would be the behaviour of the firms. When these assumptions are made, there is not much sense attached to the word heterogeneity: 'There are firm differences but there is no essential autonomous quality to them' (Nelson 1991, p. 64).

More efforts are needed to analyse the determinants of firms' advantages and their interactions with internationalisation processes.

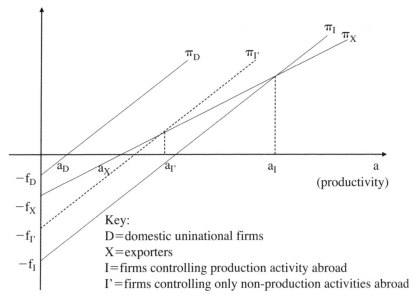

Key:
D=domestic uninational firms
X=exporters
I=firms controlling production activity abroad
I'=firms controlling only non-production activities abroad

Source: Adapted from Helpman et al. (2004).

Figure 3.1 Productivity differences, profit schedules and international involvement of firms

In this respect, useful insights can be derived from international production literature.

3.4 INTRA-INDUSTRY HETEROGENEITY: EXPLAINING FIRMS' ADVANTAGES AND INTERNATIONAL INVOLVEMENT

We shall focus first on some of the key concepts and ideas introduced by Hymer, providing a rich background for the modern analysis of intra-industry heterogeneity and internationalisation. Second, we shall highlight some more recent qualifications to the concept of ownership advantage in the new international environment. Third, attention will be given to the origins of firms' advantages and to their interactions with international operations.

3.4.1 Hymer's Heritage

One might date the first elements for the analysis of firm level advantages and of their implications for international involvement back to Hymer

(1960). He put forth the idea, later subsumed by other scholars including the above noted trade theorists, that firms need to be endowed with some distinctive asset to overcome the costs and risks of international operations. These comprise costs of communication and acquisition of information in a context of less favourable treatment given to foreign companies by the host governments and the costs and risks of exchange rate fluctuations. Such extra costs and risks imply what he called the 'liability of foreignness', something that local counterparts do not suffer as they are already active in the host market. The existence of a specific advantage explains why, in spite of these extra costs, a firm can decide to do business abroad and expect to compete successfully against local counterparts. An important insight, not fully developed in subsequent literature, is the link between the existence of such advantages, market structure and firm behaviour. On the one hand, in Hymer's view it is market imperfections that determine a competitive advantage over rivals. On the other hand, he suggests that the exploitation of advantages in foreign markets enhances firms' market power and thus increases the overall level of imperfections in the market. This line of argument has two important implications for the analysis of heterogeneity and international involvement. First, it implies that firms engaged in foreign activities abroad differ from non-internationalised ones as they have distinctive advantages enabling them to face international markets. The greater the involvement in international markets, the greater the 'liability of foreignness' and the greater the advantages needed to overcome them. This intuition has been incorporated, *inter alia*, in recent trade theories. Second, it suggests that advantages are only partially exogenous. In Hymer's theory, advantages are partially beyond firms' control in that they originate from market imperfections, but it is the (endogenous) choice to internationalise that generates new market power and reinforces market imperfections.

3.4.2   The Changing Nature of Ownership Advantages

Both insights from Hymer's seminal contribution have received increasing attention in the international production literature. The former idea, that internationalised firms differ from non-internationalised ones in terms of some specific advantage, has been reconsidered in the light of changes in the economic environment. In fact, it is widely acknowledged that globalisation has been increasing its intensity and geographic reach since Hymer's original contribution. From this perspective, it would be limiting and misleading to maintain that ownership advantages are necessary to overcome merely the costs and risks of doing business abroad. In fact the only firms not sustaining such costs and risks are local uni-national firms. While juxtaposing internationalised firms to purely domestic firms was an acceptable approximation of the real world in the early phases of multinational expansion when Hymer was writing, it is no longer so. Specific advantages are more and more needed to compete against other MNFs (or parts of other multinationals) in the international markets they serve. They must all bear the costs and risks of doing business internationally, but they each require some distinctive edge vis-à-vis one another.[38] Competition among multinationals thus goes hand in hand with their diversity. Multinationals need some distinctive capabilities in order to compete against other multinationals (or parts of other multinationals), and the competitive process itself contributes to differentiate them over time (Cantwell and Narula 2001). This aspect of intra-industry heterogeneity, which we shall identify as diversity across and within multinationals, will be the subject matter of Chapter 4.

Let us turn back to the aspect of intra-industry heterogeneity we have been considering so far – diversity between firms according to their degree of international involvement (domestic sales vs. exports vs. FDIs). In this case, the line of argument we have just developed has a straightforward implication as well. That is, the intensity of global competition affects differences in the advantages of firms, and hence contributes to differentiate their performances and their international operations. If internationalised firms need to have some distinctive advantage to face competition from local rivals, their advantages must be even stronger if competition comes from other international rivals. One might thus expect differences to be sharper – with multinationals exhibiting much higher productivity and innovation than exporters, and the latter largely outperforming uninational firms – in sectors which are characterised by particularly fierce international competition.

3.4.3 The Origins of Ownership Advantages

As recalled in section 3.4.1, a second important issue raised by Hymer has to do with the origins of ownership advantages. Dunning (1977) has partially incorporated Hymer's concern for this issue in his eclectic paradigm. On the one hand, he singles out a whole set of country, sector and firm-specific factors underlying ownership advantages of multinationals. On the other hand, and even more interestingly, he highlights that not only ownership advantages determine the actual degree of international involvement of a firm. What really makes the difference is how these advantages combine and interact with what he calls *locational advantages*, which reflect the attractiveness of a given host economy; and with *internalisation advantages*, which depend on market imperfections and failures. Therefore, in Dunning's framework ownership advantages are not fully exogenous because all factors affecting international business – including these advantages – are seen as mutually interdependent. In a nutshell, his approach also provides a key to analysing intra-industry diversity, as it envisages a number of possible combinations of advantages leading to an extremely large variety of outcomes in terms of internationalisation strategies and performances.[39]

Other contributions have attempted to explain the origins of ownership advantages and of firm diversity more explicitly. One way to address this issue is to assume that firms intentionally invest to accumulate knowledge as a means of increasing their competitiveness relative to their rivals in the final product market. By reducing unit costs below those of others in the same industry, firms with higher technological capabilities (hence exhibiting some distinctive advantages) may both increase their margins and reduce prices, thus expanding their international market shares (Cantwell 1989; Cantwell and Sanna Randaccio 1993). By contrast, 'firms with the fewest or weakest ownership advantages in general hold their position more easily in domestic markets than in international markets owing to government support, consumer loyalty, the closeness of local business contact and so forth' (Cantwell 2000, p. 39). This view, which is often referred to as 'technological accumulation approach', thus sheds some light into the black box of heterogeneity. Firms will differ in their international involvement according to their endogenous choices to invest in competence creation and innovation.

However, this is only part of the story. The choice of internationalisation modes also interacts with the cycle of utilisation and generation of technological advantages. Given the partially tacit nature of knowledge developed by firms, its exploitation and use tends to require robust organisational devices and the creation of internal networks within firms, especially when technology is applied in different and (culturally and institutionally) distant markets (Cantwell 1989; Kogut and Zander 1993; Vaccà and Zanfei 1995).

Furthermore, a growing albeit less established literature has emphasised that internationalisation, and particularly production and R&D investments abroad, can be a fundamental means of gaining access to complementary knowledge sources.[40] *Ex ante* advantages, resulting from a firm's history of technological accumulation, will provide guidance for further research as well as abilities to absorb external complementary knowledge, wherever this may be available. The dynamic process of knowledge accumulation through internationalisation has been identified in the literature as 'asset seeking' (Dunning 1993; Dunning and Narula 1995; Narula and Zanfei 2005) or 'home base augmenting' (Kuemmerle 1999), or 'technology sourcing' FDI (Driffield and Love 2003). As discussed in Part I, these strategies will generally require the combination of internal network development within multinational firms, with external networks involving partners active in the specific local markets in which foreign affiliates are active (Zanfei 2000).

To summarise, there are three distinct albeit complementary elements to the view of heterogeneity and international involvement we have just recalled. First, differences in firms' efforts to accumulate knowledge determine differential edges over rivals, and discriminate internationalised firms from non-internationalised ones. Second, the international exploitation of knowledge accumulated implies some degree of retention of technology within firm boundaries as well as some interaction with external users and suppliers. Third, the international expansion through wholly owned subsidiaries and through external networks with local firms and institutions creates the conditions for the global absorption and generation of further knowledge. This will eventually reinforce the competencies of internationalising firms.

Two important caveats apply here. On the one hand, internationalisation strategies need not be alternative to one another. Global competitors may well engage in exports, FDIs, and contractual arrangements simultaneously. This is apparent if one takes the view that firms are indeed collections of competencies, hence exhibiting distinctive high level competencies in some technology as well as weaknesses in others. This view is consistent with the evolutionary approach to the theory of the firm (Nelson and Winter 1982) and to its applications to international production (Cantwell 1989; Kogut and Zander 1993). If one adopts this approach, there is no need to consider different modes of internationalisation as mutually exclusive, as they serve distinct but complementary purposes in knowledge exploitation and accumulation.

On the other hand, internationalisation may also evolve in time independently of technological advantages. The choice of internationalisation modes is influenced by the gradual acquaintance of firms with foreign contexts, with their social and institutional characteristics, and with the managerial and organisational problems of conducting business abroad (Johanson and Wiederheim-Paul 1975). This process is largely endogenous and path dependent, and will be influenced by the pre-existing knowledge of foreign markets and of international operations, and by the outcomes of each move as firms get gradually engaged into internationalisation.[41] This view has affinities with a rather extensive literature on market entry strategies which we have considered also in Part I of this volume. The basic idea is that internationalisation is itself associated to a process of reduction of uncertainty about foreign markets. As firms become engaged in international operations uncertainty is reduced, and firms will become more prone to commit resources to further international operations. The prediction is that international involvement will presumably start with exports, then proceed with licensing, continue with more complex inter-firm agreements, and subsequently lead to FDIs (Johanson and Vahlne 1977; Gatignon an Anderson 1988; Gomes-Casseres 1989; Hennart and Larimo 1998). This view may be criticised as too deterministic, and because it disregards important dynamic efficiency considerations which might underlie the choice of a given internationalisation mode (see Part I on this criticism). It remains true that the selection of internationalisation strategies is not only correlated to the level and dynamics of technological capabilities of firms, but also to the evolution in time of their capacity to deal with foreign markets. This ability is certainly different from the (technological) capability to introduce new (or improved) products or processes.

3.5   A SYNTHESIS OF VIEWS ON HETEROGENEITY AND INTERNATIONAL INVOLVEMENT

The different streams of literature we have reviewed in sections 3.3 and 3.4 can be organised into three sets of testable hypotheses (see Table 3.1 for summary of these views).

First, the self-selection mechanism emphasised in trade models (the more firms are productive, the deeper their engagement in international markets) is reinforced by the technological accumulation literature. In addition, the latter strand of literature sheds some light on the process through which technological advantages are created and strengthened. The relationship between firm advantages and internationalisation here becomes a two-way link, which can be described as follows. In an environment of heterogeneous firms, the more strategically oriented actively invest to accumulate advantages. This will imply greater capabilities to compete internationally. As part of the knowledge accumulated is tacit, this will also imply a greater need to retain some technology internally, thus increasing engagement in international markets. As a consequence firms are in a better position to absorb foreign knowledge, new advantages will be created and heterogeneity will also increase. As Cantwell (2000, p. 29) posits it: 'By extending its own network, each firm extends the use of its unique line of technological development; and by extending it into new environments, it increases the complexity of its development.'

Trade theories and technological accumulation approaches can thus be seen as partially overlapping and complementary. The former could even be subsumed as a special case of the latter, from this perspective. We shall identify this way of interpreting the two-way link between intra-industry heterogeneity and international operations as *Heterogeneity-Mark I*: the

Table 3.1   Views on heterogeneity and international involvement

Label	Antecedents	References	Prediction
Heterogeneity Mark I	Hymer, 1960 Dunning, 1970	*Technological accumulation approaches:* Cantwell, 1989, 2000 Narula and Zanfei, 2005 *New Trade Theory:* Helpman et al. 2004	Two-way positive correlation between (innovative and economic) performances and international involvement
Heterogeneity Mark II	Nelson, Winter, 1982	Cantwell, 1989 Kogut and Zander 1993	The wider the portfolio of competencies, the more extensive the range of international operations undertaken simultaneously
Heterogeneity Mark III	Johanson, Wiederheim-Paul, 1975	Johanson and Vahlne, 1990 Gomes-Casseres, 1989 Hennart and Larimo, 1998	Two-way positive link between experience of foreign markets and international involvement

degree of international involvement is positively correlated to innovative activity and productivity of firms.

Second, as argued in section 3.4, a view of firms as a collection of competencies entails that different modes of internationalisation can be adopted simultaneously, for any given level of productivity. The hierarchy of performance levels assumed under the Heterogeneity Mark I hypothesis (the higher the economic and innovative performances the deeper the international involvement) should then be reconsidered. This would lead to a different, partially alternative view of the link between diversity in performances and diversity in international involvement, which we may dub as *Heterogeneity Mark II*: the wider the portfolio of competencies of firms, the greater the variety of international operations in which they will be simultaneously engaged, regardless of their technological levels.

Third, other streams of literature we have reviewed emphasise that the transition from one internationalisation mode to another may occur independently of firms' efforts to accumulate technological competencies. To the extent that learning about foreign markets and international practices is important, this would not be captured by a correlation between innovative performances and international involvement. The role of these kinds of knowledge assets would perhaps be better captured by the level and evolution of productivity. In fact, knowledge of markets or abilities to manage international operations – which may translate into productivity improvements – can be used to engage in international operations or to increase involvement in a foreign market. One may venture to say that a correlation between productivity and internationalisation might reveal that firms with a deeper involvement in foreign markets could achieve higher productivity levels because they utilise a better knowledge of these markets and of international management practices. It may thus be useful to identify this further set of hypotheses as *Heterogeneity Mark III*: A deeper international involvement is associated with greater experience in foreign markets and with higher capabilities for managing international operations. This might be reflected in a positive correlation between international involvement and productivity, for any given level of R&D and innovation.

The discussion above has two important implications for empirical analysis. On the one hand, both innovation and productivity should be placed at centre stage when considering the relationship between heterogeneity and international strategies. On the other hand, one should consider that firms' international involvement can further reinforce their advantages and hence contribute to generating heterogeneity.

3.6   EMPIRICAL STUDIES ON HETEROGENEITY AND INTERNATIONAL INVOLVEMENT

Several studies have produced evidence on the relationship between firm heterogeneity and internationalisation modes. However, most of them have focused on firm diversity either in terms of productivity or in terms of innovation, but they do not examine them both. Moreover, the large majority of these works analyse the relationship between either economic or innovative performances and individual internationalisation strategies. This is the case of the extensive literature on export and firm productivity, which has documented that exporters tend to outperform non internationalised firms. Clerides et al. (1998) (for Columbia, Mexico and Morocco), Aw et al. (1998) (for Taiwan), Bernard and Jensen (1999) (for the US), all find evidence that the direction of causation runs from productivity to export status, hence signalling a self-selection process of the most efficient firms into export markets.

Some studies provide evidence concerning the different productivity profiles associated with alternative internationalisation strategies. Most of them can be considered as a partial test of the view that we have identified as Heterogeneity Mark I in section 5 of this chapter. Helpman et al. (2004)

test their own theory using data of US affiliate sales and US exports in 38 countries and 52 sectors. These authors find evidence that sector/country-specific transport costs and tariffs have a strong negative impact on export sales relative to sales of foreign affiliates, in line with earlier results obtained by Brainard (1997). They also find that more heterogeneity leads to significantly more FDI sales relative to export sales. Their measure of heterogeneity is firm size, according to a recurrent albeit controversial practice in economics literature. While identifying a relationship between size and productivity may be reasonable to simplify the analytical treatment in a theoretical model, empirical work has shown that this is a rather poor proxy.[42] Several other studies have directly addressed the prediction of Helpman et al. (2004) that differences in productivity should correspond to different foreign market entry modes. Head and Ries (2003) use several indicators of performance to differentiate firms in a sample of 1,070 large Japanese companies classified in 17 two-digit industries in 1991. These indicators range from sales to value added, and total factor productivity. They find that domestic firms, exporters, and firms investing abroad exhibit the predicted hierarchy in performance levels (from the lowest to the highest performance) only when using sales data, while much weaker support is found for the theory when using direct measures of productivity. Furthermore, consistent with the criticism recalled above, Head and Ries (2003) find only a weak correlation between firm size and productivity. However, they observe that among overseas investors, more productive firms span a wider range of host-country income levels, reflecting higher capabilities for penetrating different markets.[43] Girma et al. (2004) compare sales, productivity and profitability of purely domestic firms, domestic exporters and domestic multinationals with specific reference to Ireland for the year 2000. They utilise a non-parametric approach based on the principle of first order stochastic dominance, and find that the distribution for multinationals dominates that of other domestic firms, while they do not find clear differences in plant performance between domestic exporters and non-exporters. Girma et al. (2005) apply the same non-parametric technique to UK data and find consistent evidence that the productivity distribution of multinational firms dominates that of exporting firms, which in turn dominates that of non-exporters. While these studies do not generally address the issue of how internationalisation modes affect productivity, a few contributions find that increasing degrees of learning are associated with increasing commitment to international operations. In particular, Kraay (1999) for China and Castellani (2002a) for Italy find that a higher share of foreign to total sales are associated with larger productivity gains to exporting firms. Barba Navaretti and Castellani (2004) apply matching estimators to a sample of Italian firms investing in foreign production for the first time and show that such firms experience a higher growth both in productivity and in gross output after becoming multinationals than a counterfactual of national firms. Consistent with the idea that higher commitment to foreign operations should determine higher learning effects, Castellani (2002b) finds that firms investing in commercial (and other non-production) activities abroad do not experience the same positive effect as firms setting up production abroad.

Some empirical works explore the relationship between performance and internationalisation using innovation data. This helps overcome the general criticism that applies to studies based on productivity measures, whenever data on physical quantities are not available. These works also shed some light on what we called Heterogeneity Mark I, although from a different perspective. However, as in the case of works on productivity, most of these studies focus on how innovation is associated with individual modes of internationalisation. A number of empirical contributions have assessed the impact of different innovation measures and export propensity, as in the case of Wakelin (1998) for the UK, Sterlacchini (2002) and Basile (2001) for Italy. Fewer works have provided evidence on the relationship between innovation and other modes of foreign market entry. Fors and Svensson (2002) examine the impact of R&D investments on foreign sales of Swedish multinationals. Frenz and Ietto-Gillies (2005) focus on the relationship between the degree of multinationality of UK firms (measured in terms of the number and geographic spread of subsidiaries) and their innovative behaviour. Basile et al. (2003) build an indicator of foreign expansion of Italian firms and find that firms' innovative activities are important determinants of the degree of involvement in international operations. Criscuolo et al. (2004) use a data set similar to the one used in the empirical analysis that we shall illustrate in the next section and test for the role of global engagement in UK firms' innovation, controlling for knowledge inputs. Their results are consistent with the idea that a higher propensity to innovate in multinational firms can be attributed to better access to internal and external stocks of knowledge.

Several studies based also on case histories examine how different managerial skills and organisational capabilities affect the evolution of international involvement in time. These works thus shed some light on the view we have identified in the previous section as Heterogeneity Mark III. Johanson and Wiederheim-Paul (1975) offer a detailed analysis of four Swedish based firms active in different industries (Sandwick AB, Atlas Copco, Facit-Electrolux and Volvo). They observe that these firms' involvement in international markets followed a linear sequence from exporting, to independent sales agents, commercialisation affiliates and finally manufacturing affiliates. They emphasise that this process goes hand in hand with firms' knowledge of foreign markets accumulated through direct experience of specific contexts, as well as with more generic experience in internationalisation practices.[44] This evidence is largely consistent with the market entry literature reviewed in Part I (Chapter 1), which emphasises the role of multinational experience, usually proxied with measures of previous activity in a given country, as a determinant of further international involvement. The most frequently observed pattern is that firms start entering foreign markets with low commitment operations such as exporting, licensing and joint ventures. As multinational experience increases, these low commitment strategies become less likely, and subsidiary creation prevails (Davidson and McFetridge 1984, Gomes-Casseres 1989; Mutinelli and Piscitello 1998). It suffices here to recall that several studies have emphasised that the relationship between foreign market experience and international involvement may not be a linear one (Erramilli 1991), with high greater multinational experience often consistent with greater creation of linkages with local firms (McAlesee and McDonald 1978; Dunning 1993; Arora and Fosfuri 2000; Castellani and Zanfei 2004).

Some works also find that firms can simultaneously resort to a wide variety of internationalisation strategies, thus providing indirect support to the view we have identified in the previous section as Heterogeneity Mark II. This is especially true in the case of high technology sectors, such as several branches of electronics and chemical industries, wherein firms need to gain access to a wide variety of competencies (Arora and Gambardella 1990; Castellani and Zanfei 2002; Cantwell and Santangelo 2002).

To sum up, there is a growing empirical literature that provides partial support to Heterogeneity Mark I either in terms of innovation or productivity, and a lower number of works consistent with Heterogeneity Mark II and III. However, there is virtually no evidence on how differences in *both* productivity and innovation are associated with *alternative* modes of entry in foreign markets.

3.7 EVIDENCE ON THE HETEROGENEITY AND INTERNATIONAL INVOLVEMENT OF ITALIAN FIRMS

This section draws from complementary insights stemming from the different streams of literature we have reviewed, and provides evidence on the relationship between firm heterogeneity and internationalisation modes, with specific reference to the Italian manufacturing industry. Our focus will be on what we have identified as Heterogeneity Mark I in section 3.5. We test to what extent a deeper involvement in internationalisation corresponds to higher innovative and economic performance of firms. We shall not directly address Heterogeneity Mark II and Mark III, although some pieces of evidence will be found to be consistent with these views of the relationship between internationalisation and performances.

We introduce two main novelties in the empirical analysis of this issue. First, we extend the span of variables to capture intra-industry heterogeneity, by focusing on both productivity and measures of R&D and innovative behaviour. This marks a departure from most contributions reviewed earlier in this chapter, which have either focused on the former or on the latter type of indicators. By combining both types of measures, we can disentangle different aspects of firm performances and separately examine their links with various internationalisation modes. Moreover the available data will allow us to test to what extent heterogeneity in productivity associated with international involvement is robust to controls for innovation inputs and outputs. In other words, we shall be able to check whether improvements in economic performances occur with a deeper involvement in international markets, for any given level of innovative activities. Although the direction of causality cannot be fully tested with the available data, our analysis will shed some light on the role of international involvement in the generation of further intra-industry heterogeneity.

The second novelty of this empirical analysis will be to consider the relationship between (economic and innovative) performances and a further mode of internationalisation, i.e. the creation of non-production activities abroad, that is mainly commercialisation facilities in foreign markets. This is a sort of intermediate category between 'pure exporters' and the creation of affiliates for foreign production. We assume that along the continuum from exports to the creation of production affiliates, one should observe a higher commitment to foreign markets. The key issue here is that the creation of affiliates entails investment in a foreign country, and hence a higher (or deeper) engagement in international markets, which is also likely to be associated with higher risk. Considering also the creation of non-production affiliates will enable us to test the robustness of the theoretical prediction that a deeper international involvement is associated with higher performances (see Figure. 3.1 discussed in section 3.3). Furthermore, it will allow a more detailed analysis of the relationship between internationalisation strategies and the different performance indicators.

3.7.1 Data and Variables

As in other chapters later in this volume, we shall here use information on a data set resulting from the intersection of two different sources: the Second Community Innovation Survey (CIS2) and ELIOS (European

Linkages and Ownership Structure). The former is a survey based on a common questionnaire administered by Eurostat to firms from all European countries, which aims at assessing various aspects of firms' innovative behaviour and performances. Subject to a confidentiality agreement, we were allowed to access micro data for Italy from the survey carried out in 1997 and covering innovation occurring in 1994–96.[45] Innovation data were complemented with ownership, multinationality and economic performance data from ELIOS data set developed by the University of Urbino, Italy, which combines information from Dun & Bradstreet's *Who Owns Whom* and Bureau Van Dijck's *Amadeus* (see the Appendix for more details on the two data sources). The sample resulting from this matching comprises 778 domestic-owned firms operating in the Italian manufacturing industry. Exploiting information on exports, available from the CIS, and information on subsidiaries controlled abroad, available from ELIOS, we broke down the sample distinguishing between firms serving *only* the domestic market (DOM MKT), firms serving foreign markets *only* through exports (EXP), and two types of multinational firms, namely those that control *only* subsidiaries carrying out non-production (mainly sales) activities in foreign markets (MNF1) and those which control at least one production subsidiary abroad (MNF2).[46] While MNF1 *do not* control any foreign production activities, this group does include 156 out of 164 firms which are engaged also in exporting. Furthermore, of the 121 firms carrying out international production (MNF2) 117 are also exporting and 79 are engaged in other non-production activities abroad. In other words, firms tend to resort to more than one internationalisation mode, and moving along the *continuum* from DOM MKT to MNF2, commitment to foreign markets increases. Although our focus is on Heterogeneity Mark I, one should note incidentally that the existence of a large number of firms simultaneously resorting to two or more of the internationalisation strategies identified here, is roughly consistent with the view we labelled as Heterogeneity Mark II.

As illustrated in Table 3.2, approximately one-half of the sample firms serve foreign markets only through exports, 21 per cent control non-production activities abroad and 16 per cent are multinational firms controlling foreign production. A relatively small proportion of the sample is not internationalised. It is rather clear from the large number of average employees that our sample is biased against small firms and is very likely to under represent non-internationalised firms. This bias derives from the fact that *Who Owns Whom* (from which we draw information on ownership and multinationality) has a large coverage of firms belonging to groups of two or more firms, while it does not cover small independent firms. However, the sectoral distribution of the sample firms turns out to be not significantly different from the Eurostat universe of firms over 50 employees, and the coverage of multinational firms appears to be very accurate.

3.7.2 Patterns of Productivity, Innovation and Internationalisation

Following recent models in international trade theory as well as previous developments in economic literature, in the previous sections we have argued that firms involved in exporting activity can be expected to outperform purely domestic firms, while multinational firms should reach higher performance than the former.

We here discuss some evidence consistent with this view, which we have labelled Heterogeneity Mark I. In Table 3.2 we report the mean size, productivity and innovation of firms serving only the domestic market (DOM MKT), firms serving foreign markets though exports (EXP) and multinational firms, distinguishing firms controlling only non-production activities (MNF1), and firms engaged in international production (MNF2). Such basic statistics support the idea that increasing commitment to international activities are associated with larger firm size, higher productivity[47] and propensity to innovate, and higher intensity in *intra muros* R&D

Table 3.2   Internationalisation, innovation and productivity in Italy: distribution of the sample and basic statistics, 1996

	N.	Firms (%)	Employees	Labour productivity	'Approximate' TFP	TFP
DOM MKT	98	13	435	73.0	0.97	1.00
EXP	395	51	393	76.8	0.96	1.01
MNF1	164	21	1511	79.3	1.00	1.06
MNF2	121	16	1756	88.7	1.09	1.12
Total	778	100	881	79.0	0.99	1.04

	Share of firms (%)			R&D intensity (%)		
	Innovating products	Innovating processes	Carrying out R&D	Total R&D	Internal R&D	External R&D
DOM MKT	28	40	34	1.9	0.2	1.7
EXP	59	59	65	2.5	0.7	1.7
MNF1	69	66	73	3.0	0.9	2.1
MNF2	80	78	89	3.1	1.2	1.8
Total	60	61	66	2.6	0.8	1.8

expenditures. Further support to this hypothesis can be drawn from Figures 3.2 and 3.3 where the cumulative distributions of TFP and intra-muros R&D intensity for the four groups of firms are compared.[48] In particular, productivity in multinational firms with foreign production dominates all the other groups of firms for almost any value of the cumulative distribution; MNF1 dominate EXP and the productivity of firms serving only the domestic market lies at the left hand side of the other groups for at least half of the distribution. While the ordering in the distribution of internationalised firms closely matches the Heterogeneity Mark I view, the productivity of DOM MKT is not constantly lower than in all other cases, as we would expect. However, we believe that this is due to the fact that, as mentioned earlier, our sample is biased in favour of large firms. As purely domestic firms are usually smaller in size, this bias is likely to reduce the dampening effect that small firms tend to have on the productivity of this group of firms. A similar pattern can be observed for the distribution of *intra muros* R&D intensity, with the expected ordering of curves from multinationals to uni-national firms.

However, the differences we have illustrated so far might well reflect a number of firms' characteristics that affect productivity, innovation and internationalisation, such as the size and age of the firm, the sectoral and

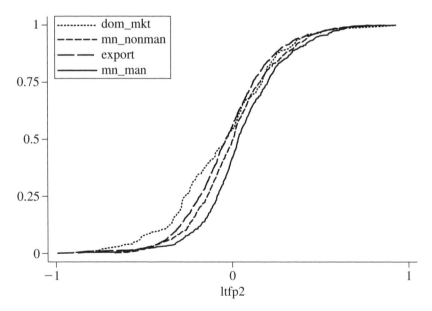

Figure 3.2   *Cumulative distribution of the log of TFP in Italy by firm type, 1996*

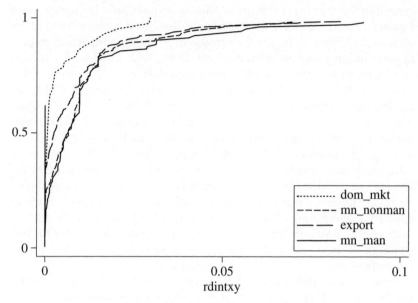

Figure 3.3   Cumulative distribution of the intra-muros R&D intensity in Italy by firm type, 1996

geographical composition. In order to take these sources of heterogeneity into account, we rely on parametric analysis. We ran regressions of various measures of productivity and innovative behaviour on three dummies identifying DOM MKT, MNF1 and MNF2, using the largest group (EXP) as baseline category and controlling for other exogenous characteristics of firms, such as sector and geographic location dummies, age of the firm and dummies for the size class. Coefficients on the three dummies reflect percentage differences in productivity and innovative behaviour of the various groups relative to exporters.

Results of regressions reported in Table 3.3 confirm that both economic and innovative performances vary according to firms' engagement in international markets, with a few important qualifications. First, estimates for all measures of productivity suggest that multinationals with manufacturing activities abroad perform better than multinationals with only non-production activities abroad, and the latter outperform both exporters and purely domestic firms. No differences in productivity emerge between exporters and purely domestic firms in our sample, but this might reflect the bias in favour of large companies we have already mentioned earlier. Second, multinationals controlling production affiliates abroad exhibit the highest *intra-muros* R&D efforts and innovative output; while multinationals with

Table 3.3 International involvement and performances in Italy, 1996–2000

Dependent variable Estimation method	(1) OLS	(2) OLS	(3) OLS	(4) PROBIT§	(5) PROBIT§	(6) PROBIT§	(7) TOBIT	(8) TOBIT	(9) TOBIT
MNF1	0.109**	0.101**	0.061**	0.171**	0.137**	0.210**	0.010*	0.007**	0.007
	(4.52)	(4.31)	(4.77)	(2.99)	(2.45)	(3.78)	(1.78)	(2.08)	(1.47)
MNF2	0.057**	0.089**	0.029**	0.077	0.044	0.056	0.007	0.001	0.007
	(2.80)	(4.62)	(2.63)	(1.53)	(0.90)	(1.21)	(1.28)	(0.27)	(1.64)
DOM MKT	-0.018	-0.014	0.008	-0.305**	-0.147**	-0.245**	-0.017**	-0.019**	-0.009
	(0.55)	(0.46)	(0.39)	(4.81)	(2.42)	(4.06)	(2.44)	(4.00)	(1.47)
Constant	0.038	-0.173**	-0.018				0.009	-0.017**	0.009
	(0.61)	(3.03)	(0.49)				(0.83)	(2.55)	(0.99)
Observations	3026	2937	3025	778	778	778	778	778	778
Test on coefficients									
MNF2 – MNF1	0.05*	0.01	0.03**	0.09	0.09	0.15**	0.00	0.01*	0.00
p-value	[0.06]	[0.64]	[0.02]	[0.12]	[0.12]	[0.01]	[0.56]	[0.09]	[1.00]

Baseline category: Exporters. All regressions are estimated controlling for the age of the firm, sector, region and size dummies. Robust t-statistics in parentheses below estimates. Asterisks denote confidence levels (**: $p < 0.05$; *: $p < 0.10$)
§ Marginal effects are reported
Dependent variables:
(1) Log of Labour productivity
(2) Log of 'Approximate' TFP
(3) Log of (estimated) TFP
(4) = 1 if the firm introduced a product innovation in 1994–1996
(5) = 1 if the firm introduced a process innovation in 1994–1996
(6) = 1 if the firm carried out R&D in 1994–1996
(7) Total innovation expenditures in 1996 as a share of turnover
(8) *Intra-muros* R&D in 1996 as a share of turnover
(9) External R&D in 1996 as a share of turnover

non-production subsidiaries abroad do not exhibit innovative activities different from mere exporters. Non-internationalised firms appear to invest the least in R&D and to innovate less than exporters. It thus appears that a higher involvement in international activities is associated with greater R&D and innovation. Our results broadly confirm the idea put forth by the technological accumulation literature which we have included in Heterogeneity Mark I. Moreover, the observed productivity premium of firms with non-production affiliates relative to pure exporters is consistent with the literature we have dubbed as Heterogeneity Mark III. We refer here to the knowledge of foreign markets, facilitated by the availability of commercialisation facilities abroad (a factor favouring higher economic performances) even in the absence of innovation.

However, no strong causal interpretation can be given to these findings. In fact, even if we control for structural characteristics (such as age, size, sector and location of each firm), our set of dummies are likely to pick up some unobserved, firm-specific characteristics such as managerial ability, which might affect both the internationalisation mode and innovative activity (or productivity). Unfortunately, the fact that our set of internationalisation dummies are time invariant does not allow us to apply panel data techniques, while no good instrumental variable could be constructed with the available data to alleviate this endogeneity problem. Given these constraints, we are forced to interpret the coefficients for our explanatory variables in Table 3.3 as simple differences in means, conditional on sector, age and location characteristics.

In Table 3.4 we circumvent this problem by estimating the effect of internationalisation status on productivity, controlling not only for structural characteristics but also for innovation outputs (captured by two dummies indicating the introduction of process and product innovation) and inputs (such as *intra* and *extra muros* R&D intensity and two dummy variables indicating technological co-operation with Italian and foreign counterparts). By so doing we are able to separate the internationalisation–productivity relationship from the innovation–productivity linkage. In the first column of Table 3.4 we test whether the observed heterogeneity in terms of productivity is robust to controls for innovation outputs (captured by two dummies indicating if a firm had introduced process and product innovation) and inputs (such as *intra* and *extra muros* R&D intensity and two dummy variables indicating a firm's involvement in technological co-operation with Italian and foreign counterparts). Results of this test confirm the ranking in TFP of multinational firms, exporters, and non-internationalised firms. The second column of Table 3.4 also confirms that the heterogeneity in the propensity to innovate of the four groups of firms persists even controlling for innovation inputs.

Table 3.4   Differences in performances of Italian firms: the role of international involvement and innovative behaviour, 1996–2000

Dependent variable estimation method	Log of TFP OLS	Product innovator (dummy) PROBIT[§]
MNF1	0.050**	0.141**
	(3.89)	(2.28)
MNF2	0.024**	0.069
	(2.21)	(1.29)
DOM MKT	0.023	−0.273**
	(1.10)	(3.55)
Intra-muros R&D intensity	−0.393	8.260**
	(1.30)	(3.73)
Extra-muros R&D intensity	−0.322**	5.253**
	(2.09)	(6.49)
Product innovator dummy	0.042**	
	(3.24)	
Process innovator dummy	−0.005	
	(0.38)	
Technological co-operation with	0.029**	0.169**
national counterparts	(2.05)	(2.37)
Technological co-operation with	0.043**	0.200**
international counterparts	(2.99)	(2.42)
Constant	−0.080	
	(0.79)	
Observations	3025	759
R-squared	0.17	
Test on coefficients		
MNF2–MNF1	0.03*	0.07
p-value	[0.06]	[0.27]

Baseline category: Exporters. All regressions are estimated controlling for the age of the firm, sector, region and size dummies. Robust t-statistics in parentheses below estimates. Asterisks denote confidence levels (**: $p < 0.05$; *: $p < 0.10$)
[§] Marginal effects are reported

The results of Tables 3.3 and 3.4 shed some light on the relationship between ownership advantages and internationalisation. As discussed earlier (sections 3.3 and 3.4), firms' involvement in foreign activities can be associated with both *ex ante* and *ex post* advantages. In other words, the more firms are engaged in international markets, the more they need to be endowed with some immaterial assets, such as superior technology, enabling them to face their competitors and overcome the costs and risks of carrying out their operations abroad. But a higher involvement in international activities may be also associated with learning and technology sourcing, thus further reinforcing their ownership advantages. As we have noted already, given the limitations of our data, it is not possible to identify the direction of causality (from performance to internationalisation or vice versa), nor whether one of the two effects prevails. However, these results do show that a higher involvement in international activities is associated with higher productivity, holding constant at least some of the most important sources of technological advantages. Two interpretations can be offered here. On the one hand, this result supports Heterogeneity Mark I, reflecting the fact that firms which are more rooted in foreign contexts may be better positioned to gain access to foreign sources of knowledge. On the other hand, it may reveal the importance of foreign market experience acquired through international operations, which affects firms' economic perform-ance, whatever their innovation. The latter interpretation would be consis-tent with Heterogeneity Mark III.

Finally, when we turn to heterogeneity in R&D efforts and innovative outputs, our results highlight that it is R&D *intra-muros* (and not R&D *extra-muros*) that makes the difference between multinationals with pro-duction activities and all other categories of firms. This is a key feature of multinationals: they are more likely than other firms to be able to develop autonomously new products and processes, but they also have more absorptive capacity to gain access to external sources of technology.

3.8   CONCLUDING REMARKS

The chapter has highlighted how intra-industry heterogeneity is associated with different internationalisation modes. We have shown that, starting from an initial emphasis on sector- and country-specific patterns of inter-nationalisation, there has been an increasing attention in the literature on differences in performances across firms within national and industrial boundaries, and on how these relate to their degree of international involvement. We have identified three different and partially complement-ary views of the issue of intra-industry heterogeneity and international-isation. First, what we have called Heterogeneity Mark I, which combines a long tradition in the theory of international production with more recent developments in international business and trade literature. The prediction here is that there will be a two-way correlation between the ranking of firms in terms of economic and innovative performances, and the degree of their involvement in internationalisation. Second, a Heterogeneity Mark II is identified, based on the hypothesis that firms are a collection of competen-cies. This view implies that a variety of internationalisation modes may be simultaneously adopted by firms, especially in dynamic industries characterised by complex technologies. Third, Heterogeneity Mark III is defined according to which international involvement results from the gradual acquaintance of firms with foreign markets. Consistent with this view one may observe that international involvement increases over time, hand in hand with economic performances, largely independent on the technological level of firms.

We have reviewed a wide, albeit still underdeveloped empirical literature on firm diversity and internationalisation. Most recent studies have focused mainly on Heterogeneity Mark I. Moreover, they have largely limited their attention to either economic or innovative performances, never combining the analysis of how they both relate to international involvement.

With specific reference to Italian manufacturing firms, we test the view identified as Heterogeneity Mark I, while, due to data limitations, only impressionistic evidence is provided to support the other two views. We find that firms with a high engagement in foreign activities also exhibit better economic and innovative performances. In particular, companies with the highest international involvement, namely firms with production activities abroad, are characterised by both the highest productivity premiums and the highest R&D efforts and innovative performances. However, Italian multinationals with a lower commitment to foreign markets, i.e. with only non-production activities abroad, do show levels of productivity that stand between those of multinationals with production activities abroad and those of mere exporters, but they do not innovate more than the latter.

These results might have important policy implications. In fact, an increase in the share of firms carrying out some production activities abroad is likely to be associated with an increase in technological capabilities, and especially *intra-muros* R&D activities. Besides, we found evidence that a higher commitment to foreign markets is *per se* associated with higher efficiency of Italian firms, even controlling for innovation inputs and outputs. This further reinforces the conclusion that the creation of production activities abroad can represent a fundamental channel for the creation of innovation opportunities in this country.

4. Heterogeneity across and within multinational firms

4.1 INTRODUCTION

In Chapter 3, we highlighted that MNFs differ from exporters and from uni-national firms in terms of economic and innovative performances. Moreover, we introduced a distinction across multinationals. In fact we separated firms controlling production activities abroad from firms controlling non-production facilities only, and showed that this distinction is also associated with some diversity in performance. In this chapter we shall focus on other aspects of heterogeneity across multinationals and introduce a further dimension, that is, diversity within multinationals.

To address the issue of *heterogeneity across multinationals*, we shall use a metaphor introduced in Part I of this volume: each MNF acts as a distinct *bridging institution*, connecting in a specific way different economic and innovation systems (of origin and of destination). By so doing, each multinational company absorbs and utilises different sets of capabilities and of innovative opportunities, and combines its own knowledge base with the external assets to which it has access abroad. From this perspective, constraints and opportunities that MNFs meet in their (national, regional or sectoral) systems of origin and destination, as well as the intensity and geographic spread of the connections they are able to create with different systems are fundamental sources of heterogeneity. In fact, through their specific (internal and external) networking strategies, multinationals are able to build up their competitive strengths and to differentiate their economic and innovative performances.

The second key aspect of heterogeneity we shall address in this chapter is *diversity within multinationals*. As discussed in Part I of this book, the evolution towards a double network structure entails that an increasing number of units belonging to the MNF are involved in the creation, adoption and diffusion of innovation. However, this does not imply that all units are equally involved in this process: knowledge tends to accumulate in some units more than in others. The distribution of competitive advantages tends to be uneven within organisations in general, and within multinationals in particular. As we shall see, various factors contribute to this differentiation, including proximity, agglomeration forces, co-ordination costs and tensions for the strategic control of knowledge.

The importance of these distinctions becomes apparent when considering how the presence of foreign multinationals affects the performances of a given economy. In fact, policies devoted to attracting inward FDIs are usually based on the presumption that foreign owned firms outperform domestic owned ones, and they would bring superior technologies into the country increasing its overall performance. However, our analysis will highlight that comparing foreign and domestic firms implies a careful evaluation of differences *across MNFs*.[49] On one hand, incoming multinationals may differ according to their country of origin, level of internationalisation and entry mode. On the other hand, part of the domestic owned firms are themselves multinationals, each exhibiting a specific pattern of internationalisation and distinctive performances. Furthermore, a comparative analysis of foreign and domestic owned multinationals in a given economy also requires that differences *within multinationals* are examined. In fact firms having their headquarters abroad are by definition foreign affiliates of a multinational group while those belonging to a domestic owned multinational may either be parent companies or national affiliates. This *per se* implies that these firms have different possibilities to tap into the knowledge accumulated by the multinational corporation in which they operate, and are exposed differently to opportunities to generate new knowledge as well.

Thus, while it may be true that foreign companies outperform domestic firms as a whole, this underscores important composition effects. There might exist domestic firms in a better position than foreign multinationals in terms of the creation, adoption and diffusion of economically useful knowledge. From a public policy perspective, it follows that increasing the share of foreign owned firms may not be the most effective strategy for enhancing the productivity and innovation of the economy as a whole. Evaluating the direct contribution of foreign companies to the technological level of the economy requires a closer analysis of the characteristics and performances of both the incoming and the domestic firms. Whether or not multinationals also create spillovers for domestic economies is a separate issue, treated in Part III of this volume.

The remainder of this chapter is structured as follows. Section 4.2 examines the nature and determinants of heterogeneity across multinationals, while section 4.3 addresses the issue of heterogeneity within multinationals. In section 4.4 we provide some evidence on both aspects of intra-industry diversity (across and within multinationals), with specific reference to foreign and domestic firms active in Italy. Section 4.5 concludes.

4.2   HETEROGENEITY ACROSS MULTINATIONALS

One way of conceptualising heterogeneity across multinationals is to suggest that each MNF has a distinctive way of connecting different economic and innovation systems. Here we shall recall only some of the key aspects characterising MNFs as *bridging institutions*, which helps to differentiate them from one another in terms of their innovative and economic performances (see Part I for some discussion on this view of the multinational company). In a nutshell, what is distinctive about each multinational is the combination of three sets of factors: the characteristics of the economic and innovation *system of origin* relative to the main competing systems, the number and quality of *foreign systems* in which the multinational firm is active, and the way *different systems* are connected (see Table 4.1 for a summary of the following considerations).

4.2.1   Sources of Heterogeneity I: Systems of Origin

Two separate issues should be examined here: first, how the systems of origin affects FDIs and multinational expansion, and second, how the characteristics of this location impacts on innovation and productivity of MNFs.

The role of national features as determinants of FDI patterns is only partially captured in standard Hecksher-Ohlin models which focus on *factor endowments*. A pure H-O view would predict net outflows from countries rich in capital and skilled labour countries and large inflows to countries poor in capital and skilled labour. However, most national patterns of FDIs cannot be explained in terms of factor proportion models. The real world is better described as one in which only the richest most capital intensive countries have net outflows, intermediate countries exhibit the largest FDI inflows, and two way investments is substantial in all advanced economies.

The limited empirical support received by the standard H-O approach thus suggests considering national traits other than mere factor proportions as determinants of multinational operations (Caves 1996, Ch.2). While general equilibrium models have been able to explain horizontal FDIs by incorporating new hypotheses on product differentiation, scale economies and market size (Markusen 2002, Brainard 1993, 1997), other streams of literature have addressed the issue of systems of origin in a more direct and comprehensive way. The eclectic framework developed by Dunning (1977) includes a variety of country specific factors which he groups under the general labels of 'level and structure of resource endowments', 'size and character of markets' and 'government policies', with a particular emphasis on policies towards foreign direct investment, innovation and industrial concentration. Several contributions have paid increasing attention to source-country attributes as important differentiating factors. Hence 'national' and 'regional' models of internationalisation are identified.

Building on Linder (1961), who first suggested that countries will export those goods for which they have a large national market, Vernon (1966) provides a widely cited framework which best describes the US patterns of multinational expansion in the 1950s and 1960s. We discussed Vernon's contribution in some details in Chapter 3. Suffice it here to recall that in his model US firms will take advantage from proximity to a particularly *rich and dynamic demand* for consumer goods at home. This will, in fact, ensure effective communication with customers, facilitate the understanding of user needs, and create distinctive opportunities for new product development. Proximity advantages can be exploited first through national sales, then through exports (when foreign demand also grows), and finally via FDIs (when technology matures and the threat of local production emerges).

From a different perspective, Franko (1976, Ch.4) argued that the *small national markets of* some European countries created a constraint to growth and risk diversification of firms, forcing the most successful companies to heavy foreign direct investment. With reference to other more sizeable European countries, he highlighted that the *scarcity of raw materials coupled with their high level of industrialisation*, fuelled backward vertical integration through foreign direct investment (Franko 1976, Chapters 2 and 3). Japan's late and slow involvement in the post-World War II process of FDI growth is illustrative of the impact of *institutional* factors characterising that country. These include cultural and organisational aspects, which made integration difficult with Western countries, and the role traditionally played by trading companies as substitutes for FDIs (Yoshimo 1975; Tsurumi 1976). By the same token, cultural proximity and government intervention to support the restructuring of manufacturing activities (particularly through the promotion and planning activities of the Ministry of Trade and Industry), favoured the redeployment of Japanese maturing industries towards South Eastern Asian countries (Yoshihara 1978) after World War II.

The country specific characteristics are at centre stage in the literature on the *national innovation systems* (NIS) (Nelson 1993; Lundvall 1993; Edquist 2005). Some contributions to this stream of literature highlight how national systems of origin not only affect the international expansion of manufacturing activities, but also the global generation, adoption and diffusion of technology. Although innovation is generally acknowledged to be less internationalised than production (Patel and Pavitt 2000), there is also a widespread agreement on the fact that global flows of technology are increasing, signalling that national innovation systems are becoming more open and intertwined. This trend is highlighted by Carlsson (2003) who reviews a number of empirical studies on the internationalisation of innovation systems, adopting various levels of analysis[50] and focusing on different patterns such as R&D activities carried out by MNFs across national boundaries, international technical alliances, cross-border technology transfer, international trade of capital goods and flows of scientific and technical personnel. Carlsson also reports wide differences between countries in the rate and types of globalisation of their NIS, with smaller countries exhibiting larger flows of scientific and technological knowledge and embodied technology crossing their borders. See Part I of this volume for more details on these differences in the degree of internationalisation of technology by country of origin.

The prevailing argument emerging from this stream of literature is that there are more national factors *inhibiting* the internationalisation of technology than *favouring* it. Niosi and Bellon (1996, p.156) suggest that there are impediments to cross-border integration of innovation systems due to 'different natural factor endowments, cumulative effects of industrial organisation and specialisation, different national stocks of knowledge, different national economic and political institutions'. Institutional specificities and cultural and organisational ties are particularly emphasised as important limitations to the free international deployment of technology.[51] Foray (1995) shows that the path-dependent nature of institutional arrangements in the field of intellectual property right protection is an obstacle to the international standardisation of these regimes, and puts a brake on global technology integration. Diversities in higher education systems also create difficulties for the circulation of knowledge within the European Union (Gregersen and Johnson 1997). Furthermore, national innovation systems can be expected to contribute to the inertia of firms in their decisions to internationalise R&D activities and to gain access to foreign knowledge. From the latter perspective, Narula (2003) stresses that firms face high costs of integrating into the host location's system of innovation as opposed to the low marginal cost of maintaining their embeddedness in their home location's innovation system. This helps explain the inertia of firms in their decisions to locate their R&D abroad and source knowledge outside their home countries. Using PACE data on knowledge source evaluation by R&D managers of large companies active in Europe, Arundel and Geuna (2004) provide evidence of a similar inertia in the field of international sourcing of public knowledge. More generally speaking, 'while institutions are important for the formation and functioning of particular innovation systems, they may also, by their very nature, impede internationalisation of innovation systems' (Carlsson 2003, p.16).

However, this is only part of the story. Institutional settings characterising a specific national context may not only create barriers and limitations to firms' globalisation of technology, they may also act as fundamental *inducement mechanisms*. Institutional bottlenecks can be expected to stimulate a creative reaction, pushing firms to exploit innovation opportunities outside national borders, as existing norms and rules prevent them from doing so at home.[52] This type of inducement mechanism helps explain the internationalisation of US telecommunications operators in the post-divestiture phase of the second half of the 1980s. Restrictions imposed on diversification appear to have spurred the so-called 'Baby Bell' companies to set up international co-operative agreements to exploit technological and market opportunities they could not gain access to in the national arena (Zanfei 1993). In a similar vein, one could interpret the patterns of internationalisation of the US pharmaceutical industry as a consequence of export restrictions impeding to commercialise new drugs not yet approved for sales in the US – even if the regulatory agency in the recipient country had already approved the product for marketing. This provided US firms with a significant incentive to exploit technological and market opportunities through either direct investments or licensing agreements (Swanson 1986). Deregulation of domestic air transportation in 1978 apparently had a positive impact on internationalisation of innovation in the US aircraft industry. Early institutional change in the US has pushed airline service providers to lower quality levels to keep costs down, and hence reduced the propensity of manufacturers to take advantage from interactions with local users (air carriers). This may have helped focus manufacturers' attention towards technical co-operation with foreign customers and manufacturers as a compensating mechanism (Mowery 1988).

Using the term 'institutional factors' more extensively, differences in cultural and organisational approaches can also be expected to affect innovative behaviour in multinationals and influence the rate and direction of international technology transfer. For instance, Lam (1997) argues that approaches to the organisation of knowledge and technical work are very different in Japanese and British electronics firms. J-firms are characterised by multifunctional project teams with a high degree of cross-functional knowledge integration in product development, while B-firms exhibit a sequential approach wherein product development is organised along the principle of clear division of labour and product specialisation. These organisational diversities, which are deeply embedded in divergent skills, work roles and careers of engineers, may impact on international knowledge sharing and transfer between firms originating from these countries.

The J approach tends to create a greater deal of tacit knowledge which is not amenable to codification, and can only be effectively transmitted among members with common knowledge and shared 'coding schemes'. An important implication of this analysis is that the two types of firms can be associated with different degrees of tacitness and hence transferability of knowledge, also across firm boundaries, making collaboration with other parties (including local counterparts) more difficult in the case of J-firms than in the case of B-firms.

To summarise, by shifting the attention away from mere factor endowment one can single out a variety of home-country characteristics affecting multinational expansion and its links to innovation and productivity. Proximity to a dynamic demand in the country of origin may generate distinctive advantages to be exploited by firms through production abroad. A small national market or a binding resource scarcity at home may spur firms to internationalise as a compensation strategy. Acquaintance with institutional and cultural factors at home relative to the costs of taking roots in a foreign context helps explain the inertia of international production and of the geographic dispersion of technology in particular. However, country-specific institutional and cultural constraints at home can also act as inducing mechanisms as they create a compelling pressure to exploit technological opportunities abroad. One can thus expect that MNFs' economic and innovative performances will be heavily affected by the specific mix of opportunities, constraints and inducing mechanisms characterising their system of origin.

4.2.2   Sources of Heterogeneity II: Foreign Systems

A second set of differentiating factors is made up of foreign systems in which multinationals are active. For the moment let us set aside considerations as to how these systems are connected, which we shall briefly deal with in section 4.2.3. In this section we focus on the specific advantages deriving from the number and quality of locations in which a firm operates. A similar perspective is adopted by Harris and Robinson (2002, p.209 fn4). They incidentally observe that foreign plants benefit from participation in a multinational network, and that 'different types of networks – perhaps linked to different countries – will have different advantages'. Proceeding deeper in this direction, here we maintain that, first, an important source of MNF diversity is the specific *mix of location advantages* a firm can leverage, according to where it is actually active. Second, the *number and variety of foreign locations* may *per se* differentiate the performances of MNFs, regardless of whether these locations are individually advantageous to operate in.

The impact of *location advantages* on multinational performances can be examined in the light of a rather extensive literature on geographical patterns of FDI. This literature generally focuses on host country (and host region) determinants of location decisions. Local production costs, institutional characteristics and externalities can induce firms to direct their investments towards certain areas more than others. For the purpose of the present analysis, this viewpoint can be easily reversed. The key issue here is how firms differ in terms of locational choices, and how this translates into firm-specific advantages (Dunning 1998). From this perspective, MNFs can be expected to be better off the greater their presence in countries and regions where the cost of production factors (labour, skills and raw materials) are relatively low, especially in the case of vertical investments. This is also true where foreign market size is large, thus allowing greater plant level economies of scale, especially in the case of horizontal investments (Barba Navaretti et al. 2005 for a review). Multinational advantages are also affected by national and regional policies, including market protection, horizontal infrastructural policies as well as more direct promotion of incoming investments (Dunning 1993; Wheeler and Mody 1992; Dunning and Wymbs 1999).

New economic geography has also stressed the importance of agglomeration economies deriving from the presence of other local or foreign firms in the same geographical area that tend to attract FDIs, although the impact of these variables are admittedly non-linear (Fujiita et al. 1999; Head et al. 1999). By extension, the literature on the internationalisation of technology has emphasised the advantages stemming from spatial agglomeration of innovative activities in explaining the localisation of R&D FDIs (Cantwell and Iammarino 2003; Verspagen and Schoenmakers 2004; Mariani 2002). This line of research highlights that distance hampers the exchange of tacit knowledge, thus spurring firms to localise close to spatial areas where they can enjoy technological externalities and spillovers (Boschma and Lambooy 1999; Martin 1999; Dunning and Wymbs 1999). The implication for heterogeneity is straightforward. Performances will differ according to locational patterns because these will determine a distinctive exposure to agglomeration economies (see section 4.3 for further discussion of agglomeration factors).

Both technological and more generic agglomeration economies tend to be cumulative: geographic concentration of activities attracts further investments, increasing the attractiveness of a given location, up to a point at which congestion problems arise. This dynamic process implies that firms will be attracted to regions where agglomeration economies are high, thus contributing to increase local externalities and further improving their own performances. Among other externalities, firms will develop knowledge of local and international partners and this will eventually increase their ability to select other advantageous locations. The more firms are active in high level regions, the better their economic and innovative performances and the higher the likelihood that they take root in other high level regions.

Most of the considerations above on the links between location advantages and heterogeneity could be easily reframed in the context of innovation system literature. MNFs' performances not only reflect the characteristics of innovation systems of origin, as discussed in section 4.2.1, but also the features of innovation systems of destination. That is, the set of institutions, infrastructures, and relationships between actors in a given economy affects, *inter alia*, the performances of foreign affiliates active there.[53] Hence, MNFs differ according to the range of foreign innovation systems they deal with.

So far we have suggested that the location of activities matters as a source of distinctive advantages. These advantages can be actively created through the firm's strategic decisions to locate in specific areas. However, the *extension* and *geographic dispersion* of *multinational activities* may *per se* be a source of advantages, even regardless of how attractive the *individual* locations are.[54]

The number and variety of systems connected through multinational links can directly and positively affect productivity and innovation through a variety of channels. First, they are associated with intensive *learning processes*. The extension and geographic spread of international activities allows firms to explore and select among a wide range of knowledge sources and of technological opportunities, thus establishing a spatially (and sectorally) diffuse system for the creation of new competencies (Dunning 1998; Cantwell and Piscitello 2000; Zander 1999; Patel and Vega 1999). Learning opportunities may derive both from contacts with a variety of local R&D capabilities, and from interactions with a large number of users yielding specific application experience.

Second, a large number and variety of foreign markets increases the possibility of *spreading the risk* associated with innovation, as a failure to commercialise a new product or process in one country may well be compensated by a success in another. This is part of a more general strategy of risk diversification which can more easily be carried out by MNFs thanks to the geographic spread of their activities (see Ietto-Gillies 2005, ch.15, for a review).

Third, the number and variety of links to foreign markets are fundamental means for gaining *experience of international markets* themselves. On the one hand, increasing the number of systems connected might increase generic capabilities for further internationalisation, and hence reinforce advantages of the same sort we have discussed earlier in this subsection.

On the other hand, expanding the variety of markets in terms of geographic, economic and cultural distance is likely to generate greater exploratory capacity (Castellani and Zanfei 2004). This can be an important vehicle for increased innovation and productivity through technological diversification.

The number of countries where a multinational is active will also have a more indirect impact on performance. One important effect is on the bargaining power of MNFs towards labour and other stakeholders (Cowling and Sugden 1987; Sugden 1991; Peoples and Sugden 2000; Ietto-Gillies 2005). Moreover, the existence of units located in multiple markets will facilitate a number of price and non-price competitive strategies (e.g. aggressive transfer pricing, cross-hauling, price discrimination, excess capacity manoeuvring) (Caves 1996, ch.4). The key point here is that, when used to support these policies, the number and variety of foreign markets will not necessarily impact positively on innovation, nor improve the general efficiency of the firm and its productivity. In some circumstances they will even affect them negatively. This might, for instance, be the case of market pre-emption policies based on predatory pricing in one market sustained by higher prices in others. This could reduce competition with possible negative impacts on innovation in the post-paradigmatic phases of technology development. As well, policies used to increase the bargaining power of the firm against labour or vis à vis suppliers or partners might hinder innovation if this creates a business climate not favourable to innovation, e.g. reducing mutual trust or the informal circulation of ideas. It thus appears that, when these policies are used *in isolation*, their impact on productivity and innovation is likely to be null or negative.

By contrast, some of these policies could be usefully *combined* with other measures aimed at improving efficiency and enhancing technology development and competence accumulation, hence positively supporting innovation strategies. To illustrate, let us consider the use of retaliation threats to reduce the likelihood of opportunistic behaviour combined with technological cooperation strategies: the multinational can credibly threaten to damage a partner in market A (for instance by adopting aggressive price strategies) if it deviates from agreements made in market B. The credibility of this threat helps to stabilise the alliance as it increases the costs of deviating from a cooperative behaviour (Kogut 1989b). A more stable framework for collaboration will eventually support the intentional effort of a firm to invest and cooperate in technological development (Bureth et al. 1997). Under similar circumstances the number and variety of markets are used directly to pursue objectives which would *per se* be irrelevant to innovation (enabling aggressive pricing strategies) but can also be utilised indirectly to sustain innovative processes (by enhancing technological cooperation).

4.2.3   Sources of Heterogeneity III: How Firms Interact with Different Systems

The means utilised to connect the system of origin with the other systems are also important sources of heterogeneity across MNFs. The manner in which firms resort to internal or external linkages certainly differs across industries – with implications for the evolution of sectoral systems of innovation (Malerba 2005). However, significant variation can be expected also within industries, as a result of both firm-level structural characteristics such as size and resource endowments, and strategic choices of individual companies.[55]

Linkage creation affects MNFs' behaviour and performances in a number of ways. First, it is widely accepted that the creation of subsidiaries, and of foreign R&D labs in particular, is positively related to innovation. The expansion of internal networks is a fundamental vehicle for the adaptation and improvement of technology according to local demand (Mansfield et al. 1979; Lall 1979; Warrant 1991), for the monitoring of technology development carried out elsewhere (Miller 1994; Florida 1997), and for the absorption of locally available knowledge (Almeida 1996; Cantwell and Noonan 2002).

Second, external linkages can affect innovation too. Various studies show that networks provide access to more diverse sources of information and capabilities than are available to firms lacking such ties, and, in turn, these linkages increase the rate of innovation of firms, especially in high technology industries (Teece 1992; Powell and Grodal 2005). Case studies carried out on large samples of manufacturing firms emphasise that innovation is more likely to emerge in the presence of long term, intimate linkages with local firms due to the fact that trust and cognitive understanding require time to develop (Godoe 2000; Andersson and Forsgren 2000; Vinding 2002). Powell et al. (1999) emphasise that network centrality among biotechnology firms results in more patenting. Furthermore, while network experience had a positive influence on patenting, the rate of increase diminished with additional experience, suggesting possible diminishing returns from network connectivity.

Third, informal links matter both within and across firms. Tsai and Ghoshal (1998) found that social ties led to a higher degree of trustworthiness among business units within a multinational electronics company, inducing extensive exchanges of resources and ideas and contributing to product innovation. Saxenian (1994) observed a wide sharing of proprietary knowledge among engineers in Silicon Valley, creating a fertile, innovative climate and often attracting multinationals to locate there in order to gain access to strategic knowledge.

Fourth, the combination of link types impacts on innovation as well. A balance of formal and informal ties is important both within and across firms. Ruef (2002) found that individuals taking part in heterogeneous networks, comprising both strong and weak ties, are more likely to be regarded as innovative by peers, as compared with individuals belonging to more homogeneous networks. Rosenkopf and Tushman (1998) found similar patterns of co-evolution of formal and informal relationships in their research on expert communities in the area of flight simulation. Complementarities are also found between internal and external links. Some of the technological opportunities created by expanding internal networks can be further explored and exploited by means of external networks. As a consequence, the creation of new subsidiaries often paves the way to licensing agreements, strategic alliances and joint ventures with local and international counterparts (Cantwell 1995; Sachwald 1998; Castellani and Zanfei 2004). But the causal link also runs the other way, from the development of external networks to the growth of internal networks. Knowledge accessed through external networks can also create opportunities for expanding the internal network locally or in other markets (see Part I for further discussion on the complementarity and substitutability between internal and external networks).

It thus appears that multinationals are most likely to perform differently according to the nature, intensity and composition of their internal and external network strategies. In other words, the way MNFs bridge economic and innovation systems is not neutral, and contributes to generate intra-industry heterogeneity.

4.3 HETEROGENEITY WITHIN MULTINATIONALS

As anticipated earlier, a further often neglected level of analysis concerns heterogeneity within multinationals. To simplify, we shall concentrate on the role played by three units or aggregates of units composing the MNF: the parent company, foreign affiliates and national affiliates. In our terms, a parent company (PC) is a firm controlling ownership of at least one enterprise located in a different country (i.e. the host economy). We assume this participation to allow a majority or *de-facto* control over this enterprise located abroad, and identify the latter as one of its foreign affiliates (FAs). A PC is assumed also to contribute to the assets of firms located in the same country (i.e. the home country), and identify these as national affiliates (NAs).[56] The set of PC and all of its affiliates (FAs, and NAs) constitutes a multinational firm (MNF). We shall use the terms MNF, multinational group or multinational corporation interchangeably. The direct,

Table 4.1   Heterogeneity across multinationals

Source of heterogeneity	Impact on internationalisation and performance	Main references
Systems of origin		
Rich and dynamic demand at home	Product innovation lead time, export and market seeking FDI	Vernon 1966
Small market at home	Market seeking FDIs and scale economies	Franko 1976
Scarcity factors (raw materials, labour, skills, land) at home	Resource seeking FDIs, vertical integration advantages and redeployment	Franko 1976 Ozawa 1979 Wakusagi 1994
Inertia of National Innovation Systems	Globalisation of technology inhibited	Narula 2003 Carlsson 2003
Institutional bottlenecks at home	Cooperation affecting the rate and direction of technical change	Zanfei 1993 Lam 1997
Foreign systems		
Attractiveness of locations	Factor cost advantages Plant-level economies of scale Efficiency of local infrastructure Agglomeration economies Technology sourcing	Beckman and Thisse 1986 Markusen 2002 Dunning 1993 Fujita, Krugman and Venables 1999 Dunning and Narula 1995
Number and variety of locations	Learning opportunities Risk spreading Multinational experience Bargaining power	Cantwell 1995 Castellani and Zanfei 2004 Ietto-Gillies 2002 Cowling and Sugden 1978
Modes of interaction		
Internal network	Adaptation to local demand Monitoring of foreign technology Absorption of foreign technology	Mansfield et al. 1979 Florida 1997 Almeida 1996
External network	Exploratory capacity Technological diversification Learning by interacting	Teece 1986, 1992 Cantwell and Piscitello 2005 Bureth et al. 1997
Informal networks	'Atmosphere' conducive to innovation	Tsai and Goshal 1998 Saxenian 1994
Combination of links	Cumulative learning advantages	Ruef 2002 Narula and Zanfei 2005

non-intermediated, participation in foreign activities is the distinctive
feature of our definition of parent company. A PC may well be itself controlled by other companies having the same or different nationality of
origin.[57] We preferred not to associate the term parent company with the
ultimate level in an ideal chain of controlling entities, because we are more
interested in focusing on those manufacturing units responsible for taking
direct decisions on international activities rather than the top level wherein
financial and administrative activities are normally concentrated.

To analyse economic and innovative diversity within multinationals one
needs to evaluate at least three issues: (i) why and to what extent technology is transferred to and created by peripheral units of the MNF including
its foreign affiliates; (ii) why and to what extent should the performances of
foreign affiliates differ from those of parent companies of a multinational
group; and (iii) why and to what extent should the performance of foreign
affiliates differ from those of national affiliates belonging to a multinational
group.

Let us analyse these issues in some detail (see Table 4.2 for a summary of
the following discussion).

4.3.1   The International Dispersion of R&D Activities: A Reappraisal

Tackling the first issue implies a careful examination of arguments for and
against the international dispersion of innovative activities. This was done
at length in Chapter 1, to which the reader should refer. Suffice it here to
recall that R&D and innovation are traditionally expected to be geographically concentrated in the home country of multinationals and controlled
by the parent company, with subsidiaries playing primarily a role in the
adoption of centrally created technology. This view, largely associated with
the product cycle hypothesis (Vernon 1966), was supported mainly by US
economists and based on US evidence from the early post-World War II
period. The underlying theoretical reasons have to do with economies of
scales in the R&D function; with technological agglomeration advantages
that lead firms to locate their R&D where other firms already carry out
innovative activities as a means of gaining access to more tacit knowledge;
and with learning advantages related to demand dynamics thus enabling
firms to innovate more where there is a richer and faster growing market for
new products. The empirical literature we have reviewed in Part I of this
book, confirms that a large fraction of R&D is geographically concentrated
in the home locations (Patel and Pavitt 1991; Patel 1996) and that technology is transferred from parent companies to foreign affiliates more than the
other way around (Fors 1997). However, at least three facts contrast with
the traditional product life-cycle view. First, there are significant differences

across firms, sectors and countries. In fact, European multinationals exhibit a long history of relatively high R&D internationalisation compared with US based ones (Cantwell 1995). Moreover knowledge flows from subsidiaries to parent companies appear to be significantly higher in some technological categories, such as in the case of multinationals active in the fields of computing and communication technologies (Singh 2004). Second, the share of innovative activities carried out abroad by firms has been increasing significantly over the past decades for all firms, including US based ones (Creamer 1976; Dunning 1994). Third, patterns of geographic concentration of R&D, which still occur in the proximity of parent companies of multinationals, tend to be replicated in highly advanced regions in which MNFs locate their most innovative affiliates (Cantwell and Iammarino 2003; Verspagen and Schoenmakers 2004).

As discussed in Part I of this book, these patterns of R&D internationalisation reflect a combination of asset exploiting and asset seeking motives (Dunning and Narula 1995; Kuemmerle 1999). On one hand, as firms create new affiliates to exploit their ownership advantages in foreign markets, they increasingly need to perform some R&D locally to adapt products and technologies to specific applications and user needs. It is foreign demand that attracts these R&D investments abroad. On the other hand, foreign R&D is needed to gain access to and utilise local technology and competencies, wherever these are available. It is thus foreign knowledge and related infrastructures that attract these R&D investments abroad. While both investment motives justify some internationalisation of innovation, it has been noted that asset seeking investments lead to regional clustering of R&D activities (Verspagen and Schoenmakers 2004, pp. 25–26). In fact, as knowledge is often hard and costly to codify (although there are differences across industries in this respect), its absorption requires a close interaction with localised sources of technology, and is facilitated by proximity. Hence asset seeking multinationals are more likely to locate their R&D in the vicinity of local innovative activities, and contribute to technological agglomeration processes.

To summarise, the organisation of innovative activities of multinationals is changing, and foreign affiliates are increasingly involved not only in the adoption but also in the creation and diffusion of new products and technology. The international dispersion of innovation goes hand in hand with both asset exploiting and asset seeking investments. To the extent that asset seeking strategies are increasing[58] in intensity, the international dispersion of R&D will be geographically oriented. In other words, technological activities of multinationals take place in an increasing number of locations both within the country of origin and abroad, but not all regions are equally attractive for asset seeking R&D investments. We thus observe a transition from the clustering of innovation in a few regions, in which parent companies of large multinationals were typically located, to the clustering of innovation in a larger number of regions. These are the regions wherein proximity advantages and technological agglomeration economies can be more easily reproduced and exploited by firms, including foreign affiliates of MNFs.

Given this general trend, there are intra-industry differences in the organisation of innovative activities of multinationals (and in the role of FAs in R&D and innovation). A number of differentiating factors have been highlighted in the literature and are briefly recalled below (see Part I of this book for further discussion):

Constraints and incentives to the transfer of knowledge   These include spatial distance, differences in language, outlook, norms and culture, and even simply time zone, which may create severe communication problems and misunderstandings (Buckley and Carter 2004). By contrast, the transfer of knowledge is positively related to the similarity of activities carried out by parent companies and subsidiaries (Andersson et al. 2003), and to the length of activity of affiliates in the host location, which increases the acquaintance of the MNF with the local economy and increases the incentive to commit strategic resources to it, including R&D (Gomes-Casseres 1989). Furthermore, the ICT has made it easier for firms to access and combine geographical dispersed competences and resources. This contributed to diversify and internationalise corporate technological profiles (Santangelo, 2001)

Constraints and incentives to the adoption of knowledge   New technology originating elsewhere within the MNF may turn out to be incompatible with local standards and user needs. Furthermore, foreign affiliates are often forced by host country governments to source at least part of their inputs and technology locally, thus reducing the rate of adoption of knowledge from parent companies. Finally, not all foreign affiliates possess the 'absorptive capacity' – most often associated with firm size and human capital endowment – needed to adopt technology from parent companies, and from other parts of the MNF (Teece 1977; Cantwell 1995; Gupta and Govidarajan 2000).

Knowledge creation mandates   Pressures in this field are exerted by parent companies as well as by foreign affiliates.[59] On one hand the likelihood of a competence creating mandate is positively affected by the richness of the local resource pool and negatively affected by the local presence of other technological leaders, which will either exert control over scarce resources (gravitational pull) or create dynamic barriers to entry and increase the costs of competition in local markets (oligopolistic deterrence) (Cantwell and Mudambi forthcoming; Cantwell and Santangelo 2002). On the other hand, the extent to which affiliates play a role in knowledge creation is less the result of discretion by central units, and more difficult to revoke, when they control assets vital to the rest of the MNF (Mudambi and Navarra 2004).

4.3.2   Comparing the Performances of Parent Companies and Foreign Affiliates

The second issue to tackle is diversity between foreign affiliates and parent companies. We have highlighted that under specific circumstances, foreign affiliates will play a key role in the innovative activities within MNFs. Can foreign subsidiaries outperform parent companies, which are by definition responsible for multinational strategies including a large part of R&D activities? There are important reasons for answering this question negatively.

First, foreign affiliates incur high fixed costs of learning how things are done in the host country. This implies a lower efficiency of their plants relative to the parent company, unless the local market is large enough to fully exploit economies of scale (Caves 1996, p. 58). As an example of the learning costs foreign affiliates have to deal with, Harris and Robinson (2002, p. 211) stress that 'it may take a considerable time to overcome such factors as cultural barriers to entry'. In a similar vein, Gomes and Ramaswamy (1999) emphasise the costs of managing culturally distinct markets and diverse human resources. Consistently with these views, Dunning (1988) notes that in the 1950s US manufacturing affiliates in the UK recorded lower labour productivity than those of their parent plants, due to lack of experience in management and labour attitudes. More recently, Dunning (1998) recalls that more than one interviewee has gone as far as to claim that US affiliates only really prospered since their management had become British.

Second, foreign affiliates are less exposed to technological agglomeration economies than parent companies. As we have mentioned earlier, most R&D and patenting is geographically concentrated in a few highly agglomerated areas at home, where the parent company and satellite R&D labs are located, and it is geographically concentrated in a few dynamic areas abroad – also where the most innovative FAs are located. However, not all FAs are located in dynamic areas and take advantage of and contribute to externalities characterising these areas. A multinational company may have different FAs in a given country, some of which will be highly innovative and active in the most dynamic regions, whereas other FAs (most likely located elsewhere in the same country) might well be mere importers of technology from home for use in local market production.[60] For instance,

MNFs often locate low value added plants in government assisted peripheral regions (Harris 1991; Shaver and Flyer 2000), especially when products are in their mature stage of development (Harris 1988). By contrast, a parent company will tend to be highly innovative either because they directly carry out first class R&D activities, or because they have immediate access to innovation of nearby research labs. One may thus conclude that while parent companies are almost by definition at the centre of technological agglomerations and take direct advantage from them (in terms of dynamic economies of scales, cross-fertilisation and other externalities), not all foreign affiliates of an MNF in a given sector will gravitate towards highly dynamic areas and will benefit from technological opportunities and spillovers. All else being equal, the agglomeration factors we have examined thus push in the direction of creating an advantage for parent companies relative to foreign affiliates.

Third, foreign affiliates are in less of a position to gain access to the global knowledge network of the MNF. Parent companies are likely to enjoy a relative advantage here too, even though the issue is more complex. In fact, they govern the entire network of foreign affiliates and potentially convey all the knowledge streams originating from different locations where asset seeking strategies are being carried out. In other words, while it is true that foreign units not only have access to technology transferred from PCs, but also to local knowledge, what remains specific to the PC is their role as 'technology organiser' (Cantwell 2001), or 'architect' (Tallman and Fladmoe-Lindquist 2002). This role enables them to regulate the flow of knowledge available abroad that is transmitted and utilised within the MNF. In a similar vein, Siler et al. (2003, p. 18) observe that 'despite the evolution of MNFs towards the establishment of more independent subsidiaries, the parent firm continues to serve as the most active creator and diffuser of knowledge within the corporation'. The extent to which technology is transferred from foreign locations towards parent companies is subject matter for empirical research.[61] It remains true that parent companies are in a position to gain access to at least part of the knowledge assets generated or adopted locally by potentially all foreign subsidiaries. It is much less so in the case of an individual FA active in any single country, which will not generally gain access to knowledge generated or adopted elsewhere by other units of the MNF's internal network as quickly and effectively as the PC will. This asymmetry has to do with both organisational and strategic reasons. From an organisational point of view, 'horizontal' knowledge transfers between FAs located in different countries or regions may not be easy to organise within complex multinational networks. Obstacles to transnational and cross-regional knowledge transfers even within a firm may be due to the diversity of incentive structures and to communication problems, which in turn reflect the specific environment in which they are active (Jaffe and Adams 1996; Szulanski 1996). The strategic reasons relate to the intentional effort made by parent companies of MNFs to prevent unwanted information leakages and to avoid loosing control over strategic assets. Overall, organisational and strategic factors constraining horizontal knowledge circulation are consistent with the findings of studies which show that knowledge transfer between R&D labs located in different countries are the least likely to occur (Warrant 1991; Siler et al. 2003; Foss and Pedersen 2004). Given this lack of horizontal circulation of knowledge, new assets accessed in one country can reach FAs in another country only or primarily if: (a) they are themselves transferred back to the parent company from the FA located in the source country; (b) they are evaluated correctly at the parent company level; and (c) they get transferred to the FA located elsewhere. This implies that the probability that knowledge generated by asset seeking strategies reaches the parent company is higher than the probability that this same knowledge reaches an individual FA other than the one that originated it.

Altogether the examined factors appear to push in the direction of the higher economic and innovative performances of parent companies relative to FAs. However, one needs to take into account that comparing average performances might downplay the important role of knowledge complementarities. Particularly when technologies are complex, it may be more relevant that FAs enrich the spectrum of MNF competencies rather than the fact that they outperform PCs. A further caveat: while it may be an acceptable generalisation that parent companies will outperform FAs as a result of extra costs of learning, agglomeration and asset seeking tensions, it is also true that the action of these factors will be mediated by the more general environment in which these firms are active. MNFs may create new subsidiaries in order to open a technological window or plug into a higher level innovation system. This could determine a faster learning process for the FA with respect to the parent company. This process can persist and lead the FA to outperform the parent company at home, especially if the reverse technology transfer mechanisms do not work perfectly.

4.3.3   Comparing the Performances of Foreign and National Affiliates

Let us finally focus on the third issue anticipated in the introduction of section 4.3, that is, diversity between foreign and national affiliates of multinationals. There are different, partially conflicting forces which affect the relative distribution of advantages here. On one hand, proximity matters in technology and innovation. This would generally facilitate national subsidiaries relative to foreign subsidiaries in receiving spillovers from technological activities carried out at the parent company level or in nationally based R&D labs (usually located within, or close to, the parent company itself). We have shown that part of the knowledge generated at the central level is transferred through national and international communication channels within the MNF. Since a large component of technology is tacit, its transfer requires the mobility of researchers whose costs are positively related to geographic distance. Furthermore, the functioning of informal mechanisms of knowledge transmission is certainly facilitated by a commonality of language, jargon and habits which typically characterise affiliates located within the same country (Buckley and Carter 2004). These proximity factors would thus seem to create some advantages to the NAs relative to FAs, which would translate into better performance for the former.

On the other hand, there are strategic reasons why FAs may be expected to have, on average, greater access to knowledge than NAs. First, in spite of the proximity reasons facilitating the transmission of knowledge to NAs, PCs are most likely to be willing to transfer more relevant technology to FAs as a means to overcome the extra costs and risks they face in foreign markets. Second, FAs are in a better bargaining position relative to national affiliates to gain access to relevant technology generated at the central level and in other *loci* of knowledge creation within the MNF. In fact, FAs have direct control of the foreign market which would be harder and costlier to serve by other means, given the high sunk costs associated with the creation of a subsidiary in that market and given information asymmetries concerning the characteristics of demand and of application needs. In other words, subsidiaries that control knowledge and other assets vital to the rest of the MNF will be able to accumulate a high bargaining power (Mudambi and Navarra 2004, p. 399). The greater their bargaining power, the higher the likelihood that they will gain access to relevant knowledge originating from the PC. Of course, both sunk costs and information asymmetries may also be significant in the case of affiliates active in the home market, giving rise to a bargaining power issue here too. However, we may submit that both problems (sunk costs and information asymmetries) are higher in the case of foreign subsidiaries. More generally, the bargaining power issue is made more dramatic by the fact that foreign affiliates are more costly to substitute for in case of failure or opportunistic behaviour than a national production facility. Third, FAs are more highly motivated to innovate due to their exposure to greater challenges and opportunities within the foreign context, and they are in a unique position to gain access to locally available knowledge. While some of this knowledge may be available by means of arm's length transactions through licensing agreements which do not have to be signed at the local level (and are therefore a strategy available to subsidiaries located back home as well), its tacit component requires different organisational devices (such as more robust agreements with local firms) as well as informal interactions with indigenous parties. This privileged access to local knowledge, together with the greater environmental stimuli to innovate, can *per se* positively impact on economic and innovative performances of FAs relative to national affiliates. Such an advantage will last at least for the transitory period in which the new technology developed locally is 'decontextualised', i.e. converted from its application-specific state into bits of knowledge that can be more generally understood and applied to different contexts (Arora and Gambardella 1994; Becattini and Rullani 1993). Knowledge accessed locally might not even be transferred back at all if it stemmed from co-operation with local counterparts and, as such, circulates according to contractual constraints (Zanfei 2000; Buckley and Carter 2004). Under these circumstances, locally accessed knowledge may not be made available to the rest of the MNF, not because the FA is not willing to transfer it back but because it is temporarily or permanently constrained not to do so (see Part I of this volume for more discussion on the constraints to the transfer of knowledge within the multinational). An important qualification to be made here is that the NA might receive from the FA even less than other units of the MNF. The reasoning is similar to the one we have developed in subsection 4.3.2 above: as horizontal transfers are largely constrained (although not absent), most of the knowledge flows from the FAs, if any, are likely to reach the PC first and thereafter be eventually redistributed through the network. The implication is that, the privileged access of foreign affiliates to knowledge available in a foreign market may translate into a temporary or even permanent advantage over national affiliates in terms of productivity and innovation. Apart from these constraints to the transfer of technology, the FA may be willing to use locally generated knowledge strategically to strengthen its own bargaining power as a means of gaining access to further knowledge generated at home and elsewhere within the MNF. This will of course reinforce the advantage of FAs relative to national affiliates.

Whether foreign affiliates will outperform national affiliates in a given industry will then depend on which of the examined forces prevails. That is, whether proximity to national research labs is more or less relevant than proximity to a foreign source of knowledge, combined with bargaining power factors and other strategic considerations. To the extent that the evolution towards a double network structure takes place as discussed in Part I of this book, one might expect that the balance would lean in favour of foreign affiliates, outperforming national affiliates in terms of productivity and innovation.

Once again, similar to our discussion concluding subsection 4.3.2, some caveats apply. Here too, the effects of the examined forces will be mediated

Table 4.2   Heterogeneity within multinationals

Type of heterogeneity	Determinants of heterogeneity	Main references
Dispersion of innovation activities	Constraints on knowledge transfer Constraints on knowledge adoption Knowledge creation mandates	Buckley and Carter 2004 Teece 1977 Cantwell and Mudambi 2005
Diversity between Parent Companies and Foreign Affiliates	Costs of learning about the host country Exposure to technological agglomeration Access to global MNF network	Caves 1996 Dunning 1988 Harris 1991 Singh 2004 Cantwell 2001
Diversity between Foreign and National Affiliates	Proximity to home sources of knowledge Transfer of assets to overcome local costs and risks Bargaining power Exposure to local sources of knowledge	Buckley and Carter 2004 Mudambi and Navarra 2004 Cantwell 1995 Zanfei 2000

by the more general factors referring to the characteristics and relative technological strengths of the systems in which FAs and NAs are located. Moreover, when FAs and NAs of different multinational groups are compared, the characteristics of the multinational groups they belong to should be also considered, especially in terms of their degree and geographic spread of internationalisation.

4.4   HETEROGENEITY ACROSS AND WITHIN MULTINATIONALS: EVIDENCE FOR ITALY

This section applies a large part of the conceptual framework developed in this chapter to shed some light on intra-industry heterogeneity across and within multinationals with specific reference to the Italian case. Using firm level data on innovation and productivity, we shall follow four main steps. First, we shall compare performances of foreign and domestic owned firms as a whole. This is perhaps the most commonly adopted level of analysis (e.g. Veugelers and Cassiman 2004 and Balcet and Evangelista 2005). It is, however, the least informative of the real role of multinationals in a given economy, as stated in the introduction. The second step will be to distinguish within the domestic component of the Italian economy those firms which are themselves multinationals. We shall emphasise that both foreign and domestic owned multinationals outperform Italian uni-national firms, while no significant difference seems to exist on average between the two categories of MNF. It is thus multinationality rather than foreignness that appears to make the difference in terms of innovation and productivity (see Doms and Jensen 1998; Criscuolo and Martin 2003; Frenz and Ietto-Gilllies 2005 for a similar distinction across domestic owned firms). The third step will be to make the comparison more precise, and distinguish between parent companies and national affiliates of domestic multinationals, comparing them with foreign firms – which are by definition foreign affiliates of MNFs rooted in different countries. This will allow us to carry out a detailed analysis of heterogeneity within multinationals, that is to see how economic and innovation performance differs according to the position companies occupy within multinationals. Finally, we shall provide some evidence that the characteristics of the home and foreign systems connected by MNFs are associated with performance differences among FAs, hence contributing to heterogeneity across multinationals.

4.4.1 Data and Specification

The empirical analysis presented below is based on the same dataset we utilised in Chapter 3 and in other parts later in this volume, resulting from the intersection of two different sources: the Second *Community Innovation Survey* (CIS2) and ELIOS (*European Linkages and Ownership Structure*). See the Appendix for a detailed description of the data. The former source, assessing various aspects of firms' innovative behaviour and performances in 1994–96, was accessed subject to a confidentiality agreement with the Italian Bureau of Statistics, Istat.[62] Innovation data were complemented with ownership, multinationality and economic performance data from ELIOS dataset developed by the University of Urbino, Italy, which combines information from Dun & Bradstreet's *Who Owns Whom* and Bureau Van Dijck's *Amadeus*. For the purpose of this part of the analysis we used a sample of 903 firms active in Italy which resulted from this matching. Balcet and Evangelista (2005) utilise part of the same dataset to characterise innovative patterns of foreign owned firms in Italy. Our work differs from the latter because we do not only compare foreign owned firms (i.e. affiliates of foreign multinationals located in Italy) with national firms as a whole, but also with different categories of domestic owned companies. As anticipated, we break down the subset of domestic firms, distinguishing between uni-national firms and two different categories of domestic multi-nationals, namely parent companies (PC) and national affiliates (NA) of the same MNF.[63] Figure 4.1a and 4.1b provide a graphical representation of the sample and of its various subsets of firms.

To summarise, out of the 903 sample firms (all active in manufacturing sectors in Italy) 321 are foreign owned firms (i.e. foreign affiliates of multi-nationals based in a different country) denoted as FA and 682 are domes-tic owned firms (DOM). Within this latter group, 310 are not part of any multinational group. Out of the 276 firms which are part of a multinational group (MNFGRP), 121 are parent companies (PC), identified in section 4.3 as firms participating in at least one company abroad[64] while 151 are national affiliates of domestic owned multinationals (NA).

Table 4.3 provides some further details on the sectoral composition of firms, their size together with the main indicators of their technological activities as expressed in terms of total factor productivity[65], the share of innovative firms, and product to process innovation ratio in each of the examined subsamples. Suffice it here to notice three important features of

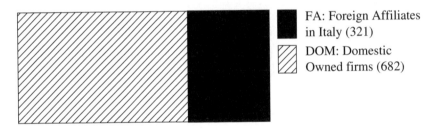

Figure 4.1a   Domestic and foreign owned firms in Italy: the sample composition

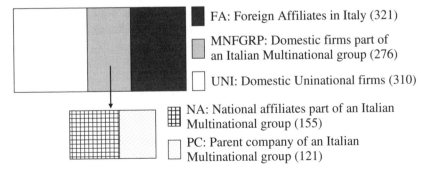

Figure 4.1b   The sub-sample of domestic owned companies in Italy

Table 4.3   Differences across and within multinationals in Italy: descriptive statistics, 1996

	UNI	FA	MNFGRP	PC	NA	TOTAL
N. firms	310	321	276	121	155	903
%	*34.3*	*35.5*	*30.6*	*13.4*	*17.2*	*100*
By OECD tech class						
Low tech	37.7	17.1	25.4	25.6	25.2	26.8
Medium–Low tech	27.1	24.6	23.6	24.8	22.6	25.2
Medium–High tech	30.3	46.7	38.4	43.8	34.2	38.8
High tech	3.9	11.5	8.0	5.8	9.7	7.9
	100.0	100.0	100.0	100.0	100.0	100.0
By Pavitt sectors						
Science Based	20.3	34.0	23.2	25.6	21.3	26.1
Scale Intensive	41.3	40.5	37.3	36.4	38.1	40.0
Specialised Suppliers	9.7	16.5	16.3	19.8	13.5	14.2
Supplier Dominated	27.7	9.0	18.5	18.2	18.7	18.4
	100.0	100.0	100.0	100.0	100.0	100.0
Avg. TFP	4.08	6.02	7.07	7.01	8.02	6.02
Avg. N. employees	298	714	1375	1716	1078	785
N. product innov.	159	224	184	97	87	567
Share in total firms (%)	51.3	69.8	66.7	80.2	56.1	62.8
N. process innov.	170	204	188	94	94	562
Share in total firms (%)	54.8	63.6	68.1	77.7	60.6	62.2
Product/process innov.	0.94	1.10	0.98	1.03	0.93	1.01

the examined sample. First, the sampled firms are relatively large in size, certainly larger than the average firm in the universe of manufacturing firms in Italy, but the distribution of firms by low–medium–high technology classes substantially corresponds to the specialisation of Italy's industry – with a high overall weight of low (and medium)-tech firms.[66] Second, the share of science based (and high-tech) activities is slightly higher in the case of affiliates of foreign owned multinationals (FAs) than it is the case of domestic firms. This largely corresponds to the sectoral distribution of foreign affiliates as recorded by available statistics produced by the Reprint Dataset and ultimately published in OECD's *Measuring Globalisation* for Italy (Cominotti and Mariotti 2002; OECD 2002). Third and finally, foreign owned manufacturing affiliates (FAs) do appear to be systematically more productive and more innovative than domestic uni-national firms (UNI), and the former also have a higher product to process innovation ratio than the latter. However, the scenario becomes much more blurred once we compare foreign affiliates to the other categories of domestic owned multinational firms.

Table 4.4   Indicators of firm performance and innovative behaviour

Variable	Description	Source
Performance		
VAL	Log of the Labour Productivity of firm i	ELIOS
TFP	Log of the TFP of firm i	ELIOS
Innovation		
INPDT	=1 if firm i introduced product innovation in 94–96	CIS2
INPCS	=1 if firm i introduced process innovation in 94–96	CIS2
RTOT	=1 if firm i spent any money in R&D activities (both *intra* and *extra muros*)	CIS2
PAT	=1 if firm i applied for at least one patent in 94–96	CIS2
CO_NAZ	=1 if firm i had some technological cooperation with Italian counterparts in 94–96	CIS2
CO_INT	=1 if firm i had some technological cooperation with foreign counterparts in 94–96	CIS2

Of course, data in Table 4.3 only allow for rough comparisons without any controls. For a more precise analysis we shall make use of multivariate techniques. In particular, we shall first estimate the following expression:

$$y_i = \alpha + \beta\, FA_i + Z_i'\gamma + \varepsilon_i$$

where y denotes a measure of firm performance or a characteristic of its innovative behaviour (see Table 4.4), Z is a vector of controls such as firm age, sector, region and size dummies, while FA is a dummy taking a value of 1 for affiliates of foreign multinationals in Italy. Within this context, β represents the difference in performance or innovative behaviour of foreign owned firms relative to domestic-owned firms. This will allow us to proceed with step 1 of the empirical analysis: whether and to what extent foreign firms outperform domestic firms as a whole. Next, we will move to step 2, and identify within the group of domestic firms, those firms which are are part of an Italian multinational. The estimated equation will take the following form:

$$y_i = \alpha + \beta\, FA_i + \delta_1 MNFGRP_i + Z_i'\gamma + \varepsilon_i$$

where *MNFGRP* is now a dummy taking a value of 1 for all firms being part of an Italian multinational firm. In this, and in the following specifications, the baseline category becomes the group of uni-national firms (UNI).

We then extend this specification in order to test whether it makes any difference being a parent company or a national affiliate of a domestic manufacturing multinational group. In other words, we estimate:

$$y_i = \alpha + \beta\, FA_i + \delta_2 PC_i + \delta_3 NA_i + Z_i'\gamma + \varepsilon_i$$

In this case, β can be interpreted as before, δ_2 captures differences in performance or innovation in the parent companies of Italian multinationals, while δ_3 measures differences in performances of national affiliates of Italian multinationals – the baseline remaining domestic uninational firms. This equation will be used to proceed with step 3 as mentioned earlier: whether and to what extent FAs outperform Italian PCs and NAs.

4.4.2   Patterns of Productivity and Innovation Across and Within Multinationals

The results from Table 4.5a deal with step 1 of the empirical analysis. Consistent with conventional wisdom, foreign owned firms appear to be more productive than domestic firms as a whole, once controls are made for size, age, region and sector. However, there seems to be a lot of variation in the productivity of domestic firms, such that the (positive) coefficient on FA turns out to be not significantly different from zero. Significant differences emerge in the propensity to patent (lower in FAs). As discussed in this chapter, comparing FAs with all domestic firms with the entire domestic owned component of the economy would make little sense. It would be wrong to imply that increasing the share of foreign owned firms as opposed to any other domestic company enhances the efficiency of the system. In fact, an important composition effect is to be accounted for, namely, the existence of domestic owned firms that are themselves multinationals. Once we introduce a control for Italian firms belonging to a multinational group (MNFGRP), in Table 4.5b it turns out that both FAs and MNFGRPs outperform domestic uni-national firms in terms of productivity and exhibit higher propensity to innovate products. However, it is multinationality, rather than foreignness, that matters in terms of productivity and innovation premiums. In fact, testing the difference between the coefficients on FAs and MNFGRPs we can assess to what extent productivity and innovative behaviour differ when considering foreign and domestic multinationals active in Italy. Our evidence strongly suggests that firms belonging to Italian multinational groups are more productive and exhibit a higher propensity to carry out innovative activities (such as R&D, patenting and technological cooperation) in Italy. Similar results have been obtained in the literature with reference to other countries, although from data either on productivity or innovation (Doms and Jensen 1998; Criscuolo et al. 2004). At this stage, our analysis further confirms and reinforces what has emerged in the empirical literature, using both types of data.

Table 4.5c allows us to proceed to step 3 of our empirical analysis concerning differences in performance according to the position of firms within multinational groups. Several interesting results emerge here. First, it becomes apparent that parent companies of domestic owned multi-nationals not only outperform domestic uni-nationals, but also tend to outperform foreign firms. This is a neat result, in terms of both innovation and productivity. Second, the same does not apply to the case of national affiliates of Italian multinationals, which do exhibit a productivity premium relative to foreign firms but generally perform worse than both PCs and FAs in terms of innovation. These two results seem to suggest that a sort of hierarchy exists, according to which PCs outperform both FAs and NAs. The comparison between FAs and NAs is less neat, although there is evidence that foreign affiliates innovate more particularly in terms of new products. One should be careful with generalisations, particularly when comparing firm units belonging to different multinationals (PCs and NAs of Italian multinationals and FAs of multinationals with their home base outside Italy). However, we find some consistencies with the line of argument we followed in this chapter. The prevalence of PCs over FAs seems to confirm the importance of both agglomeration pressures and tensions for the control of knowledge sources which we have identified in section 4.3.2. As regards the comparison between FAs and NAs, our discussion in section 4.3.3 had already indicated possible trade-offs between proximity factors, favouring NAs due to their geographic closeness to PCs and the nearby R&D labs in the home country, and the greater stimuli to innovate and higher bargaining power which would instead favour FAs rather than NAs. The fact that, according to our data, FAs appear to be more innovative than NAs seems consistent with the importance of the latter set of factors. FAs are more stimulated from exposure to more challenges and opportunities in a different context and they enjoy a better bargaining position by means of which they obtain technology from the PC due to the exclusive control they have over a foreign market. However, the fact that NAs exhibit a higher productivity than FAs has a number of possible explanations. Of course, the observed productivity differences might have to do with market power, scale effects or other factors which we do not properly control for. Nevertheless, they may also be consistent with the higher (cultural and geo-graphical) proximity of NAs relative to foreign affiliates in general, which facilitates the transfer of such immaterial assets as managerial practices

Table 4.5a Differences in performance and innovation: foreign vs. domestic firms in Italy, 1996–2000

	VAL	TFP	INPCS	INPDT	PAT	RTOT	CO_NAZ	CO_INT
FA	0.015	0.023	–0.078	0.139	–0.204**	–0.034	–0.130	0.137
	(0.016)	(0.015)	(0.097)	(0.099)	(0.103)	(0.104)	(0.111)	(0.110)
N. obs.	3545	3417	903	903	903	903	903	903

Estimated equation: $y_i = \alpha + \beta\, FA_i + Z_i'\gamma + \varepsilon_i$

Baseline category: domestic owned firms

All regressions are estimated with a constant and controlling for age of the firm, sector, region and size dummies. Standard Errors in parentheses below estimates. Asterisks denote confidence levels (* p<0.1, ** p<0.05, *** p<0.01)

Table 4.5b Differences in performance and innovation: comparing foreign firms with domestic multinationals and with uni-national companies in Italy, 1996–2000

	VAL	TFP	INPCS	INPDT	PAT	RTOT	CO_NAZ	CO_INT
FA	0.088***	0.103***	−0.022	0.251**	−0.198	0.129	0.105	0.399***
	(0.020)	(0.018)	(0.113)	(0.115)	(0.124)	(0.118)	(0.139)	(0.145)
MNFGRP	0.139***	0.152***	0.114	0.230*	0.010	0.363***	0.401***	0.433***
	(0.021)	(0.019)	(0.118)	(0.119)	(0.129)	(0.126)	(0.140)	(0.149)
N. obs.	3545	3417	903	903	903	903	903	903
Tests on coefficients								
FA − MNFGRP	−0.051	−0.049	−0.136	0.021	−0.208	−0.234	−0.296	−0.034
p-value	(0.007)	(0.005)	(0.235)	(0.859)	(0.080)	(0.064)	(0.017)	(0.783)

Estimated equation: $y_i = \alpha + \beta\,FA_i + \delta_1 MNFGRP_i + Z_i'\gamma + \varepsilon_i$

Baseline category: domestic owned uni-national firms
All regressions are estimated with a constant and controlling for age of the firm, sector, region, and size dummies. Standard Errors in parentheses below estimates. Asterisks denote confidence levels (* $p<0.1$, ** $p<0.05$, *** $p<0.01$)

Table 4.5c *Differences in performance and innovative behaviour, across and within multinationals in Italy, 1996–2000*

	VAL	TFP	INPCS	INPDT	PAT	RTOT	CO_NAZ	CO_INT
FA	0.088***	0.102***	−0.015	0.262**	−0.195	0.142	0.111	0.402***
	(0.020)	(0.018)	(0.113)	(0.115)	(0.124)	(0.118)	(0.139)	(0.145)
PC	0.145***	0.134***	0.304*	0.520***	0.161	0.740***	0.530***	0.607***
	(0.025)	(0.024)	(0.159)	(0.162)	(0.158)	(0.189)	(0.170)	(0.174)
NA	0.133***	0.169***	−0.008	0.040	−0.128	0.157	0.298*	0.264
	(0.026)	(0.024)	(0.135)	(0.138)	(0.154)	(0.144)	(0.162)	(0.176)
N. obs.	3545	3417	903	903	903	903	903	903
Tests on coefficients								
FA − PC	−0.057	−0.032	−0.318	−0.258	−0.356	−0.598	−0.419	−0.204
p-value	*(0.012)*	*(0.144)*	*(0.039)*	*(0.102)*	*(0.017)*	*(0.001)*	*(0.007)*	*(0.180)*
FA − NA	−0.045	−0.067	−0.006	0.222	−0.067	−0.015	−0.187	0.138
p-value	*(0.067)*	*(0.003)*	*(0.962)*	*(0.107)*	*(0.650)*	*(0.920)*	*(0.211)*	*(0.375)*
PC − NA	0.012	−0.034	0.312	0.480	0.290	0.583	0.231	0.343
p-value	*(0.671)*	*(0.226)*	*(0.072)*	*(0.007)*	*(0.097)*	*(0.004)*	*(0.191)*	*(0.060)*

Estimated equation $y_i = \alpha + \beta FA_i + \delta_1 PC_i + \delta_2 NA_i + Z'_i \gamma + \varepsilon_i$

Baseline category: domestic owned uninational firms

All regressions are estimated with a constant and controlling for age of the firm, sector, region and size dummies. Standard Errors in parentheses below estimates. Asterisks denote confidence levels (* p<0.1, ** p<0.05, *** p<0.01) and organisational procedures and may translate into higher productivity even in the absence of new product or process technology.

A third set of results worth mentioning is illustrated in Table 4.5c. This table illustrates that while PCs of Italian multinationals do not exhibit any different propensity to set up international technology alliances relative to foreign multinationals, they have a much higher propensity to cooperate with national counterparts (and with local suppliers and universities in particular).[67] This might have important implications to the extent that linkage creation is a key channel for the generation of positive spillovers to other domestic firms. This view, originally put forward by Hirschman (1958) with reference to all categories of investment creating new demands for inputs and/or new opportunities for downstream activities, has usually been applied to the case of foreign direct investment (see, *inter alia* Rodriguez-Clare 1996). However, empirical evidence is scarce and most often based on indirect linkage measures. In the case of Italy, we find direct evidence of higher linkage creation for investment by domestic multinationals than is the case of foreign investors (see Part III for more discussion on this aspect).

Comparing Italian PCs with FAs in Italy has the drawback that we might mix up the effects of heterogeneity within MNFs, with the effects of heterogeneity across MNFs. As discussed in sections 4.2 and 4.3, the analysis of firm and intra-firm-specific factors should be mediated with a careful consideration of the system wide factors affecting multinational strategies and hence their performances. In particular, it would be necessary to account for the geographic spread and intensity of international networks characterising the two multinational groups, the technological strengths and specialisation of the area from which the foreign firm originate relative to the area in which the domestic multinational is rooted, and the type and intensity of links the foreign firm has developed with the host economy. In any given industry, the foreign affiliate of a MNF rooted in a strong innovation system of origin may well outperform the parent company of a domestic owned firm rooted in a weaker innovation system. It is also possible that a foreign affiliate belonging to a much more internationalised multinational group might perform better than the parent company of a multinational group whose internal and external networks are less developed. Unfortunately the controls we are able to make with the available data are rough and barely illustrative of all the complexities related to all these micro and macro level factors. We partially account for the role of the systems of origin by testing whether significant differences show up when distinguishing foreign firms according to their country or geographic area of origin. In Table 4.6 we estimate performance and innovative differentials for foreign owned firms originating from European countries, the US, and from other countries (mainly from Switzerland (68 per cent) and Japan (20 per cent)). It is apparent that

Table 4.6 Differences in performance and innovative behaviour, 1996–2000, by area of origin

	VAL	TFP	INPCS	INPDT	PAT	RTOT	CO_NAZ	CO_INT
US	0.160***	0.151***	0.026	0.174	-0.202	0.015	0.070	0.439**
	(0.028)	(0.028)	(0.167)	(0.170)	(0.174)	(0.173)	(0.193)	(0.194)
EU	0.068***	0.089***	-0.040	0.278**	-0.159	0.171	0.020	0.348**
	(0.021)	(0.020)	(0.128)	(0.130)	(0.139)	(0.135)	(0.158)	(0.160)
OTH	0.021	0.052	0.027	0.389	-0.403	0.297	0.572**	0.600**
	(0.046)	(0.040)	(0.242)	(0.257)	(0.277)	(0.266)	(0.256)	(0.274)
PC	0.146***	0.135***	0.304*	0.518***	0.160	0.737***	0.527***	0.608***
	(0.025)	(0.024)	(0.159)	(0.163)	(0.158)	(0.189)	(0.170)	(0.174)
NA	0.135***	0.170***	-0.007	0.038	-0.129	0.153	0.294*	0.264
	(0.026)	(0.024)	(0.136)	(0.138)	(0.155)	(0.144)	(0.162)	(0.176)
N. obs.	3545	3417	903	903	903	903	903	903
Tests on coefficients								
US – EU	0.092	0.063	0.066	-0.104	-0.043	-0.155	0.050	0.091
p-value	(0.001)	(0.021)	(0.698)	(0.555)	(0.809)	(0.388)	(0.797)	(0.623)
US – OTH	0.139	0.100	-0.001	-0.215	0.201	-0.281	-0.502	-0.162
p-value	(0.004)	(0.020)	(0.998)	(0.451)	(0.498)	(0.340)	(0.076)	(0.579)
EU – OTH	0.048	0.037	-0.067	-0.111	0.244	-0.126	-0.552	-0.253
p-value	(0.299)	(0.339)	(0.787)	(0.675)	(0.383)	(0.647)	(0.034)	(0.349)
US – PC	0.014	0.016	-0.278	-0.345	-0.362	-0.722	-0.457	-0.169
p-value	(0.640)	(0.587)	(0.155)	(0.085)	(0.060)	(0.001)	(0.025)	(0.396)
US – NA	0.025	-0.018	0.033	0.136	-0.072	-0.138	-0.224	0.175
p-value	(0.421)	(0.547)	(0.853)	(0.460)	(0.703)	(0.470)	(0.260)	(0.385)
EU – PC	-0.078	-0.046	-0.345	-0.241	-0.319	-0.566	-0.507	-0.260

p-value	(0.002)	(0.049)	(0.038)	(0.157)	(0.049)	(0.004)	(0.003)	(0.120)
EU – NA	−0.067	−0.081	−0.033	0.240	−0.030	0.017	−0.273	0.084
p-value	(0.010)	(0.001)	(0.824)	(0.114)	(0.853)	(0.914)	(0.103)	(0.625)
OTH – PC	−0.125	−0.083	−0.278	−0.129	−0.563	−0.440	0.045	−0.007
p-value	(0.007)	(0.040)	(0.293)	(0.645)	(0.051)	(0.147)	(0.865)	(0.979)
OTH – NA	−0.114	−0.118	0.034	0.351	−0.274	0.144	0.279	0.336
p-value	(0.019)	(0.005)	(0.893)	(0.192)	(0.342)	(0.609)	(0.292)	(0.231)

Estimated equation $y_i = \alpha + \beta_1 US_i + \beta_2 EU_i + \beta\, OTH_i + \delta_1 PC_i + \delta_2 NA_i + Z'_i\gamma + \varepsilon_i$

Baseline category: domestic owned uninational firms

All regressions are estimated with a constant and controlling for age of the firm, sector, region and size dummies. Standard Errors in parentheses below estimates. Asterisks denote confidence levels (* p<0.1, **p<0.05, *** p<0.01) affiliates of US multinationals in Italy are significantly more productive than any other foreign owned firm. This is consistent with the general characteristics of US firms, reflecting their persisting technological leadership in many fields and the strengths of their innovation systems of origin. Moreover, US firms provide higher incentives (relative to EU multinationals) to transfer superior technology and managerial practices to their own affiliates, as they incur higher sunk costs to operate in Europe.[68] As illustrated in Table 4.6, the productivity premium of US-owned affiliates allows them to reach the levels of firms belonging to Italian multinationals (both PC and NA), while other multinationals exhibit significantly lower productivity than Italian ones. However, this productivity edge is not systematically associated with a higher innovative profile. US multinationals (as well as EU ones) show a significantly lower propensity to carry out innovative activities, with the exception of the propensity to engage in international technological co-operation. This suggests that US multinationals may be transferring more management and organisational skills to their Italian affiliates (which contribute to raising productivity) than innovation capabilities.

The final step of our empirical investigation tries to shed some light on the fact that multinationals may differ according to the characteristics of the foreign system to which they are connected. While our data do not allow us to address this issue thoroughly, we provide some illustrative evidence that affiliates belonging to multinational groups that tap into a larger and more differentiated set of countries reach higher performance levels. To do so, we utilised a subset of foreign affiliates active in Italy for which we could gather data on the global network of affiliates of the group to which they belong. This was possible for 71 affiliates whose parent companies are located in France, Germany, Sweden and the UK. For each multinational group these affiliates belong to, we computed two measures of the extent and variety of the foreign systems they are connected to: the network spread index, which increases with the number of countries a given group has affiliates into, and the transnationality spread, which depends both on the weight of foreign activities of a given group and the spread of its network (see Ietto-Gillies 1998 for more on these indicators). The illustrative evidence reported in Table 4.7 suggests that among the 71 sample firms the 27 with above average productivity belong to groups with more extensive and diversified global networks.

4.5   CONCLUDING REMARKS

This chapter has discussed an important and often disregarded aspect of intra-industry heterogeneity, namely, diversities in innovation and

*Table 4.7   Degree of multinationality, internal network spread and
performance of foreign multinationals in Italy, 1996*

TFP of foreign affiliates in Italy (1993–99) (*)	Number of foreign MNFs	Number of foreign affiliates	Network spread of MNFs (1)	Transnationality spread of MNFs (2)
Low	44	59	0.1756	0.1098
High	27	44	0.2082	0.1281

Source: Authors' elaborations on ELIOS dataset

(1)   network spread: number of countries where each MNF is present/total number of countries where all the examined MNFs are present (see Ietto-Gillies 1998)
(2)   transnationality spread: (foreign subsidiaries/total subsidiaries)*network spread

* Firms have been considered in the Low TFP sample if their TFP was below the mean, while high TFP firms score higher than the mean

productivity across and within multinationals. We have developed a framework with which to identify those key variables which appear to be largely responsible for these diversities. In the case of heterogeneity across multinationals the focus has been placed on the nature of MNFs as bridging institutions, each distinctively connecting different economic and innovation systems in order to create, utilise, absorb and transfer valuable knowledge. We have insisted on the role of both macro factors such as the characteristics of innovation systems connected by MNFs, and micro and meso factors such as the number, variety and type of links firms establish in order to connect the economic system of origin with other foreign systems. As regards heterogeneity within multinationals, we have discussed some of the key factors and trade-offs affecting the relative performance of units internal to the MNF, namely, parent companies, foreign affiliates and national affiliates. We have argued that, in spite of the evolution of multinationals towards a double network structure as discussed in Part I of this volume, there are powerful agglomeration forces and tensions for the strategic control of knowledge that tend to favour an uneven distribution of knowledge and technological advantages across units within multinationals. These tensions tend to favour the performances of parent companies all else being equal. Foreign affiliates in turn enjoy the benefits of stronger stimuli to innovate and greater bargaining power due to their control of distant markets, which produce a more extensive and accelerated process of knowledge accumulation relative to national affiliates.

This framework can be usefully applied to analysing differences in economic and innovative performances across and within different categories of multinationals in a given economy. We have provided some illustrative evidence with specific reference to manufacturing firms active in Italy, including locally based affiliates of foreign owned firms. We have shown that while foreign firms perform better than domestic firms as a whole, this is not the case if domestic owned multinationals are distinguished from uninational firms. Foreign firms do perform better than uninational firms, but they have lower productivity and invest less in R&D than firms belonging to domestic owned multinational groups. In particular, consistent with our analytical framework we emphasised that parent companies of domestically owned multinationals exhibit higher R&D, innovation and productivity, as well as a higher propensity to set up technological alliances with local counterparts than affiliates of foreign multinationals. As well, national affiliates of domestic multinationals appear to have productivity premiums over foreign affiliates, probably due to advantages related to proximity, such as easier access to organisational and managerial practices. However, systems of origin seem to play a role. In particular, US-owned firms outperform affiliates of multinationals from other countries and reach productivity levels similar to those of Italian multinationals. This is consistent both with a general characteristic of US firms and with the fact that firms originating from outside the EU incur higher sunk costs when doing business in a European country like Italy and need to endow their affiliates with superior technology. However, this productivity premium does not seem to translate into higher innovative profiles of US owned affiliates. In other words, there is no evidence that US multinationals have a prominent role in R&D and innovation in Italy, but they still bring in superior managerial and organisational capabilities (as reflected by their productivity edge relative to other multinationals).

The overall implication is that increasing the foreign component, relative to domestic owned firms, would *not* by itself guarantee an increase in the productivity and innovation of the system. Increasing the share of domestic MNFs might yield better results in terms of productivity and innovation than expanding the foreign presence. Nevertheless, one should avoid considering an increase of foreign owned activities as *alternative* to an increase of national firms, especially their most dynamic component – domestic owned multinationals. Expanding the presence of *both* domestic and foreign multinationals in the economy may favour a higher economic growth. While this co-existence can be problematic especially in locations where skills and other strategic resources are scarce (Cantwell and Piscitello 2005), there are at least three sets of reasons for considering the activities of domestic and foreign owned multinationals as *complementary* and playing a mutually reinforcing role in the technological evolution of an economy. First, foreign and domestic owned multinationals represent distinct and mutually complementing channels through which the economy can gain access to, and learn from, foreign knowledge sources. That is, the economy can be 'contaminated' by new ideas and technologies either by 'going abroad' to catch them through the creation of subsidiaries in foreign contexts or by letting knowledge in through affiliates of foreign owned firms (van Pottelsberghe de la Potterie and Lichtenberg 2001). Second, the proliferation of foreign and domestic owned multinational activities in a given industry could help prevent the formation or strengthening of monopolistic power, provided that appropriate policy measures at the regional, national and supra-national levels are designed (UNCTAD 2001; Zanfei 2004).[69] Third, innovative activities of foreign multinationals do not only represent a potential source of technological spillovers for domestic uninationals, but also for domestic owned multinationals. The reverse is also true – domestic multinationals may generate positive technological externalities for foreign multinationals as well. However, the presence of innovative multinationals is only a precondition for spillovers. As we shall see in Chapter 6, when examining the effects of foreign presence on performances of local firms, including domestic owned multinationals, the issue is further complicated by the fact that competition might be particularly strong, so that both parties might be very reluctant to exchange knowledge. Nevertheless, spillovers might emerge particularly in the preparadigmatic phases of technical change, when firms are generally more available to share costs and risks of innovation.

PART III

Firm heterogeneity, multinationals and spillovers

The last decades have witnessed an important change in governments' attitude towards multinational firms. While in the '60s and the '70s countries tended to discourage inward investments based on a presumption that foreign multinationals would deplete local economies, over the last 25 years, many (developed and developing) countries have reduced their restrictions to inward FDIs (UNCTAD 1999; UNCTAD 2005). More importantly, it is all the more frequent that (national and regional) governments support investment promotion agencies and grant special tax concessions and financial incentives to foreign multinationals (Hanson 2001). This different attitude is largely the result of the changing view of the role played by MNFs in knowledge creation and dissemination that we have illustrated in Part I of this volume. Multinationals are less and less seen as 'quasi-colonial' institutions that exploit technological advantages on a global scale, by monopolising markets and appropriating rents in host economies (Hymer 1960; Vernon 1966). Instead, the role of MNFs as key players in the global generation, adoption and diffusion of technology is increasingly recognised.

Consistent with this view, in Part I of this volume we have provided some evidence of MNFs as institutions evolving towards a *double network structure*, where foreign affiliates are increasingly involved in innovative activities and in external relationships with host country firms and institutions, while in Part II we have focussed on the differences in productivity and innovation between MNFs and other firms operating in Italy. In particular, we have illustrated that multinationals are more productive and innovative than exporters and uni-national firms. This would support the idea that increasing the share of MNFs in the economy would provide a positive *direct effect* on the rate of innovation and productivity growth. However, we have also submitted that attracting foreign multinationals would not *per se* increase the performances of the economy. In fact, MNFs differ in terms of their technological profiles, and foreign-owned multinationals may not outperform the most dynamic component of the host economy, such as the domestic-owned multinationals. This induced us to pose the dilemma whether promoting foreign investment is really more effective than favouring the expansion of domestic owned multinationals. In this part of the volume, we shall continue along this line and take into account the *indirect effects* of MNFs. In particular, we shall discuss the extent and conditions under which MNFs determine productivity spillovers to local firms.

In Chapter 5 we shall introduce the literature on spillovers from multinational presence. The theoretical arguments and the main results of the empirical literature on the external effects of multinational presence on the host country will be reviewed. It will be shown that the evidence is still rather mixed, and in many cases host country firms do not seem to benefit from multinational presence. We shall then illustrate different streams of empirical research which have tried to tackle this problem. These include: the attempt to improve on the measurement of productivity and the specification of the external effects; the choice to look for spillovers mainly along the vertical value chain and across industries; and the analysis of the role of technological gaps between foreign and domestic firms, and of local companies' absorptive capacity as key factors favouring the creation of spillovers within the same industry. The latter stream of research will be taken as a useful point of departure for the study of how spillovers differ according to the characteristics of both foreign and domestic firms.

We shall build on this idea in Chapter 6, arguing that not every multinational firm is a good source of externalities, and not every domestic firm is equally well placed to benefit from multinationals. By so doing we draw implications from the analysis of intra-industry heterogeneity carried out in Part II, for the study of intra-industry spillovers. Using firm level data on ownership structure and performances of Italian firms, we shall show that spillovers for domestic companies are greater if foreign affiliates are more R&D intensive and if they have been established in Italy for a long period of time. Consistently with results of Part II, we shall posit that the degree of international involvement is a good proxy for a firm's absorptive capacity. We shall thus show that exporters benefit more from foreign multinationals than non-internationalised firms. However, as we shall see, the latter benefit from the expansion of domestic multinationals in their home country. This result indicates that the expansion of domestic multinationals can be a source of spillovers for their home countries. Moreover, their spillovers accrue to different categories of local firms, as compared to those created by foreign multinationals. Our results thus suggest that domestic and foreign MNFs may play a complementary role as sources of spillovers, accruing to the benefit of uni-national firms and exporters respectively.

5. Multinational firms and spillovers: theoretical, methodological and empirical issues

5.1 INTRODUCTION

In Part II of this book we highlighted the fact that multinational firms tend to be different from non-multinational firms, both in the home and the host countries. In particular we saw that affiliates of foreign multinationals and firms belonging to domestic multinational groups are larger, exhibit higher productivity, and have a higher propensity for innovation, for carrying out R&D and for engaging in technological cooperation. This has a *direct effect* on the home and host countries where they operate: average productivity and innovation in a given country increase as the share of activities due to multinationals in the economy rises. This has to do with the fact that multinational firms bring in a bundle of assets which might not be available locally, such as technologies, market and employment opportunities, capital, and management skills (Barba Navaretti and Venables 2004). This kind of direct effect might be relevant *per se*, justifying, for example, a significant increase in public incentives to attract foreign multinationals which we have witnessed in the last decades both in developed and developing countries (Hanson 2001). However, multinationals also determine significant pecuniary and technological externalities affecting the behaviour and performance of other domestic firms. This occurs through various channels such as: competition, imitation and demonstration, worker mobility and spin-offs, backward and forward linkages, and other forms of inter-firm cooperation (Blomström and Kokko 1998). In this chapter we present the theoretical arguments supporting such external effects of foreign multinationals on host countries (sections 5.2 and 5.3), and discuss recent evidence on the effects of foreign multinationals on productivity of domestic firms (section 5.4). In this discussion of the empirical evidence we first focus on some methodological issues concerning the estimation of total factor productivity (TFP) and specification of the FDI externality, then we review some empirical studies that analyse conditions favouring productivity spillovers. More specifically we consider the literature on vertical (or inter-industry) spillovers as opposed to intra-industry (or horizontal) spillovers, and on technology gaps and absorptive capacity as factors affecting horizontal spillovers. At this stage we do not address the effects on the home economy of domestic firms investing abroad. In the next chapter (section 6.4) we will return to this aspect by looking at the differential spillover effects of foreign and domestic multinationals on productivity of Italian firms.

5.2   EFFECTS OF MULTINATIONALS ON HOST ECONOMIES: TECHNOLOGICAL AND PECUNIARY EXTERNALITIES

As mentioned earlier, multinational firms can determine important technological and pecuniary externalities on domestic firms. *Technological externalities* occur whenever the output of a firm depends not only on the factor of production utilised, but also on the output (and utilisation of inputs) of another firm or group of firms (Meade 1952). The technological nature of such external effects stems from the fact that they directly affect a firm's production function. However, since they are often the result of an involuntary exchange of knowledge and ideas as well as new (or improved) organisational and managerial practices between firms, they are also referred to as *knowledge spillovers* (Krugman 1991). In our case, such externalities are the unpredicted consequences of incomplete contracts where knowledge is transferred from multinationals to local firms beyond the scope of a market transaction and for which the former does not receive any specific compensation. For example, local assemblers or licensees could learn more on the outsourced production process than the multinational firm would wish to, and domestic firms could reverse engineering products and technologies introduced by foreign firms into the local market. Similarly, organisational and managerial practices might spillover to domestic firms by simple personal interactions among people working for different companies (Barba, Navaretti and Venables 2004).

   However, external effects take place also through the market mechanism and are referred to as *pecuniary externalities* (Scitovsky 1956). In this case, the action of a firm (or a group of firms) affects the price of inputs used in production by another firm, which buys on the market a cheaper factor of production. For example, the growth of an industry allows both economies of specialisation and labour market economies which in turn lower the prices and raise the quality of inputs used in production (Krugman 1991).[70] In many instances pecuniary externalities arise from the creation of new

markets. For instance, an increase in local market demand stimulates the
provision in the local economy of public goods (such as educational institutions and other infrastructures) as well as private goods (including new,
knowledge intensive products and services) acquired through market transactions by domestic firms.[71] As we shall discuss at length in this section,
multinational firms can determine significant pecuniary externalities for
domestic firms. They can provide a pool of trained workers available for
domestic firms, stimulate the creation of a market for local inputs, raise the
demand for infrastructures and other public goods, and affect the degree of
competition and market prices.

5.3 CHANNELS FOR THE CREATION OF EXTERNALITIES

In most cases it is difficult to disentangle pecuniary and technological externalities since both arise through the same basic channels: *competition, imitation and demonstration, workers' mobility* and *spin-offs*, and *backward and
forward linkages*. Let us discuss how these channels work.

5.3.1 Competition

As we just mentioned, the first channel for the creation of externalities is
competition. MNFs tend to concentrate in industries characterized by relatively high entry cost and inefficiency determined by the limited contesta-
bility of markets.[72] As they can normally rely on superior technology and
other proprietary advantages, multinationals are in a position to overcome
such barriers, to contribute to their creation, and to substantially affect the
degree of competition in the host country (Hymer 1960; Kindleberger 1969;
Caves 1974). This will determine a number of consequences on profitability
and efficiency of domestic firms. First, there will be a negative product
market competition effect. The entry of multinational firms contributes to
reduce prices and squeeze indigenous firms' profit margins and forcing them
up their downward sloping average curve. This will push the less efficient
firms, which will not be able to make any positive profits, out of the
market (Aitken and Harrison 1999). While from the point of view of overall
efficiency this selection process can increase welfare, exit of national
firms might not be a desired outcome from the national policy maker
perspective.[73]

Second, the increased competition causes a typical pecuniary externality
on firms in upstream and downstream industries, which will benefit/suffer
from any drop/increase in prices and product quality, determined by the

entry of foreign firms. In particular, if MNFs enter into upstream industries, they will probably crowd out domestic competitors, but, to the extent that they sell at lower prices, they will also provide cheaper inputs to local firms.[74] This represents a pecuniary externality, which raises profits in downstream industries and induces a catalyst effect for the entry of local firms (Markusen and Venables 1999). This in turn might feed back to the upstream industries, by increasing demand for inputs and determine a further positive pecuniary externality. The net effect on the economy will depend on the balance between the positive and negative externalities and on the ability of MNFs to monopolise the input producing industry. Whenever multinationals enter downstream industries, they may cause negative externalities by crowding out their domestic competitors and, to the extent that they have market power vis à vis local suppliers, they might induce a fall in the price of inputs. However, if they source inputs locally, they are also likely to determine some positive externality. This is the backward linkage channel for spillover, which we will address later in this section.[75]

Third, competition will also determine a labour hoarding effect.[76] In fact, there is evidence that multinationals tend to pay more for labour of a given quality than local firms (Lipsey and Sjoholm 2004). They might do so for several reasons. One is that workers have a preference for locally-owned employers. Multinationals are perceived as more 'footloose' than domestic firms, and this might motivate a request for a wage premium which would ensure against the higher likelihood of loosing the job. A different motivation for paying higher wages, would be that MNFs might wish to reduce employee turnover, because they invest more in training than domestic-owned firms, or because they fear the leakage of their technological advantages if employees move to other employers (Fosfuri et al. 2001). Finally, foreign firms may pay higher wages to attract good workers, because of a lack of knowledge of the local labour market. Therefore, to the extent that multinationals will bid for higher salaries, they will displace domestic competitors, which, in turn, will either pay higher wages or hire less productive workers. In both cases the labour hoarding effect determines a negative pecuniary externality.

Finally, the increased competition could determine an incentive for domestic firms to react to the competitive threat posed by foreign multinationals and invest to become more efficient and innovative, in order to maintain their market shares. For example, in the case of Japanese multinationals' entry into the UK market in the 1980s, it has been found that in most cases indigenous firms reacted to this competitive threat by improving product quality and diversifying their product portfolio (Dunning 1988). Strictly speaking this cannot be considered an external effect, as the increase in firms' efficiency would be determined by their own strategy and investment and not by the behaviour of other firms. However, it highlights an important aspect of the effects of multinationals on domestic firms, which will show up again when we discuss other channels through which externalities occur. In fact, in most cases such effects require a substantial effort on the part of the domestic firms in order to benefit from the presence of multinationals. They need to invest in R&D, accumulate absorptive capacity, introduce organisational and managerial innovations and upgrade the skill profile of their workers.

5.3.2 Imitation and Demonstration

Further channels for the creation of externalities are *demonstration* and *imitation*. To the extent that foreign multinationals bring in products, technologies, organizational and managerial practices not available in the host economy, they can demonstrate that a production technique is feasible in a given socioeconomic context (Jenkins 2005) and act as models that domestic firms can imitate, through reverse engineering, industrial espionage and informal contacts (Mansfield and Romeo 1980). Alfaro and Rodriguez-Clare (2004) report the case of a simple innovation introduced by a multinational firm in the *maquila* sector in Honduras: they provided a free breakfast to employees half an hour before the start of the morning shift. This not only provided incentives for workers to show up on time, but also helped to improve their productivity. This simple idea rapidly spread to other domestic firms in the sector, increasing their overall productivity. Different examples come from the practices of information exchange and open labour markets in the Silicon Valley. As Tom Wolfe (quoted in Saxenian (1994)) described it:

> Every year there was some place, the Wagon Wheel, Chez Yvonne, Rickey's, the Roundhouse, where members of this esoteric fraternity, the young men and women of the semiconductor industry, would head after work to have a drink and gossip and brag and trade war stories about contacts, burst modes, bubble memories, pulse trains, bounceless modes, slow-death episodes, RAMs, NAKs, MOSes, PCMs, PROMs, PROM blowers, PROM blasters, and teramagnitudes, meaning multiples of a million millions.

These informal conversations served as important sources of up-to-date information about competitors, customers, markets and technologies. Domestic firms and multinationals could then benefit from these pure knowledge spillovers. The case of Texas Instruments (TI) in India further illustrates how demonstration can improve the performance of domestic firms. Before the entry of TI in India, domestic firms, like TCS, Infosys and

Wipro were mainly involved in on-site services, i.e. they supplied software professionals who worked on clients' premises on a temporary basis. TI's business model, centred on the use of a powerful communication facility and high-end offshore R&D activities, has been imitated by those Indian companies who are now offering mostly offshore services. It is interesting to note that TI has shared organizational knowledge on process control, reporting and review (critical in the offshore model) with Indian firms and helped them to build their capabilities (Giarratana et al. 2004).

As the examples suggest, externalities channelled through demonstration and imitation effects are mostly knowledge externalities. However, one needs to mention that even in these cases, not every domestic firm is equally well placed to benefit from such spillovers. In fact, information is not always freely available on the shelf and firms must invest in absorptive capacity in order to evaluate and utilise it (Cohen and Levinthal 1989; Rosenberg 1990; Arora and Gambardella 1990). Furthermore, imitation may require substantial R&D investments and engineering efforts.

5.3.3　Worker Mobility and Spin-offs

A third important channel for externalities is the *mobility* of workers and the related creation of *spin-offs*. It is widely documented that multinationals tend to employ a higher share of skilled workers (see, for example, Lipsey and Sjoholm 2004) and there is some evidence that multinationals are important providers of training activities (ILO 1981). Whenever those trained workers decide to leave the multinational firm and start their own business or move to a local company, they will bring along what they have learned and create a positive externality for the receiving firm (Fosfuri et al. 2001). To some extent this is a pecuniary externality, since multinationals increase the supply of trained workers, thus lowering the price of these inputs. In absence of this exogenous shock to labour supply, one may think that the domestic firms could either decide to train their workers or hire new workers from abroad (or from a different labour market). In both cases, the quality-adjusted price of such inputs would probably be very high. However, to the extent that the salary received by the moving worker does not incorporate all his/her knowledge,[77] the hiring firm receives an additional positive knowledge externality. This process has been widely documented by case studies and other qualitative works. Spin-offs in the software industry is one example of this. Sands (2004) shows that more than 30 per cent of the founders of a sample of 52 Irish software firms started in the period 1981–2002, were previously employed by multinational firms. Interviews carried out by Giarratana et al. (2004) to some of those firms reveal also that technical expertise is less relevant for spin-off firms than managerial skills and 'business sense'. For example, DLG services (now Transware), a firm specialised in localisation software development and testing, was set up in 1996 by a Lotus' former employee. The founder and managing director of DLG reported that his experience had helped his staff in DLG to learn optimal organisational and management practices from Lotus, such as project management and relational marketing capabilities. Another case is Anam, a start-up established in 1999 by three former employees of Siemens Ireland and Logica which supplies wireless Internet platforms for electronic commerce. The founders brought in both technical expertise in wireless products accumulated at the Irish Siemens Internet Security subsidiary, but also expertise in the area of general and international business management, as well as project and product management (Giarratana et al. 2004).[78]

5.3.4 Backward and Forward Linkages

The creation of *backward and forward linkages* with local firms is also an important channel through which pecuniary and technological externalities from multinational firms arise. This issue has a long tradition of studies dating back to Hirschman (1958) and Lall (1978) and recently revived by Rodriguez-Clare (1996) and Markusen and Venables (1999). Multinational firms may enter into a foreign country by setting up plants in upstream industries, where intermediate inputs are produced, or in downstream industries, mainly producing final goods. In both cases they tend to crowd out domestic competitors (see section 5.3.1), but are likely to induce forward (in the former case) and backward (in the latter case) linkages, which can in turn determine second order positive effects on the domestic competitors. The forward linkage mechanism hinges on the fact that MNFs might reduce prices in upstream industries, reducing costs (and increasing profitability) of domestic firms in downstream industries. This raises demand in such industries, and this in turn increases the incentives for domestic firms to start intermediate input production. When MNFs enter into the downstream industries they have to decide where to source their inputs from. They can decide to produce these inputs internally, to import them from their suppliers in other countries, or to buy them from local suppliers. To the extent that MNFs source locally, backward linkages will take place. In fact, multinationals will raise demand and incentives to domestic firms' entry in upstream industries producing intermediate goods. This should increase variety and lower prices of such inputs and create a pecuniary externality for MNFs and domestic firms producing final goods. Therefore, on the one hand, MNFs entry in downstream industries induce domestic firms' exit due to product market competition, but on the other hand, the backward linkage effect might increase profitability due to the lower price of inputs and induce by domestic firms' entry in upstream industries.

However, while the pecuniary externality mechanism can be very important, significant knowledge transfer can also occur between MNFs and their local counterparts. For example, in most developing countries MNFs have access to cheap labour and raw materials, but suppliers seldom meet their quality standards. In these cases multinationals may choose to assist their counterparts in reaching their requirement level through various actions: (i) *information* on markets, regulations, pricing, exporting, location of production; (ii) *technical* assistance on product design, quality control, factory outlet, labour and inventory management; (iii) *financial, management* and *procurement* assistance. In this perspective Lall (1978, pp. 216–17) has referred to such linkages as 'those relationships between TNCs and domestic enterprises trading with them that have led the latter to respond, positively or otherwise, to technological, pecuniary, marketing or entrepreneurial stimuli provided by the former. A "linkage" in this sense is clearly different from a normal transaction in a competitive market'.

A recent issue of the World Investment Report, published by the United Nations Conference on Trade and Development (UNCTAD 2001) provides a number of examples which illustrate this process. For example, when the French company Saint Gobain decided to set up a floating glass plant in Chennai (India), local suppliers where disorganised and lacked the ability to reach minimum standards. Saint Gobain set up specialised teams to develop suppliers three years before starting production operations. The teams worked with suppliers to develop cost and business models, to train a largely illiterate labour force, to educate firms in management concepts, and to help them to obtain loans. In four years 80 per cent of raw material requirements were supplied by indigenous firms, which also began supplying other firms in India (UNCTAD 2001, p. 144). Similarly, in Mexico, IBM could not find any supplier of packaging materials, therefore assisted the local firm Ureblock to start producing such inputs. Now Ureblock has a 200 m^2 building in the IBM plant and its responsibilities in the production process range from cleaning the final product, to labelling, packaging and final delivery to IBM distribution department (UNCTAD 2001, p. 254). The case of Quang An, a supplier of plastic bottles for Unilever's plant in Hanoi (Vietnam) provides an interesting example of the importance of own investments by the suppliers and the potential pecuniary externality for other firms. When in 1997 Quang An became a supplier of Unilever, quality standards, sampling procedures and analytical test methods were established and staff training provided. Furthermore, the assurance of a steady business volume also allowed Quang An to invest in new equipment. The linkage relationship with Unilever allowed not only a six-fold increase in turnover in three and a half years, but also improved its capabilities and enabled it to become a supplier to other multinational and local firms in Vietnam (UNCTAD 2001, p. 146). Providing training and finance to suppliers is another important area where multinational firms can play a key role. For example, in the case of Intel Malaysia, suppliers are trained and coached both within the firm and through the Penang Skills Development Centre (PSDC), an independent institution which packages and delivers training courses contributed by Intel and other foreign affiliates in Penang (UNCTAD 2001, p. 149). This creates an important pecuniary externality in the area, since, as we argued above, it creates a market of trained workers which can be hired both by multinational and local firms.

The case of Toyota in Thailand illustrates the role of multinationals in financing their suppliers. During the economic downturn following the East Asian financial crises, in order to prevent the bankruptcy of their first-tier suppliers, Toyota Motor Thailand provided some 1.6 billion baht through advance payment revolving funds, dead stock purchase schemes at cost, and advance payments for tooling expenses (UNCTAD 2001, p. 146).

While an improvement of supplier performances has been observed in many developing countries, recent studies report some evidence that also when multinationals source in advanced countries, they can induce a quality and efficiency improvement in their local counterparts. For example, evidence from the UK suggests that some relevant transfer of knowledge flows from multinational firms to their local suppliers occurred, and this transfer substantially improved productivity and product quality of upstream producers (Potter, Moore and Spires 2003). Similarly, a survey on foreign affiliates in Northern Ireland shows that knowledge transfer activities are a very frequent event and at least 50 per cent of the managers of the surveyed firms stated that such transfer had a positive impact on their suppliers competitiveness in terms of price, quality or delivery conditions (Crone and Roper 2001). Evidence consistent with technology transfer from foreign subsidiaries to local firms has also been found by Veugelers and Cassiman (2004) using the Community Innovation Survey data from Belgium, even if this result seems to hinge on the fact that foreign subsidiaries have a higher propensity to acquire technology internationally than local firms.

However, in developed countries (and increasingly in developing countries too) a different trend has been observed in the last few decades. As we argued in Part I of this book, multinational firms are increasingly involved in exploiting their international network to tap into different scientific and technological domains, as well as extracting and levering knowledge from their various worldwide users . From this perspective, there exists a two-way flow of knowledge between the foreign affiliates, their suppliers and other counterparts in host countries. Multinationals do not only establish links for transferring technical expertise, skills, and management practices, but also set up cooperative ventures wherein each party has something to learn. This has important implications for spillovers. In fact, when such linkages are set up one may envisage a great deal of horizontal cooperation between competitors. This is the case of electronics firms cooperating on a common technological development project in the Silicon Valley and competing fiercely in the product market. Another example is the case of car makers sharing R&D as well as other types of investments, then competing with differentiated products incorporating the same components. For example Toyota, which started up a European plant in France in 2001, has recently agreed with the French car maker PSA Group (owner of the trademarks Peugeot and Citroen) to develop jointly a new model of economy car aimed at the bottom of the market which will be produced in a new plant in Poland. Within the agreement, Toyota took charge of the manufacturing aspect of the joint venture project, while one of PSA's key responsibilities was the purchasing of components. However, while the two companies cooperated in the early stages of design, production and input supply, they will compete in the product market with three different models (Toyota Aygo, Citroen C1 and Peugeot 107) which will share 80 per cent of their components and will be produced by the same Polish plant (*Automotive News Europe*, 27 June 2005).

As we have seen from the examples above, backward and forward linkages can arise when multinational firms decide to produce locally. In these cases, new business opportunities arise for local suppliers, both upstream and downstream (in the case of assembly and distribution activities). This larger market allows the exploitation of economies of scale, specialisation and division of labour in suppliers' activities. Furthermore, knowledge transfer can occur, both unintentionally and purposefully, and the quality and efficiency in upstream and downstream production can improve. To the extent that foreign multinationals source locally, one can expect a positive effect along the supply chain (vertical spillovers), which is mainly due to knowledge externalities and scale effects, as well as a positive impact on the other firms competing downstream with multinationals (horizontal spillovers) which will benefit from the higher variety of input suppliers and from their increased efficiency (Rodriguez-Clare 1996; Hirschman 1958). In other words, multinational firms determine a pecuniary externality for their competitors. By creating (or extending) the local market for inputs, the price will drop, and usually the quality of supplies will improve, for all firms buying a given input, not only for the multinational firm. This effect emerges rather neatly from some of the examples above. In the case of Saint Gobain in India, four years after the suppliers development programme started, several firms were already selling to other firms in the country.

Moreover, when multinationals set up backward and forward linkages with local firms, pecuniary and knowledge externalities can arise, to the advantage of both suppliers and competitors of the foreign affiliate. On the contrary, if inputs are imported and local suppliers are displaced, multinational firms can cause negative effects for their upstream and downstream counterparts. In this respect, evidence that the share of inputs sourced locally would be lower in the case of foreign multinationals than in the case of domestic firms has created pessimistic views as to the likely spillover effects from FDI through backward linkages (McAlesee and McDonald 1978; Potter et al. 2003; UNCTAD 2001). However, Alfaro and Rodriguez-Clare (2004) show that if we account for the fact that foreign firms tend to use more materials per unit of labour, the linkage effect of multinationals is higher relative to domestic firms. They propose a measure of linkage propensity obtained from the share of inputs bought locally in relation to labour employed.[79] Using this measure they suggest that the linkage effects of multinationals in Brazil, Chile, Mexico and Venezuela have been higher than the corresponding effects of domestic firms, even if the proportion of inputs bought locally in relation to total inputs used has been lower. Furthermore, they find that the extent of local linkages increases with the age of the foreign affiliates, suggesting that the more embedded the multinational firms are in the local context, the higher the potential for spillovers. These results are consistent with evidence from a survey on multinationals and their suppliers in the UK (Potter et al. 2003) where it is found that the extent of supplier upgrading increases as they have longer term relationships with foreign affiliates.

5.3.5   A Taxonomy of Channels for The Creation of Externalities

To sum up, in this section we have argued that multinational firms can have external effects on host country firms and we have sketched the types of externalities and the main channels through which they take place. First of all, we have noticed that both pecuniary and knowledge externalities can arise, and in many instances the former effects can be more significant than the latter. This has important implications for public policy and empirical work, as knowledge externalities have the effect of extending the production frontier, pecuniary externalities affect mainly the profit function of domestic firms. We have also pointed out that such externalities occur through four basic channels (competition, imitation and demonstration, labour mobility and spin-offs, backward and forward linkages), where pecuniary and knowledge externalities play different roles. In particular, bearing in mind that any taxonomy has its own limitations and at the risk of oversimplifying a complicated issue, one can try to rank the different channels according to the importance of pecuniary versus knowledge externalities. In Table 5.1 we provide a visual representation of our taxonomy. From our theoretical discussion and from the examples we have drawn from the literature, competition seems to affect domestic firms mainly through pecuniary externalities, while, at the other extreme, when local firms imitate or demonstrate foreign technologies, products and management practices, knowledge externalities seems to be more relevant. In the case of labour mobility and spin-offs, we have identified substantial pecuniary externalities, but in most cases some (unpaid for) knowledge flows also occur. Finally, linkages seem to entail both pecuniary and knowledge externalities.

An important qualification on the nature of the externalities need also to be done. These effects are by no means automatic and in most cases domestic firms have to sustain extra costs in order to benefit from multinational presence (although this extra cost does not necessarily correspond to a direct payment to the MNF for the supply of some specific assets). In particular, they need to accumulate absorptive capacity and invest in R&D, skilled workers and organisational practices. These efforts are likely to vary across the different channels. Demonstration effects and labour mobility probably require the lowest effort, while domestic firms may need to make significant investments in order to benefit from imitation, competition and linkages. In particular, when we look at knowledge externalities, domestic firms need to devote substantial resources to their relations with foreign affiliates. From this perspective, one can think of multinationals as a potential source of externalities 'with entry costs': each MNF generates different spillover opportunities, which can be appropriated by those firms which are willing or capable to pay for the required fee. We shall further develop on this view in Chapter 6, where the issue of heterogeneity of multinationals and of domestic firms will be reconsidered in the analysis of spillovers.

Table 5.1   A taxonomy of channels and types of externality

Channels	Pecuniary Externality	Knowledge Externality	Local firm effort
Competition	***	*	**
Imitation/Demonstration	*	***	*
Labour Mobility	***	**	*
Linkages	***	***	***

5.4   EMPIRICAL EVIDENCE ON SPILLOVERS FROM MULTINATIONAL FIRMS

While recognising that multinationals can affect the behaviour of local firms through various types of externalities and different channels, empirical work has hardly been able to identify the relative importance of pecuniary and knowledge externalities, as well as of competition, imitation, labour mobility and linkages. The main approach used in this extensive empirical literature has been to search for an aggregate (or net) effect of the presence of multinationals on productivity of domestic firms in the same sector. As we shall show in section 5.4.3 of this chapter, some efforts have been devoted to investigating the conditions favouring positive effects which, to some extent, can be correlated with the different channels illustrated above.[80] Most studies in this literature refer to such effects as technological spillovers from foreign direct investments (or multinational firms), but it is well understood that these effects can only partially be attributed to pure technological externalities (Breschi et al. 2005).

Early empirical works on spillovers from multinational firms relied on cross-sector data and usually specified an equation for the value added per employee due to domestic-owned firms in a sector as a function of the share of activities accounted for by foreign owned firms in the same sector (defined as the foreign presence ratio), controlling for other sectoral characteristics. These studies generally found a positive association between the foreign presence and domestic productivity (see for example Caves 1974; Blomstrom 1986) and interpreted this evidence as consistent with productivity spillovers from multinational firms. Aitken and Harrison (1999) showed that those studies suffered from a severe specification error, which derived from the fact that, as we have seen in previous chapters of this book, the theory of the multinational firm suggests that such firms emerge in knowledge-intensive sectors. If this is the case, a positive association between the foreign presence and domestic productivity might simply reflect the fact that foreign multinationals are attracted towards high productivity industries in the host country. This endogeneity problem is likely to yield upward biased estimates of the spillover effect of multinational firms. In order to address the question of whether multinationals determine productivity spillovers on host country firms, this specification issue must be addressed. Scholars could partially solve the endogeneity problem described above, by controlling for industry dummies in cross-sectional regressions; and more effectively by exploiting the longitudinal dimension of firm-level data which became increasingly available in the recent years, as to account for sector or firm-level fixed effects. Furthermore, the availability of more detailed data allowed for the estimation of a production function, leaving the researcher the choice of analysing the effect of foreign presence on labour productivity or on TFP. Most empirical works in the last decade chose the second route and modelled the effect of foreign presence in an augmented production function framework of the following form:

$$Y_{ij} = A_{ij} (FP_j, Z_{ij})F(X_{ij}) \tag{1}$$

where output of firm i in sector j, Y_{ij}, is expressed as a function of a vector of inputs (X), and firm's productivity (A) which shifts the production function upwards. In turn, productivity can be explained by a number of firm and sector characteristics (Z) and by the external effect determined by the activity of foreign multinationals, usually captured by the foreign presence ratio (FP), obtained by aggregating activities of foreign firms in sector j as a share of activities of all firms in the sector.

$$FP_j = \frac{\sum_{i \in j} FOR_i * K_{ij}}{\sum_{i \in j} K_{ij}} \tag{2}$$

where FOR takes value 1 if firm i is foreign-owned and K denotes a measure of firm's activity (such as capital stock or employment).

Assuming a Cobb-Douglas form for the function F(.), recent empirical works on productivity spillovers from multinationals used the following log-linear specification:

$$\log(Y_{it}) = \alpha \log(K_{it}) + \beta \log(L_{it}) + \gamma \log(M_{it}) + \log(A_{it}) \tag{3}$$

where upper case letters denote output (Y), capital (K), labour (L) and materials (M), while A_{it} is a productivity term which is modelled as:

$$\log(A_{it}) = \delta FP_{jt} + \phi Z_{it} + \eta_i + \varepsilon_{it} \tag{4}$$

where FP is defined as above, Z is a vector or firm and sector specific controls, η is a individual fixed effect and ε is an error term.

Using this sort of specification most recent works tend to find no evidence of spillovers from multinational firms. Görg and Greenaway (2004), building on a previous work by Görg and Strobl (2001), review 33 empirical papers on productivity spillovers on developed, developing and transition economies. They highlight that most recent panel data studies, which corrected for the endogeneity bias illustrated above, tend to find evidence of non-significant (or even negative) productivity spillovers. These results have been interpreted as evidence that multinationals have the incentive to minimise technology leakages to competitors, thus negative competition effects might offset positive technological and pecuniary externalities.

The current empirical literature attempts to investigate this issue more carefully. We can probably identify two main directions of research, which converge in a better understanding of the effects of multinationals on domestic firms productivity. One is addressing specification and measurement issues, including the correct identification of production function parameters and a correct specification of the foreign externality. We review some of these efforts in section 5.4.1. and 5.4.2. A second stream of research, which we review in section 5.4.3, addresses the conditions which eventually favour positive spillovers. Within this line of research, the literature has placed considerable emphasis on vertical vs. horizontal spillovers, and on the role of technology gaps vs. absorptive capacity in favouring spillovers.

5.4.1 Empirical Evidence I: Issues on the Estimation of Productivity

As mentioned earlier, the increasing availability of detailed firm-level data has allowed recent research to test for FDI spillovers within the context of 'augmented' production functions. While this offers the possibility of more flexible and richer specifications, it poses the problems of the correct identification of the production function parameters. Reviewing the literature on the estimation of production functions and on the measurement of productivity is beyond the scope of this study.[81] Nevertheless, it is worth devoting some attention to those aspects which bear more relevance in the literature on FDI spillovers reviewed here. The first issue concerns the *correct identification of the output elasticities of the different factors of production*, i.e. the production function parameters for labour, capital and material use. The problem is that the use of inputs tends to be correlated with productivity. For example, more productive firms tend to be larger and use a higher quantity of factors in production. Slightly more technically, productivity is unknown to the econometrician, i.e. it corresponds to the error term, but firms know their productivity when they decide how much input to use. Therefore, the amount of input used is likely to depend on the firm's productivity level. In these conditions, a correlation between regressors (inputs) and the residual (productivity) arises. OLS estimates of elasticities on the various inputs will then be over- or underestimated and so will be the estimated productivity, which might capture the badly measured contribution of inputs to output, rather than 'true' productivity. The availability of panel data allows to partially workaround this endogeneity problem by applying fixed effect estimators. Using within-group estimators or first-differences one can control for the correlation between the time invariant component of productivity and the use of inputs. For example, using fixed-effects models, one can control for the fact that more productive firms tend to be larger and use more inputs, or that sector specificities simultaneously determine the level of productivity and the level of inputs used (e.g. firms in capital intensive industries are usually more productive and use systematically more capital than labour intensive firms).

However, the fixed-effect solution does not solve for the endogeneity occurring when a shock to productivity induces firms to adjust their input use. For example, introducing a new organization of labour or a new material requirement planning system will increase firms' productivity and this is likely to lead to lower use of inputs. To control for this further source of endogeneity, instrumental variable estimators must be applied. Blundell and Bond (1999) noted that to the extent that productivity exhibits some degree of persistence one could apply the GMM estimators for dynamic panel data, proposed by Arellano and Bond (1991) and Blundell and Bond (1998), to obtain estimates of the production function parameters. This approach has been followed by some recent empirical works on multinational firms and productivity (Damijan et al. 2003; Barrios and Strobl 2002; Benfratello and Sembenelli forthcoming; Griffith 1999). However, such dynamic panel estimators may suffer from the weak instrument problem and biased estimates might be obtained – especially in short panels and when individual responses are very heterogeneous.

A different strategy for obtaining unbiased estimates of the production function parameters is to apply the semi-parametric procedure proposed by Olley and Pakes (1996) (OP). They argue that if firms' investment decisions can be expressed as a function of their capital stock and respond monotonically to productivity shocks, one could invert the investment function and express productivity as a function of investments and of the capital stock. Using a third-order polynomial approximation to this unknown function as a control in the estimation of the production function, one can obtain an unbiased estimate of the labour and material elasticities, while the capital coefficient can be recovered in a second step of the estimation routine.[82] One of the limitations of the Olley and Pakes procedure is that, in order to ensure invertibility of the investment function, they require firms to make positive investments every year: this condition does not necessarily hold in actual firm-level data and would cause dropping a number of observations. Levinsohon and Petrin (2003) (LP) notice that the proxy for productivity shocks can also be based on intermediate inputs and that this solution solves the zero investment problem, since it is very likely that firms register a positive use of materials every year. Furthermore, they argue that in the presence of adjustment costs a proxy based on the use of intermediate inputs may be more appropriate, since these are likely to react more rapidly than investments to productivity shocks. The OP and LP approaches to productivity measurement have become increasingly popular in recent works on FDI spillovers (Smarzynska Javorcik 2004; Blalock and Gertler 2004; Schoors and van der Tol 2002) and have now set the standard for the current literature.

A different issue related to the estimation of productivity which is likely to affect the measurement of FDI spillovers on domestic firms' productivity, concerns the possibility of computing a *different production function for every sector*. In fact, if one allows the output elasticities of capital, labour and materials to vary across industries, the impact of FDI on productivity can be very different. In particular, imposing common input elasticities for all firms will result in an overestimation of productivity for firms and sectors which have higher returns to inputs. For example, if in a given sector the 'true' return is higher than the one estimated on the whole economy, an increase in input use in that sector will determine a growth in output higher than one would expect from the estimated production function, and this difference will then wrongly be considered productivity gain. To the extent that foreign presence is correlated with sectoral returns to scale (i.e. multinationals are attracted to higher return to scale industries) the estimated external effect will likely be biased. An analytical illustration of how such a bias could arise is relatively straightforward. Let's assume, for simplicity, an augmented log linear production function with only one input X, with a sector-specific elasticity (β_j), and a foreign presence term (FP).[83]

$$y_{it} = \beta_j x_{it} + \delta\, FP_{jt} + u_{it} = (\beta + \beta_j^*)x_{it} + \delta\, FP_{jt} + u_{it} \tag{5}$$

where β_j^* is the difference between the economy wide return to input x (β) and the sector-specific elasticity. If one estimates a common production function for all sectors, $\beta_j^* x$ enters the error term.

$$y_{it} = \beta x_{it} + \delta FP_{jt} + v_{it} = \beta x_{it} + \delta\, FP_{jt} + (\beta_j^* x_{it} + u_{it}) \tag{6}$$

To the extent that FP is correlated with sector specific returns to scale β_j^*, one is likely to obtain a biased estimate of δ. In particular, if multinational firms are concentrated in increasing returns to scale industries, δ might pick up a positive correlation with the error term and turn out upwardly biased. Admittedly, this problem could be mitigated by controlling for fixed effects. However, this argument suggests that, whenever possible, one should estimate production functions sector by sector, in order to avoid possible biases in the estimation of external effects from multinational firms. Unfortunately, the limited sample size in actual data often constrains the researcher to economy-wide production functions.

5.4.2   Empirical Evidence II: Identification of the External Effects

With regard to specification issues, let us now discuss how foreign presence should be identified when measuring the impact of multinationals on domestic firms. We have noted elsewhere (Castellani and Zanfei 2002, 2003) that using the foreign presence ratio might yield downward biased estimates of the 'true' externality from foreign multinationals. The basic idea is that there is no clear theoretical motive to use such a ratio, as an explanatory variable for the log of TFP. If one is interested in testing the role of external effects on firms' productivity, he/she would estimate a production function of the following form:

$$y_{it} = \alpha k_{it} + \beta l_{it} + \gamma m_{it} + a_{it} \tag{7}$$

with y, k, l, m and a denoting the log of output, capital, labour and total factor productivity respectively. External effects can be captured by specifying productivity as a function of a measure of sectoral activity, like fixed capital. This would yield the following equation:

$$a_{it} = \theta \log(\sum_{i \in j} K_{ijt}) + u_{it} = \theta k_{jt} + u_{it} \tag{8}$$

where

$$u_{it} = \eta_i + \varepsilon_{it}$$

The parameter θ will capture the externality accruing to each firm i from aggregate activity in their sector j. For example, a similar specification is used in Basu and Fernald (1995), who estimate the role of external effects in US industries. The more general way one would introduce different sources of externalities would be to add them multiplicatively in the productivity term. Then, if we were to introduce foreign firms as a specific source of externality, we could augment (8) by plugging in a term for the aggregate activity of foreign firms in sector j

$$a_{it} = \theta k_{jt} + \delta \log(\sum_{i \in j} FOR_i * K_{ijt}) + u_{it} = \theta k_{jt} + \delta f_{jt} + u_{it} \tag{9}$$

Adding and subtracting δk_{jt} on the RHS one can rewrite (9) as

$$a_{it} = \delta f p_{jt} + (\theta + \delta) k_{jt} + u_{it} \tag{10}$$

The first term on the RHS of equation (10) ($fp_{jt} = \log(F_{jt}/K_{jt})$) is now the foreign presence ratio used in most existing works. However, the simple specification that we derived from an augmented version of standard models with externalities highlights that usual estimates of δ implicitly impose that $\delta + \theta = 0$. The point here is that this is not such an innocent restriction, since it imposes that an increase (decrease) in F_j and K_j in the same proportion will have an impact on domestic productivity that is equal in magnitude but opposite in direction. In other words, the restriction entails that either a positive spillover generated by foreign activities is exactly counterbalanced by a negative spillover of total activities; or, symmetrically, that a positive spillover generated by total activity is exactly counterbalanced by a negative spillover of foreign activity. Neither of these circumstances needs to occur as a rule (even though it might be the case under specific conditions). In fact, the former statement contradicts most of existing theoretical work in the economic growth literature (e.g. Romer 1986 and Arrow 1962) and empirical findings (Caballero and Lyons 1991; Oulton 1996) which would rather suggest that increases in total activities determine positive productivity effects. On the other hand, if one is willing to accept that aggregate activity determines some positive external effect, the restriction forces spillovers from multinational activity to be negative.

Indeed, one can easily notice that imposing $\delta + \theta = 0$ will most likely cause a downward bias in $\hat{\delta}$. Taking first differences of equation (10) wipes out fixed effects and yields

$$\Delta a_{it} = \delta \Delta fp_{jt} + (\theta + \delta) \Delta k_{jt} + v_{it}$$
$$= \delta x_{jt} + \lambda z_{jt} + v_{it} \tag{11}$$

where we simplified the notation by setting $x_{jt} = \Delta fp_{jt}$, $z_{jt} = \Delta k_{jt}$, and $\lambda = \delta + \theta$. Whenever $\lambda = 0$ is imposed, i.e. z is omitted from the regression, equation (9) can be re-written (dropping individual and time subscripts) as:

$$\Delta a = \delta x + \kappa \tag{12}$$

Where $\kappa = \lambda z + v$ is the new error term. Equation (12) is a simplified version of what is estimated in most of the literature using only the FP ratio as a measure of foreign presence.[84] From textbook econometrics we obtain (Greene 1997, pp. 401–03):[85]

$$E(\hat{\delta}) = \delta + \frac{Cov(x, z)}{Var(x)} \lambda = \delta + \frac{Cov[(\Delta fp),(\Delta k)]}{Var[(\Delta fp)]} (\delta + \theta) \tag{13}$$

To the extent that the restriction imposed in the literature estimating only the FP ratio is satisfied (i.e. $\delta + \theta = 0$), no bias is produced. Otherwise, since $Var(x) > 0$, the direction of the bias is determined by two terms: (*i*) the sum of the unrestricted coefficients of externalities from foreign and aggregate sectoral activity and (*ii*) the covariance between Δfp and Δk. Therefore, if $\delta + \theta > 0$, the restriction imposed in the literature is likely to produce a downward biased externality coefficient, when Δfp and Δt are negatively correlated. This formalises an intuition put forward by Aitken and Harrison (1999, p. 610, footnote 7, our comments in squared brackets): '*if foreign plants do not adjust quickly to economic downturns, while domestic firms react immediately* [which occurs if Δfp and Δk are negatively correlated], *this would lead us to observe a rising foreign share in periods of economic decline. If productivity is procyclical* [i.e. domestic productivity growth depends on the rate of growth of the sector $(\delta + \theta > 0)$], *we would wrongly infer that foreign investment has a negative impact on domestic productivity.*'

The case of firms active in Italy is illustrative of how relevant such a bias can be, and shows that FDI externalities are markedly higher when the restriction is not imposed. In Table 5.2, we report estimates from an augmented production function, using OLS on first-differences (OLS-DIF) as derived from the specification obtained by equation (11). The sample is drawn from the intersection between ELIOS and CIS2, as described in the Appendix. For the present analysis we were forced to restrict ourselves to a

Table 5.2 Spillover effects from multinational firms in Italy, 1993–2000: specification issues

	(1) OLS-DIF	(2) OLS-DIF	(3) OLS-DIF
fp	0.041 (0.032)	0.111*** (0.032)	
f			0.105*** (0.028)
k		0.375*** (0.031)	0.276*** (0.037)
Constant	−0.018*** (0.004)	−0.027*** (0.004)	−0.027*** (0.004)
Adjusted R-squared	0.000	0.039	0.040
N. observations	3129	3129	3129

Standard errors in brackets below estimates
* p<0.1, ** p<0.05, *** p<0.01

balanced sample of 447 domestic-owned firms in Italy over the period 1994–2000.[86] The dependent variable is the log of TFP, obtained as the residual from production functions estimated for each two-digit NACE industry, using the Levinshon and Petrin approach. In column (1) we regress the log of TFP on the log of FP, which should capture FDI spillovers.[87] FP is calculated summing up (net) tangible assets, as reported in balance sheet accounts, for each foreign firm in sector j at time t, as a share of the same sum for all firms regardless of the nationality of the ultimate owner. This specification mimics what is done in most empirical works as reviewed by Görg and Greenaway (2004). Consistently with most previous findings, we find no evidence of spillovers. However, when we control for the growth in total industry activity (column 2), the externality from foreign presence turns out much larger (0.111) and now soundly different from zero. Therefore, as suggested by our simple empirical model, a specification error might have induced us to believe that foreign firms have no effect on Italian firms' productivity, while it is probably not true. In column 3 we further support our simple empirical model, by estimating equation (9) using OLS in first-differences and show that the estimated external effect from multinational firms is equivalent to the one obtained in column (2).[88] The results in column 2 should not be taken as definitive evidence of positive externalities from foreign firms in Italy. In this and in the following chapter we shall highlight a number of other issues which need to be taken into account to improve our evaluation of spillover effects. Nevertheless, findings reported in Table 5.2 highlight that using the FP ratio, as is most common in the literature, would have determined a biased estimate of spillover effects.

To sum up, our simple empirical model suggests that an omitted variable (Δk) might yield downward biased estimates of productivity spillovers from multinational companies. This helps explain the evidence of negative or non-significant impact of foreign presence on domestic firms' productivity, obtained by many studies, including Görg and Greenaway (2004).

Our concern about the use of the FP ratio as a measure of externality is shared in a few other recent empirical works. Using data on Indonesian plants, Todo and Miyamoto (2002) find positive externalities from the aggregate foreign capital but not from the share of foreign capital in the industry. Similar results have been obtained by Ruane and Ugur (2002) for Ireland. The use of the foreign presence ratio has been criticised also by Lipsey and Sjoholm (2004), who argue that such a measure might be endogenously determined if productivity spillovers expand activity in local firms. They also state, 'it is not clear why we would assume the effect from FDI to be linear in the foreign share of an industry's economic activity: spillovers are not obviously maximized at a 100 foreign ownership share'.

5.4.3   Empirical Evidence III: Conditions Favouring Positive Spillovers

Apart from the specification issues illustrated in the previous section, the general finding that there are no significant spillovers from multinational firms or host country firms in the same industry, can be the result of negative competition effect offsetting any positive (pecuniary and knowledge) externalities induced by multinationals.[89] The idea, illustrated in Figure 5.1 (adapted from Aitken and Harrison 1999), is that even if multinationals determine some positive externality which allows the domestic firms to shift their average curve downwards (from AC_{nofdi} to AC_{fdi}), the negative competition effect might force them up their new average curve cost, so one could observe no change in the actual average cost of domestic firms.

An accurate analysis of the effects of multinationals on domestic firms' productivity should be able to disentangle the various effects, but

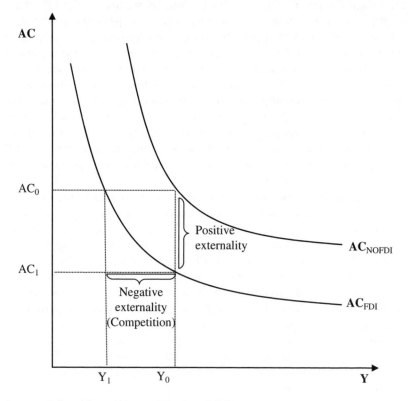

Source: Adapted from Aitken and Harrison (1999).

Figure 5.1   The opposite impact of externality and competition effects

identifying each of the individual channels through which multinationals affect domestic firms' productivity requires very detailed data, which are very difficult to collect.[90] The second best solution is to focus on the conditions under which positive externalities are likely to outweigh negative competition effects. The literature has followed two main directions. On the one hand, several contributions have emphasised that whether spillovers from multinational presence can be observed or not depends on where we look for them: they are more likely to occur across vertically related industries (vertical or inter-industry spillovers) than within the same industry (horizontal or intra-industry spillovers). On the other hand, research has focused on intra-industry spillovers, and has investigated some conditions which determine a higher potential for knowledge transfer. Within this context, considerable attention has been placed on the role played by technology gaps between foreign and domestic firms, and by the absorptive capacity of the latter.

The basic idea of empirical works searching for spillovers across industries is that we should observe lower intensity of negative competition effects and higher positive externalities along the supply chain than within the same sector. In fact, while multinationals may have a rather strong incentive to minimise information leakages to competitors, they may have an incentive to transfer some knowledge to their local suppliers, as illustrated by case histories in section 5.3. Furthermore, while within-industry competition may take a form of a market stealing effect, along the supply chain it mainly takes the form of an incentive to increase competitiveness, expanding (not contracting) market shares for upstream and downstream firms. Many recent works have addressed this type of spillover by introducing two measures of foreign presence: the standard intra-industry measure of foreign activity, which captures horizontal externalities, and a sum of the foreign presence in all the other sectors, weighted by the share of purchases from each sector (drawn from the technical coefficient in the input-output tables), which captures inter-sectoral externalities. Some studies distinguish between a measure of foreign presence in the industries that are supplied by sector j (e.g. downstream industries), which should capture the impact of multinationals through backward linkages on productivity of their suppliers, and a measure capturing the impact of forward linkages. Results unambiguously support positive inter-sectoral spillovers in the case of UK (Driffield et al. 2002), Latvia (Smarzynska Javorcik 2004), Indonesia (Blalock and Gertler 2004), Hungary (Schoors and van der Tol 2002), Czech Republic, Poland and Slovenia (Damjian et al. 2003). This bunch of converging evidence on vertical spillovers has relieved many scholars. In fact, they have supported the idea that the lack of any sound evidence of spillovers had to do with the fact that we were looking in the wrong place, i.e. within the same industry where multinationals are active, and not in upstream or downstream industries (Smarzynska Javorcick 2004). The balance between negative competition effects and other sources of positive externalities suggests that multinationals crowd out other competitors in the same sector. On the contrary, both positive externalities and lower competition should cause positive effects on productivity of domestic firms in upstream and downstream industries. However, while finding evidence of positive vertical spillover is very comforting, it is not clear why if inter-sectoral linkages occur and multinationals cause positive externalities on the productivity of their local suppliers and resellers, other domestic firms competing with foreign affiliates would not benefit from the increased variety and efficiency of upstream and downstream firms (Alfaro and Rodriguez-Clare 2004). As we have discussed in section 5.3, a larger pool of more efficient suppliers creates a pecuniary externality for other firms supplying the same inputs, most of which will be competing in the same sector of the foreign affiliates of multinational firms. In other words, theory would suggest that vertical knowledge spillovers should favour horizontal pecuniary externalities. Why then do we not find evidence of within-industry spillovers?

One explanation would be that this mechanism determines a pecuniary externality, which is likely to affect the profit (or cost) function of the domestic firms competing with the MNFs, more than their productivity. Sembenelli and Siotis (2002) using a large sample of Spanish firms over the period 1986–96 seem to go in this direction, and estimate a price–cost margin equation, rather than an augmented production function. Furthermore, they conjecture that competition effects will most likely occur in the short run, while externalities will take some time to manifest themselves. Results from their dynamic specification of firms' price-cost margins suggest that foreign presence dampens margins in the short run, but have a positive impact in the longer run. This result is consistent with the findings of some works looking at plant entry and survival rates more than productivity spillovers,[91] such as De Backer and Sleuwaegen (2003b) for Belgium and Barrios, Görg and Strobl (2005) for Ireland, where FDI discouraged domestic firms' entry in the home market in the short run, but these effects reversed in the longer run. Furthermore, Görg and Strobl (2004) show that a higher foreign presence increases the rate of UK plant survival but decreases their post entry performance.

The study by Sembenelli and Siotis (2002) on Spanish firms also finds that the negative short run effect is absent in R&D intensive industries, where foreign presence have a positive impact on domestic firms' profitability. They argue that this might have to do with the fact that in those industries technological externalities outweigh competition effects, due to the fact that the nature of knowledge might have created higher opportunities for technological externalities. However, they also note that Spanish firms in those sectors are lagging behind foreign multinationals suggesting that this might have opened up higher opportunities for catching up. Then, it is implicitly suggested that externalities do not occur automatically: one should probably look at the other 'environmental conditions', apart from competition, which favour higher externalities, including the existence of catching up opportunities and of abilities to exploit such opportunities.

A rather extensive literature has examined these conditions more explicitly, focusing on the role of technology gaps and absorptive capacity, but different views have emerged in this respect. On the one hand, scholars have argued that the lower the technological gap between domestic and foreign firms, the higher the *absorptive capacity* of the former, and thus the higher the expected benefits in terms of technology transfer to domestic firms. We label this as the 'technological accumulation hypothesis' (Cantwell 1989). The 'technological accumulation hypothesis' places the emphasis on the ability to absorb and utilise foreign technology as a necessary condition for spillovers to take place. The analysis of the responses of local firms to the entry and presence of US multinationals in European markets over 1955–75 seems to suggest that the most positive impact occurred in industries where the technological gap was small (Cantwell 1989). This is consistent with the view that relatively low technological differentials between domestic and foreign firms would grant higher ability of local economies to capture technological opportunities and to respond to the stimuli created by MNEs. Kokko (1994) focuses on 156 industries that hosted MNEs in Mexico in 1970 and finds evidence that in industries characterised by both large technological gaps and large foreign market shares, which he identifies as 'enclave sectors', local productivity growth is significantly inhibited. His idea is that in such circumstances, MNEs are able to crowd out local competitors from the most important market segments, thus reducing the likelihood that positive benefits accrue to, and are captured by, local firms. In a work on Uruguayan manufacturing plants Kokko, Tansini and Zejan (1996) find positive and statistically significant spillover effect only in the sub-sample of locally-owned plants with moderate technology gaps vis-à-vis foreign firms. They argue that small or moderate gaps, in the case of Uruguayan plants, identify cases where foreign technologies are *useful* to local firms and where local firms possess the skills needed to apply or learn foreign technologies. On the contrary, large gaps may signal that foreign technologies are so different from local ones that local firms have nothing to learn, or that local firms are so weak that they are not able to learn. Girma (forthcoming), using data on a large sample of UK firms, finds evidence supporting an inverted-U shaped relationship between absorptive capacity and FDI spillovers. Mixed results have also been found in transition economies. Measuring absorptive capacity in terms of R&D investments Damjian et al. (2003) find that in a sample of firms from the top ten transition countries, only in Slovakia it played a role in facilitating FDI spillovers. Similarly, in the case of Spanish firms, Barrios and Strobl (2002) found that firms carrying out R&D did not benefit more from foreign presence than other firms, while they provide evidence that exporters have been able to benefit more from foreign firms than non-exporters.

On the other hand, it is suggested that the larger the *technology gap* between host country firms and foreign-owned firms, the larger the potential for technology transfer and for productivity spillovers to the former. This assumption, which we label as the 'catching up hypothesis', can be derived from the original idea put forward by Findlay (1978). In his seminal contribution, technological progress in relatively 'backward' regions was formalised as an increasing function of the distance between their own level of technology and that of the 'advanced regions', and of the degree to which they are open to foreign direct investment. While this view is often thought of as alternative to the technological accumulation hypothesis, it is worth noting that the role of absorptive capacity has not been neglected in the catching up tradition. In particular, it is acknowledged that a sort of lower bound of local technological capabilities exists, below which foreign investment cannot be expected to have any positive effect on host economies.[92] Consistently with the catching-up hypothesis, Blomstrom and Wolff (1994) find evidence that the growth of gross output per employee of locally owned firms in Mexico in 1970–75, is positively related to a measure of FDIs and of initial labour productivity gap between local firms and multinationals. In the sample of UK establishments, Griffith, Redding and Simpson (2002) find that a higher foreign presence increases productivity growth of firms which are lagging behind the productivity frontier in their industry. Consistently, Haskel et al. (2002) find that UK firms in the lower end of the TFP and skill intensity distribution are able to appropriate more productivity spillovers from foreign firms than the firms which are closer to the frontier. Driffield and Love (2003) also obtain some results which are largely consistent with the catching up hypothesis. In fact they highlight that technology exploiting FDIs (proxied by investments originating from a country with a higher sectoral R&D intensity than the host country) raise productivity in the UK industry, while technology sourcing FDIs (proxied by foreign investments originating from a country with a lower sectoral R&D intensity than the host country) do not have any productivity effect. Although their analytical purpose is different, they implicitly confirm that spillovers do appear when technology gaps are high and positive, while they do not show up when technology gaps are small or negative.

The review of the empirical literature on the role of technology gaps and absorptive capacity in the generation of FDI on spillovers from multinational firms points to at least two critical considerations, each having important analytical implications. First, the contributions we have examined adopt a view of technology gaps as reflecting differences in the 'level' of knowledge and they implicitly assume that such differences capture also the degree of 'appropriateness' of technology to local industries. Indeed, the two dimensions of knowledge should be analysed separately. A well established literature (Richardson 1972; Teece 1992) has in fact highlighted that the latter refers to the 'relatedness' of knowledge (e.g. the degree of complementarity between technological assets) which might well be lacking in spite of short gaps, as measured in terms of a general technological level. This would require detailed data on the competence profile of firms, which is hardly available.

Second, scholars tend to identify high (low) gaps with low (high) absorptive capacity of domestic firms; however, the two concepts, although clearly related, are plainly different. In fact, if one takes into account the technology gap between the *average* foreign and domestic firms in a country, high gaps necessarily imply low absorptive capacity. On the contrary, when heterogeneity is allowed, the picture may change substantially. For example, looking at sectoral patterns within a country the same gap might be associated with different levels of absorptive capacity. In some sectors both domestic and foreign firms will be above the country's average absorptive capacity, and in other sectors they may be below this average. In other words, high (low) gaps can be associated with both high and low absorptive capacity.

In a previous work using a sample of firms active in France, Italy and Spain, we have investigated the role of both absorptive capacity and technology gaps in explaining the effects of multinational firms on host country firms' productivity (Castellani and Zanfei 2003). The results of that study are summarised and reconsidered here for the purpose of the present analysis. The overall sample we used contained 3,932 firms, out of which 1,950 located in France, 980 located in Italy and 1,002 located in Spain. Employment in foreign-owned firms represented slightly less than one-quarter of total employment in Italy, and between 33 and 52 per cent in France and Spain respectively (see Table 5.3 for the sectoral details of foreign presence in the three countries). For every firm located in the three countries the ultimate parent company was identified and, with this information, foreign-owned firms (when the ultimate parent company is different from the country of registration) were distinguished from domestic firms. Economic and financial data were available for a six-year time span, from 1992 to 1997. Firms for which the complete series of data was not available

Table 5.3   *Employment in foreign owned firms in a sample of French, Spanish and Italian manufacturing firms, by industry; average 1992–1997*

Industry (2 digit SIC)	Employment in foreign owned firms (% of total employment in manufacturing)			Employment in foreign owned firms/Employment in all firms (%)		
	Spain	France	Italy	Spain	France	Italy
Food and kindred products (20)	11.2	8.2	14.0	38.7	27.3	52.1
Tobacco products manufacturing (21)		0.1			100.0	
Textile mill products manufacturing (22)	0.5	1.9		12.4	31.1	
Apparel and other fabrics products (23)	0.8	1.5	0.5	17.0	25.1	2.7
Lumber and wood products (24)		0.6			16.8	
Furniture and fixtures manufacturing (25)	0.3	0.4	0.3	11.3	17.9	8.1
Paper and allied products manufacturing (26)	2.6	6.3	1.9	45.6	67.3	17.3
Printing, publishing and allied industries (27)	0.8	1.6	0.5	18.0	14.3	5.3
Chemicals and allied products manufacturing (28)	16.1	13.2	17.7	69.1	50.5	43.7
Petroleum refining and related industries (29)	0.3	1.8	0.8	32.2	30.7	43.5
Rubber and miscellaneous plastics (30)	10.4	8.8	11.2	80.3	53.4	47.1
Leather and leather products manufacturing (31)	0.2	0.6		41.9	34.8	
Stone, clay, glass and concrete products (32)	4.7	3.9	3.8	50.7	32.7	21.0
Primary metal industries manufacturing (33)	0.7	3.6	2.2	11.3	22.5	15.5
Fabricated metal products (34)	1.4	2.7	7.0	22.0	16.9	41.5
Industrial machinery and computer equipment (35)	7.2	20.1	16.9	71.7	55.2	37.9
Electronic and electrical eq. and components (36)	12.2	11.8	15.9	65.4	31.3	41.1

Transportation equipment manufacturing (37)	28.0	6.8	6.0	61.5	13.0	5.8
Measuring, analysing and controlling instruments (38)	1.7	5.4	1.0	56.2	47.7	13.4
Miscellaneous manufacturing industries (39)	0.8	0.7	0.4	47.2	26.4	27.7
Total	100.0	100.0	100.0	52.4	33.0	25.0

Source: ELIOS dataset (see Appendix)

were preliminarily dropped, thus the sample available for estimation was a balanced panel of 23,592 observations (of which 15,606 refer to domestic firms) for the three countries altogether. For each firm the fixed-effect from the estimation of a production function was computed and used as a rough measure of productivity ($TFP_i^c = \hat{\eta}_i^c$). Averaging out productivity of foreign firms in each sector (j) and country (c) ($Foreign \_ TFP_j^c = \frac{1}{N_j^F} \Sigma_{i \in F} \hat{\eta}_i^c$), the distance of each domestic firm from the average foreign firm in its sector-country was calculated, from the following ratio:

$$GAP_{ij}^c = \frac{Foreign \_ TFP_j^c}{TFP_i^c}$$

This measure varies across firms (therefore also across industries and countries) and can be used as a proxy of the productivity gap between each firm and the average (or representative) foreign firm in its sector-country. It takes values greater than 1 for firms which are less productive than the average foreign firm and the higher it gets, the larger the gap is.

The mean of TFP_i and GAP_{ij} across all domestic firms in a given country sector, produced an industry-country specific indicator of the absorptive capacity of domestic industries in France, Italy and Spain and of the average productivity gap relative to foreign firms. In Figure 5.2, some visual evidence of the relationship between absorptive capacity of domestic firms and

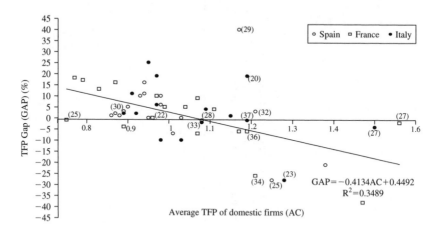

Source: Adapted from Castellani and Zanfei (2003)

Figure 5.2   Absorptive capacity and productivity gaps, in France, Italy and Spain by manufacturing industry (2-digit SIC)

technology gap. The two measures are negatively correlated, as one would expect, but only a relatively small fraction of the variance in the former is explained by sectoral variation in the latter (approximately 35 per cent, as from the R-squared reported in Figure 5.2). In fact, Figure 5.2 shows a number of interesting cases where high (low) technology gaps do not correspond to low (high) absorptive capacity. Roughly the same (null or very low) GAP characterises sectors where absorptive capacity is markedly different. In France, such cases are, for example furniture and fixtures manufacturing (SIC 25), textile mill products manufacturing (SIC 22), printing, publishing and allied industries (SIC 27), where the average TFP of domestic firms (a proxy for absorptive capacity) ranges from 0.75 to 1.56. Similarly, in Italy TFP gap is negligible in primary metal industries manufacturing (SIC 33), transportation equipment manufacturing (SIC 37), printing, publishing and allied industries (SIC 27), but absorptive capacity varies between 1.08 and 1.50. Finally, in Spain both rubber and miscellaneous plastics products manufacturing (SIC 30) and stone, clay, glass and concrete products manufacturing (SIC 32) foreign firms are 4 per cent more productive than domestic firms, but the latter exhibit TFP equal to 0.89 and 1.21, respectively. Quite symmetrically, one can observe a remarkably different TFP gap for a given level of absorptive capacity. This is the case of petroleum refining and related industries (SIC 29), stone, clay, glass and concrete products manufacturing (SIC 32), furniture and fixtures manufacturing (SIC 25) in Spain, where the average TFP of domestic firms is approximately equal to 1.2, but TFP gaps range from 40 per cent to −25 per cent. In Italy a similar pattern characterises food and kindred products (SIC 20) and apparel and other finished products made from fabrics (SIC 23) where TFP gap is respectively 20 per cent and −27 per cent.

In other words: this scattered evidence is consistent with the idea that productivity gaps and absorptive capacity are different, although related, concepts. Consistent with this view, it may well be that both the technological accumulation and the catching-up hypothesis hold at the same time.

This can be tested by interacting the foreign presence both with our measure of productivity gap of each domestic firm from the average foreign firm (GAP), and the measure of absorptive capacity (AC), as illustrated in equation (14):

$$\Delta \log Y_{it} = \alpha \, \Delta \log(L)_{it} + \beta \, \Delta \log(K)_{it} + \gamma \, \Delta \log(M)_{it}$$
$$+ \delta_1^{FR} \Delta \log(F_{jt})*FR_i + \delta_1^{ES} \Delta \log(F_{jt})*ES_i + \delta_1^{IT} \Delta \log(F_{jt})*IT_i +$$
$$+ \delta_1^{GAP} \Delta \log(F_{jt})*GAP_{ij} + \delta_1^{AC} \Delta \log(F_{jt})*AC_i +$$
$$+ \varphi \, \Delta \log(D_{jt}) + \phi \, \Delta X_{ijt} + \Delta \varepsilon_{it} \tag{14}$$

where Y, L, K and M denote output, labour, capital and materials while F and D are the number of employees in foreign and domestic firms in each sector-country. The vector of controls (X) includes the concentration in the industry, measured by the Herfindal index at the three-digits (HERF), the age of the firm (AGE) and the gap in productivity of each firm from the average foreign firm in a sector (GAP). Externalities from foreign multinationals are allowed to vary across countries by interacting $\Delta\log(F)$ with country dummies. Taking first differences wipes out any individual heterogeneity in productivity.

Results, reported in Table 5.4, suggest the TFP growth in firms whose productivity is further away from the average foreign firm in the sector will increase with the employment of foreign firms, suggesting that productivity gaps facilitates FDI spillovers, while AC does not seem to play a role in favouring spillovers. Therefore, results are consistent with the technology gap hypothesis, while the technological accumulation hypothesis is not supported. However, one needs to take into account at least two caveats. First,

Table 5.4   *The impact of sectoral foreign presence, technology gaps and absorptive capacity on domestic firms' productivity in France, Spain and Italy, 1992–1997: OLS regressions*

Dependent variable: ΔLog (real output)
Sample: Only domestic firms (all countries)

	(1)	(2)	(3)	(4)
ΔLog(F)$_{j,t}$*IT	0.034**	−0.058*	0.044*	−0.066*
	(1.99)	(1.84)	(1.94)	(1.80)
ΔLog(F)$_{j,t}$*FR	0.010	−0.088**	0.023	−0.097***
	(0.89)	(2.55)	(1.26)	(2.60)
ΔLog(F)$_{j,t}$*ES	−0.127***	−0.220***	−0.118***	−0.228***
	(6.77)	(6.60)	(5.17)	(6.09)
ΔLog(F)$_{j,t}$*GAP		0.089***		0.094***
		(3.49)		(3.97)
ΔLog(F)$_{j,t}$*AC			−0.009	0.003
			(0.64)	(0.22)
Observations	13,004	13,004	13,004	13,004
Adjusted R-squared	0.73	0.73	0.73	0.73

Source: Adapted from Castellani and Zanfei (2003)

All regressions include country-specific intercepts and input elasticities, 2–digit SIC sector dummies, time dummies, employment in domestic firms at the 3-digit SIC, and other controls as indicated in section 4. Robust t statistics in parentheses
* significant at 10%; ** significant at 5%; *** significant at 1%

the level of TFP can only imprecisely capture the 'true' absorptive capacity of the firm. Second, the relation between absorptive capacity and spillovers might be non-linear or subject to some threshold effects, that is, firms will need to reach a threshold of absorptive capacity in order to be able to reap the externalities from foreign firms. Above that threshold an increase in absorptive capacity, at the margin, does not increase benefits from FDI. This consideration might help explain the evidence we obtained for the countries examined. In the case of France, Italy and Spain, as in many developed economies, one may venture so far as to say that such a threshold is reached by the great majority of firms.

A study on Indonesian firms confirms the relevance of these two caveats. Using data on R&D expenditure as a measure of absorptive capacity and distance from the average firm productivity as a measure of technology gap Blalock and Gertler (2004) find that domestic firms with high absorptive capacity benefit more from FDI, but firms with low technology gap benefit less from foreign presence. In other words, using an appropriate measure of absorptive capacity in a country with a sufficient variability in this dimension (only 10 per cent of firms have positive R&D expenditures) they provide support both to the 'technological accumulation' and the 'catching-up hypothesis'.

5.5   CONCLUDING REMARKS

Multinational firms have both direct and indirect effects on the host economies. On the one hand, as we showed in Chapter 3, on average they have higher productivity and have a higher propensity to innovate and carry out R&D than national firms. Therefore, whenever foreign or domestic multinational firms enter or expand activities into a given country, they contribute directly to the overall performance of the economy. On the other hand, they have external effects on entry, survival and performance of other firms in the same country. In this chapter we have reviewed the literature on this second aspect and we have limited our discussion to externalities from foreign affiliates to domestic firms in the host country. Theoretical works have suggested that multinationals produce both pecuniary and knowledge externalities, and such external effects arise through four main channels: competition, imitation and demonstration, labour mobility and spin-offs, backward and forward linkages. From the theoretical point of view one can identify the different types of externalities and the different role played by the various channels in such external effects. However, empirical works have hardly been able to disentangle them, and most evidence points to the net effect of the presence of multinational firms. Although results are rather inconclusive, the more recent studies tend to find non-significant (or even negative) spillovers from multinational firms to domestic firms within the same sector. In this chapter, we have discussed two main sets of issues raised in the recent literature, which might help explain those findings.

First, we have focused on specification issues, related to the correct identification of productivity and of the foreign externality. Results from a sample of Italian firms suggest that important improvements can be achieved by allowing production functions to differ across sectors and by adopting an absolute measure of foreign activity, rather than the widely used foreign presence ratio.

Second, we examined some of the studies pointing at the conditions which eventually favour spillovers. While the available data do not allow us to discern the channels through which multinational firms affect the host economy, it is possible to evaluate under what conditions some of channels are likely to be more effective in inducing externalities. On the one hand, several studies emphasise that multinational firms are most likely to determine spillovers when dealing with their suppliers or distributors. In fact, competition effects and the incentive to prevent information leakages are lower along the supply chain than within the same industry. On the other hand, a number of empirical works concentrate on horizontal spillovers and stress the role of potential knowledge transfer, which increases with higher technology gaps between foreign and domestic firms but is also a function of the absorptive capacity of the latter. Evidence is still controversial with regard to the role of these factors. Using data from three European countries (France, Italy and Spain) we showed that it is technological gaps between foreign and domestic firms that favours positive externalities from foreign affiliates. This might be influenced by country-specific characteristics as well as the sectoral composition of foreign presence in the examined countries. More generally, these findings reflect a combination of characteristics of the multinationals and of host country firms. The former need to be strong enough to create technological opportunities for the host economy, while the latter need to be capable to capture such opportunities. In other words, not every foreign firm is a good source of externality and not every domestic firm is equally well equipped to benefit.

6. In search of horizontal spillovers from multinationals: the role of firms' heterogeneity

6.1 INTRODUCTION

In the previous chapter we stressed that most recent works did not find any sound evidence of positive intra-industry spillovers. The main theoretical explanation to these results is that multinational firms have strong incentives to prevent information leakages and have very few incentives to transfer part of their knowledge to their competitors in the host country. Furthermore, they may well push domestic firms out of the market by stealing their market share and by forcing them to produce at higher unit costs. Under these conditions, negative competition effects tend to outweigh positive externalities from the activities of foreign multinationals in the host country. However, we have also noted that a closer look at the empirical evidence reveals that positive horizontal spillovers from foreign affiliates of multinational firms to host country firms do occur under specific circumstances. In particular, a large literature has focused on the role of technology gaps and absorptive capacity in facilitating such positive externalities. In a nutshell, the technology gap hypothesis posits that in order for a knowledge transfer to occur, the foreign firm should have something to 'teach' and domestic firms should have something to 'learn'. In most studies, a high productivity gap between foreign and domestic firms is taken as a good indicator for the possible existence of such conditions. In other words, if domestic firms are far away from the technological frontier of the foreign multinationals, there is a good chance that some catching-up takes place and the potential for positive externality is likely to exceed the negative competition effect. The absorptive capacity hypothesis complements this view by postulating that for a knowledge transfer to occur the beneficiary must be capable of learning. Despite a high spillover potential, domestic firms might not be able to benefit if they do not accumulate absorptive capacity. From the theoretical point of view this is a function of the stock of knowledge of each firm, generally captured using the level of productivity, human capital or R&D investment of host country firms.

In this chapter we build on this literature by analysing the hypothesis that not every foreign firm is a good source of externality and not every domestic firm is equally well placed to benefit from the presence of foreign multinationals. The idea, which follows from the previous part of this book (Chapters 3 and 4), is that the extent to which spillover opportunities arise and can be appropriated by domestic firms depends on the characteristics of both the foreign affiliates and the domestic firms. In other words, we focus on how various aspects of firms' heterogeneity affect the realization of spillovers from multinational firms.

First, we investigate the role of *heterogeneity of foreign affiliates*, with special attention to their R&D intensity, their propensity to establish technological cooperative agreements, and the length of their presence in the host country. Second, we address the role of *heterogeneity of domestic firms*, by arguing that their degree of international involvement is a key characteristic which affects both their ability to benefit from the presence of multinational firms in their sector, and the intensity of competition. Third, we discuss how *heterogeneity across and within multinationals* affects domestic firms. In particular, we consider whether the expansion of domestic multinationals in their home market influences productivity of other domestic firms, and we compare this effect with spillovers from foreign multinationals. By doing so, we shall jointly take into account the issue of diversity among (foreign and domestic) firms belonging to different multinational groups; and the distinctive position they occupy within the transnational organisation they belong to.

The three issues briefly sketched above are investigated using firm-level data from the Elios dataset (see Appendix for a description of the data and Chapters 3, 4 and 5 for other applications) and taking into account the methodological issues raised in Chapter 5. The next sections provide a discussion of the various hypotheses and results. In particular, section 6.2 addresses the role of heterogeneity across foreign affiliates in determining spillovers to domestic firms. Section 6.3 focuses on how the international involvement of domestic firms affects absorptive capacity and competition. Section 6.4 investigates spillovers from domestic multinationals, as compared with the externalities created by foreign owned multinationals. In section 6.5 we place the issue of spillovers in a more general context, by noting that domestic firms should not only be considered as beneficiary firms, which can absorb externalities from multinational firms. In particular, we argue that technology transfers can occur also from domestic to foreign firms and the former can play an active role in stimulating the latter in the spillover generating process. Section 6.6 concludes this chapter.

6.2 HETEROGENEITY OF FOREIGN FIRMS AND SPILLOVERS

In this section, we pursue the idea that firms are heterogeneous and not every foreign affiliate provides the same knowledge opportunities for domestic firms. In particular, we put forward the idea that some characteristics of foreign firms affect the likelihood of spillovers to domestic ones. Our focus is on three key aspects which differentiate foreign affiliates: (i) the *extent of R&D activities*; (ii) the *propensity* to *establish technological cooperation*; and (iii) the *length of time* since their establishment in the host country.

6.2.1 The R&D Activities of Foreign Affiliates

Sectors which rely on technologies incorporating more codified and less appropriable knowledge will offer more opportunities for knowledge externalities (Malerba 2005). One might thus expect larger spillovers from foreign to domestic firms in technology intensive industries. Among others, Sembenelli and Siotis (2002) addressed this issue by looking at spillovers in R&D and non-R&D intensive industries in a sample of Spanish firms and find that positive spillovers occur only in the former case. This result is consistent with the idea that R&D-intensive industries offer more opportunities for knowledge transfer from foreign to domestic firms. However, as we noted in Part II of this book, inter-firm differences within the same industry can be relevant, and looking at differences across sectors might miss an important part of the story. In fact, within the same industry, we may find affiliates which carry out knowledge intensive activities at different degrees. In this line of thought, we focus on the contribution of firm-specific R&D activities of foreign affiliates to spillovers in the host country.

Traditional views on multinational firms highlight that the core activities are centralised in the home countries and knowledge and competences are developed by the headquarters and eventually transferred to foreign affiliates for exploitation in the foreign markets. However, as we have argued in Part I, an increasing share of innovative activities of multinational firms are carried out on a global scale. In Chapter 4 we also highlighted that multinationals differ in terms of international dispersion of innovative activities. The extent to which subsidiaries are involved in R&D can substantially affect spillovers from multinational firms on the host economy. First, when foreign affiliates carry out R&D activities, they bring in the host country not only technologies developed by the multinational firm elsewhere, but also new knowledge developed in their labs and incorporated in their product and processes. This provides an opportunity for imitation and learning which can favour technology transfer to domestic firms. Second, R&D activities might require inputs from, or induce technological cooperation with, domestic counterparts, where knowledge exchange between the subsidiary and domestic firms can be much more intense than in the case of supply of less knowledge intensive intermediate goods. Furthermore, while linkages for the supply of inputs are likely to involve firms operating in different sectors, R&D cooperation can also occur among competitors in the same industry. This is the case of horizontal technological cooperation taking place at the precompetitive stage. Third, pecuniary externalities through the labour market can be much more significant when R&D activities are involved. In fact, in these cases multinational firms need qualified scientists and engineers and often offer an incentive to local universities to supply such resources, which become available also for other domestic companies. The Etna Valley case can illustrate this phenomenon: when ST Microelectronics (STM) located its research labs in the area near Catania, one of the locational determinants was the supply of skilled and relatively cheap workers. However, the demand for engineers grew rapidly after the entry of STM and provided an incentive to students and the local university to pursue higher education in engineering-related fields. This further reinforced the locational advantage of the Etna Valley and stimulated the growth of a local high-tech industry (Santangelo 2004). Furthermore, R&D labs can give rise to spin-offs or worker mobility to domestic firms. All in all, we can expect the contribution to knowledge and productivity of domestic firms to be higher in the case of a scientist or a qualified engineer moving from a multinational firm than in the case of mobility of less qualified workers. In other words, when MNFs carry out knowledge intensive activities the extent of both technological and pecuniary externalities can be expected to be substantially higher and this can determine a more significant increase in domestic firms' productivity.

Considerable efforts have been devoted to studying the characteristics of the process of internationalisation of R&D and large evidence has been provided on the direct effect on the host economy determined by the different propensity to innovate of foreign and domestic owned firms.[93] Less extensive evidence has been produced in relation to the indirect impact of such innovative activities on the local economy. Among others, Holm, Malberg and Solvell (2003) find that competences of subsidiaries of foreign multinationals in Sweden favour local development by attracting other investors. Todo and Miyamoto (2002) investigate the impact of R&D activities in foreign owned firms as a condition favouring intra-industry productivity spillovers in a sample of Indonesian firms. They observe a positive impact only for the activities of multinational firms carrying out R&D in Indonesia. Marin and Bell (2004) test for productivity spillovers in a sample of Argentinian firms and find positive effects from the activity of multinationals only in the industries where foreign affiliates were significantly involved in innovative activities.

6.2.2 The Collaborative Activities of Foreign Affiliates

As discussed in Chapter 5, inter-firm linkages are an important channel through which spillovers may occur. The impact of such linkages on domestic productivity has been investigated mainly within the framework of vertical externalities. In particular, the existence of a positive effect of foreign multinationals on a domestic firm's productivity is taken as evidence of the role of backward and forward linkages (Smarzynska Javorcick 2004). However, this is only a part of the story. First, we have already noticed that some theoretical approaches suggest that backward and forward linkages should have an impact on horizontal spillovers as well on vertical spillovers (Alfaro and Rodriguez-Clare 2004). Second, backward and forward linkages are only part of a wider range of possible types of inter-firm cooperative agreements. In fact, this perspective focuses on supply contracts or licensing agreements along the vertical chain, but firms – and particularly many MNFs – may establish a large number of horizontal linkages with local firms through a variety of modes, ranging from joint ventures, strategic alliances and other non-equity type of collaborative agreements. This is the case, for example, of R&D cooperation, joint product development, co-design and standard setting. In these ventures knowledge transfer is explicit and can flow from the multinational to the local firm and vice versa. When firms set up horizontal agreements they often combine complementary but dissimilar resources (Richardson 1972), and within these ventures some knowledge can be lost and transferred to the counterparts, but this loss is 'compensated' by access to complementary assets which enrich the firm's knowledge base. In this perspective, foreign affiliates involved in technological cooperation can be an important source of technology transfer both to their counterparts and to other firms in the host country. Therefore, one may well expect that an increase in the share of foreign firms involved in cooperative ventures in the host country generates higher potential for externalities beneficial to domestic firms.

6.2.3 The Age of Foreign Affiliates

As suggested in Chapter 4, the duration of activity in a given host economy contributes to differentiating the behaviour and performance of foreign affiliates. What is worth stressing here is that the length of time since establishment can significantly reduce both 'external' and 'internal' uncertainty associated with international operations (Castellani and Zanfei 2004), and hence create a more favourable environment for spillovers. On the one hand, a lengthy experience in the local context diminishes the so-called 'external uncertainty' stemming from factors that are largely (albeit not entirely) beyond the control of individual firms, such as the variety and volatility of demand, of technological opportunities and of institutional and social conditions. Due to the unpredictability of such factors, inexperienced firms tend to overstate the risks and to understate the returns of international operations, and may consequently be reluctant to make significant resource commitments to foreign markets (Davidson 1980; Gomes-Casseres 1989). By contrast, as affiliates become more rooted in the host economy, they improve their ability to assess the costs and risks of doing business there, and to evaluate local opportunities. Therefore, they will be more available to commit resources to local markets, including strategic assets such as technology and other value added activities, thus generating more spillover opportunities for local counterparts.

On the other hand, experience is also likely to reduce 'internal uncertainty', associated with the behaviour of parties involved in economic transactions. As suggested by Robertson and Gatignon (1998, p. 520), this kind of (behavioural) uncertainty concerns the difficulty of observing and measuring the adherence of contracting parties to the contractual arrangements, and the difficulty of measuring the performance of these parties. This kind of uncertainty is critical in the absence of control mechanisms, as it is typically associated with opportunistic behaviour. A lengthy experience in the host economy is likely to diminish internal uncertainty. In fact, through a long history of relations and transactions, the parties gradually become acquainted with one another, they end up sharing goals and cultural values, and become less inclined to adopt opportunistic behaviour. In other words the length of establishment of foreign affiliates is likely to generate 'mutual trust'. This can be expected to pave the way to cooperation and to other modes of inter-firm linkages (Bureth et al. 1997; Lyons and Mehta 1997) which will eventually favour spillovers (see section 6.2.2). From this perspective, as mutual trust increases multinationals will be more willing to transfer valuable knowledge, at least in favour of suppliers. This can be reasonably expected to increase the quality and reliability of goods and services produced by the latter to the advantage of the former (Dunning 1958). MNFs might also be less worried about information leakages in favour of other local counterparts, including competitors for at least two reasons. First, as they become more trustful and trusted, multinationals will participate in a business climate of a relatively 'fair competition', wherein the rules of the game are known and shared by all parties. This will increase the likelihood that free riding and technology stealing is openly opposed by the business community, of which a long established foreign firm is perceived as a member. Second, MNFs will be less worried about knowledge leaks because they can also expect to gain access to greater flows of technology stemming from local counterparts. In fact, as mutual trust increases and as local firms augment their efficiency, knowledge flows are likely to become more and more bidirectional. In particular, local suppliers can be expected to transfer part of the knowledge they accumulate through their interaction with other client firms, including local competitors of foreign firms themselves. See section 6.5 for more discussion on the two way flow of technology between multinationals and local firms.

6.2.4 Empirical Evidence for Italy

In this section we provide some evidence that heterogeneity of foreign affiliates can affect the degree of spillovers to domestic firms. Data for this empirical investigation come from the Cis-Elios dataset illustrated in the Appendix and used elsewhere in this volume. Here we use the same balanced sample of Italian firms described in Chapter 5, which includes 447 domestic owned firms for which data on innovative behaviour (from the Second Community Innovation Survey, CISII) are available for the period 1994–1996, while output, capital, labour and material inputs observed over the 1994–2000 period are drawn from the ELIOS dataset. From the same source we gathered the year of establishment of each firm, the main sector of activity, and the ultimate owner which allows us to distinguish domestic versus foreign owned firms. We model firms' TFP as a function of foreign (F) and domestic (D) activities in the sector j where firm i operates, a firm-specific fixed effect and an error term.[94]

$$\log(A_{ijt}) = \delta_1 \log F_{jt} + \phi \log D_{jt} + \eta_i + \varepsilon_{it} \tag{15}$$

Each firm's TFP, $\log(A_{ijt})$, is obtained as the residual of a production function estimated sector by sector using the Levinshon and Petrin (2003) approach and used as the dependent variable of equation (15), where external effects from foreign and domestic activity are obtained as standard within group estimates. Results from this regression are provided in column (1) of Table 6.1, from which it turns out that, once controlling for fixed effects and for sector-specific production functions, foreign multinationals do not have any significant effect on productivity of Italian firms in the same sector. This outcome is consistent with the numerous empirical studies recalled in Chapter 5, which report null or non-significant intra-industry spillovers from multinational presence to local firms. However, in this section we have suggested that heterogeneity of foreign affiliates can matter. To test for the impact of the various characteristics of foreign multi-nationals on spillovers, we add to the general foreign externality term (F) other variables to identify specific sources of externalities. These include the involvement of FAs in R&D activities and in technical cooperation, as well as their length of establishment in Italy.

To account for the role of R&D activities of foreign multinationals we 'augment' domestic firms' productivity by an externality term where foreign capital is weighted by each foreign firm's R&D intensity (obtained from CIS2). In other words, we modify (15) to obtain:

$$\log(A_{it}) = \delta_1 \log F_{jt} + \delta_2 \log F_{jt}^{RD} + \phi \log D_{jt} + \eta_i + \varepsilon_{it} \qquad (16)$$

where

$$F_{jt}^{RD} = \sum_{i \in j} FOR_i {}^* K_{ijt} {}^* RD_i$$

and RD denotes the R&D intensity of firm i. Therefore in equation (16), δ_1 captures the external effect of affiliates of foreign multinationals *not* carry-ing out any R&D activity in Italy on domestic owned firms. The coefficient δ_2 captures the additional externality stemming from foreign firms carrying out R&D in Italy. In particular, δ_2 measures the effect of a percentage increase of capital stock in foreign affiliates weighted by each affiliate's R&D intensity. In other words, a positive sign of δ_2 indicates that increases in the stock of capital of R&D intensive affiliates has a larger impact on domestic firms' productivity than the same increase in firms with lower (o null) R&D intensity.

The hypothesis that foreign firms involved in technological coopera-tion have a higher spillover potential is tested by estimating a further modification of equation (15). Here we add to the sectoral measure of foreign capital, an additional externality caused by firms which set up tech-nological cooperation with local firms.

$$\log(A_{it}) = \delta_1 \log F_{jt} + \delta_3 \log F_{jt}^{CON} + \delta_4 \log F_{jt}^{COI} + \phi \log D_{jt} + \eta_i + \varepsilon_{it} \quad (17)$$

where

$$F_{jt}^{COI} = \sum_{i \in j} FOR_i {}^* K_{ijt} {}^* COI_i$$

and

$$F_{jt}^{CON} = \sum_{i \epsilon j} FOR_i * K_{ijt} * CON_i$$

and *COI* and *CON* are indicators which take value 1 if a firm i sets up technological cooperation with international and national counterparts respectively in the period 1994–1996, as reported by the CIS2. In these cases, δ_1 captures the impact on domestic firms' productivity of foreign firms not involved in any cooperation, while δ_3 and δ_4 measure the additional effect associated with foreign firms involved in (national and international) technological cooperation.

The impact of the length of time since establishment is investigated introducing a measure of foreign owned capital in each sector weighted by the age of each foreign firm. In other words, we modify equation (15) in the following way:

$$\log(A_{it}) = \delta_1 \log F_{jt} + \delta_5 \log F_{jt}^{AGE} + \phi \log D_{jt} + \eta_i + \varepsilon_{it} \qquad (18)$$

where

$$F_{jt}^{AGE} = \sum_{i \epsilon j} FOR_i * K_{ijt} * AGE_{it}$$

and AGE denotes the number of years since establishment in Italy of each foreign affiliate. The idea is that δ_5 estimates the effect of an increase in capital of the older firms on productivity of domestic firms. More precisely, a positive sign will indicate that a percentage increase in foreign owned capital in a sector will have a larger impact on domestic firms' productivity if it is determined by an increase of older subsidiaries than if it is accounted for by recently established subsidiaries.

In columns (2) to (4) of Table 6.1 we report results of the estimation of equations (16)–(18). From column (2) we observe that an increase in the capital stock in more R&D intensive foreign firms has a positive impact on domestic firms' productivity, while an increase in the activity of non-R&D active firms has no significant effect. In other words, these results are consistent with the idea that, within each sector, foreign firms carrying out R&D in Italy provide a higher spillover potential for the host economy than non-R&D intensive affiliates.

In column (3) we investigate the role of technological cooperation of foreign multinationals. Results seem to suggest that foreign firms involved in technological cooperative agreements with domestic counterparts have a positive impact on productivity. However, the estimated coefficient falls short of the conventional significance levels. This might have to do with the fact that the dummy variables that detect whether technical cooperation takes place are not fully satisfactory as a measure of linkage creation.

Results reported in column (4) are more sound, and they are consistent with the indication that spillovers from foreign affiliates established for a longer period of time are larger. This supports the hypothesis that as subsidiaries get rooted into a foreign context they become more willing to share their knowledge with trustworthy counterparts, or at least they might be less concerned by information leakages which might benefit domestic firms. However, the length of time since establishment in Italy is also likely to be associated with greater involvement in technological collaboration and with higher R&D intensity. In fact, as multinationals become more acquainted with the local context they also become more likely to commit strategic resources to the local markets, improve their ability to scan for local partners, and might increase the extent of cooperation. Furthermore, as we argued in Part I and in Chapter 4 of this book, the internationalisation of

Table 6.1   Heterogeneity of foreign firms and productivity spillovers in Italy, 1993–2000: fixed-effects estimation

	(1)	(2)	(3)	(4)	(5)
Log (F_{jt})	0.023	−0.023	0.033	−0.015	−0.035
	(0.023)	(0.028)	(0.025)	(0.028)	(0.032)
Log (F_{jt}^{RD})		0.098***			0.118***
		(0.035)			(0.041)
Log (F_{jt}^{CON})			0.035		0.005
			(0.025)		(0.026)
Log (F_{jt}^{COI})			−0.040		−0.052*
			(0.027)		(0.028)
Log (F_{jt}^{AGE})				0.074**	0.058*
				(0.031)	(0.034)
Log (D_{jt})	−0.045	−0.045	−0.047	−0.046	−0.054*
	(0.033)	(0.033)	(0.033)	(0.033)	(0.033)
Constant	1.917***	1.682***	1.882***	1.238*	1.336**
	(0.606)	(0.611)	(0.616)	(0.669)	(0.670)
Year dummies	yes	yes	yes	yes	yes
Observations	3576	3576	3576	3576	3576
Number of firms	447	447	447	447	447

Standard errors in brackets
* $p < 0.1$, ** $p < 0.05$, *** $p < 0.01$

R&D usually follows the establishment of production or commercial activities, but this process requires time. Therefore, it is likely that older subsidiaries show a higher propensity to also engage in R&D investments. From this perspective, the various externality terms that we have used to capture the effect of R&D, cooperation and age might have been biased by the fact the three aspects are correlated. To work this problem out, in column (6) we introduce the various sources of externalities jointly, but results remain largely unchanged.

6.3 HETEROGENEITY OF DOMESTIC FIRMS AND SPILLOVERS: THE ROLE OF INTERNATIONAL INVOLVEMENT

In the previous section we have argued that the effects of spillovers on domestic firms might differ according to some characteristics of foreign firms. In particular, we have claimed that foreign firms should have something to transfer and be willing to transfer it to domestic firms. We further maintained that these conditions are more likely to be met when foreign subsidiaries carry out some R&D, they cooperate with local firms (although this is not well measured), and are well established in the foreign country.

Here we shall look at the other side of the coin and argue that domestic firms are also heterogeneous, and different firms get different benefits from foreign presence. This section presents the hypothesis that some absorptive capacity is required to grasp the benefits of foreign presence, but will also highlight that competition effects are likely to differ across domestic firms. Absorptive capacity is most often identified as a function of R&D investments and technical efficiency of firms, which are assumed to provide guidance in the search and use of external knowledge sources (Cohen and Levinthal 1989; Rosenberg 1990). While this certainly captures a fundamental feature of firms' ability to absorb knowledge, here we shall emphasise the role of domestic firms' degree of internationalisation as a factor which can *per se* affect their accumulation of competencies and their ability to take advantage from multinational presence. In particular, we shall test whether exporters and domestic multinationals benefit more from foreign presence than non internationalised firms. There are several reasons why the degree of internationalisation can be expected to be associated with firms' absorptive capacity. First, internationalised firms are more likely to be highly innovative and productive. As stressed by theoretical and empirical works reviewed in Chapter 3, more productive and innovative firms tend to self-select into export and international production (Helpman, Melitz and Yeaple, 2004; Barba Navaretti and Castellani

2004; Tybout 2003), and their international involvement can in turn offer learning opportunities and increase productivity and innovation in the internationalised firms (Dunning 1993; Kuemmerle 1999; Narula and Zanfei 2005). In particular, as we have shown in Chapter 3, this determines a hierarchy in productivity, investments in R&D, and propensity to innovate between firms with different involvement in international activities. In particular, multinational firms outperform those internationalised firms involved only in exporting activities, which in turn do better than non internationalised firms (Girma et al. 2004; Castellani and Zanfei 2005; Criscuolo et al. 2004). This result suggests that the degree of internationalisation can be interpreted as a synthetic indicator of the productive and innovatory capacity of a firm, which in turn is a good proxy for absorptive capacity.

Second, internationalised firms not only have greater opportunities to gain access to foreign sources of knowledge, but they can also be expected to learn how to deal with such sources. In other words, through their experience in foreign markets, they will develop a specific ability to access external knowledge, i.e. a 'learning to learn' capacity. Different examples can be made of this second order learning process (Bureth et al. 1997). Perhaps the simplest illustration concerns the quality of human capital in internationalised firms. As a company increases its international involvement, one will observe a growing share of personnel with a relatively high acquaintance with foreign languages, cultures and institutions. This will eventually increase organisational flexibility and abilities to search for, evaluate, and capture external opportunities. A further step might be the development of routines and methodologies to deal with international operations which can be reused in and adapted to different contexts, reducing the cost of accessing new markets and new knowledge sources. Part of this organisational learning might be institutionalised into business units, teams and divisions specifically devoted to exploring foreign opportunities and extracting economic value from them.

The role of internationalisation as a measure of absorptive capacity has been analysed elsewhere in the literature. For example, Barrios and Strobl (2002) found that Spanish exporters benefit more from foreign multinationals than non-exporting firms. Here we take the argument a step further, distinguishing not only exporters from purely national firms, but also identifying domestic firms with control of foreign production. As we showed in Chapter 3, in the case of Italy the latter category of firms on average outperforms exporters and other domestic firms in the same sector, suggesting that multinationals have the highest absorptive capacity.

Although there are reasons to expect that absorptive capacity increases with the degree of internationalisation, it is not obvious that domestic multinationals will reap higher benefits from inward FDIs than exporters. In fact, there are at least two aspects which need to be taken into account. On the one hand, the empirical evidence highlights that the effect of absorptive capacity can be non-linear (Girma 2005). For example, one does not need to hire the top engineers to be able to incorporate a novel discovery in an existing machinery. In other words, while production of new knowledge and breakthrough discoveries requires a wide range of capabilities and substantial investments, the use of such knowledge might require much more basic capabilities. Therefore, investing in absorptive capacity above a certain threshold may not be very productive: at the margin, further accumulation of absorptive capacity will not increase the benefits from foreign presence. In this respect, the higher innovative capabilities and organizational capacities of multinational firms relative to exporters might not provide additional ability to reap spillovers from foreign multinationals.

On the other hand, competition effects might play a different role in the case of domestic multinationals. In fact, foreign multinationals might perceive them as competing more directly in international markets than mere exporters, such that there is a stronger incentive to prevent information leakages. This argument is consistent with theories of FDI in oligopolistic markets showing that firms can choose to invest in the home country of a competitor to reciprocate investment in their own home country. In other words, FDI can be the result of an exchange of threats between oligopolists from different countries (Graham 1990; Knickerbocker 1973; Smith 1987; Sanna-Randaccio 2002). To the extent that foreign and domestic multinationals take part in such an oligopolistic game in a given industry, knowledge transfers and technology sharing will be rather unlikely.

The actual impact of the degree of internationalisation of domestic firms on spillovers will then depend on the interplay of the two factors we have highlighted, namely the (positive) absorptive capacity effect, and the (negative) competition effect.

We test for the role of the degree of internationalisation as a factor affecting the ability to capture FDI spillovers by estimating the following equation:

$$\log(A_{it}) = \delta_1 \log F_{jt} + \delta_2 (\log F_{jt} * EXP_i) + \delta_3 (\log F_{jt} * PC_i)$$
$$+ \phi \log D_{jt} + \eta_i + \varepsilon_{it} \tag{19}$$

where EXP is a dummy variable taking value 1 in the case firms internationalised only through exports and PC is a dummy variable taking value 1 for parent companies, i.e. firms controlling subsidiaries abroad.

In equation (19) δ_1 indicates the externality accruing to the baseline category (non-exporting firms), while δ_2 and δ_3 measures the additional
impact of foreign presence on exporters and multinational firms.

In column (1) of Table 6.2 we report the results of the estimation of equation (19) on the sample of Italian firms illustrated in the previous section,
which suggest that the degree of internationalisation indeed affects the
capacity to benefit from foreign multinationals. The effect of an increase in
foreign owned capital is 11.9 per cent higher in the case of exporters than
non-exporting firms, while the externality benefited by domestic multinationals is not significantly different from zero at the conventional levels.
This is consistent with the fact that absorptive capacity can have a non-
linear effect and that higher competition between foreign affiliates and
domestic multinationals might prevent knowledge transfer.

*Table 6.2   Heterogeneity of domestic firms and productivity spillovers in
Italy, 1993–2000: fixed-effects estimation*

	(1)	(2)	(3)
$\text{Log}(F_{jt})$	−0.062	−0.005	−0.051
	(0.061)	(0.024)	(0.061)
$(EXP)*\text{Log}(F_{jt})$	0.119*		0.081
	(0.068)		(0.068)
$(PC)*\text{Log}(F_{jt})$	0.073		0.026
	(0.068)		(0.069)
$\text{Log}(M_{jt})$		0.027	0.116*
		(0.025)	(0.062)
$(EXP)*\text{Log}(M_{jt})$			−0.121*
			(0.066)
$(PC)*\text{Log}(M_{jt})$			−0.071
			(0.066)
$\text{Log}(D_{jt})$	−0.044		
	(0.033)		
$\text{Log}(O_{jt})$		−0.253***	−0.247***
		(0.049)	(0.049)
Constant	1.860***	4.517***	4.392***
	(0.606)	(0.816)	(0.820)
Year dummies	Yes	Yes	Yes
Observations	3576	3576	3576
Number of firms	447	447	447

Standard errors in brackets
* $p<0.1$, ** $p<0.05$, *** $p<0.01$

6.4 HETEROGENEITY ACROSS AND WITHIN MULTINATIONALS: SPILLOVERS FROM DOMESTIC PARENT COMPANIES

So far we have addressed the impact of foreign firms in host countries. This is important because foreign affiliates of multinational firms bring a bundle of tangible and intangible assets to the host countries which can contribute to innovation and productivity in the country both directly and through spillovers. Empirical studies have found that foreign affiliates of multinationals tend to outperform domestic firms, supporting the idea that expanding the activity of foreign-owned firms (i.e. attracting inward FDIs) will raise the average productivity and innovation in the recipient economy (see Chapter 4), while less robust evidence has been provided on the spillover effect of foreign multinationals on host country firms (see Chapter 5). A parallel, growing literature has discussed the role of multinationality as opposed to foreignness in explaining differences in productivity and innovation. In particular, domestic multinationals share many characteristics of foreign-owned firms in a given country and can be at least as productive, innovative, and likely to invest in R&D (Criscuolo and Martin 2003; Pfaffermayr and Bellak 2002; Frenz and Ietto-Gillies 2005; Castellani and Zanfei 2005). From this perspective, one could view domestic firms going abroad as a further source of externality for other domestic firms.

As in the case of other multinationals active in a given economy, spillovers of domestic MNFs will be influenced by the factors examined in section 6.2. Among other determinants, spillovers will depend on these firms' innovativeness, and this will in turn reflect the intensity of their R&D investments. Furthermore, spillovers will depend on the propensity of domestic multinationals to set up cooperative agreements with indigenous firms and institutions. Once again this is the same as in the case of other (foreign owned) multinationals. What is more specific of domestic MNFs and differentiates their effects on a given economy is the role of embeddedness. Domestic multinationals are generally more rooted in the economy where they have their own home base, as compared to foreign affiliates active in the same country. The former firms do not need to overcome cultural and linguistic barriers, which on the contrary can hinder the relationship of foreign owned companies with the local economy. Domestic MNFs can thus be seen as a special case in the analysis of 'heterogeneity across multinationals', characterised by a particularly high level of embeddedness and hence a higher potential for spillovers on the local economy.

A further distinctive characteristic of domestic MNFs has to do with the position they occupy in the organisational structure of the multinational group they belong to. In fact, they can either be parent companies (PC) or national affiliates (NA), while incoming multinationals are by definition foreign affiliates (FA) of a multinational group based elsewhere. This will generally determine distinctive capabilities as well as incentives to generate, adopt and diffuse knowledge. This issue has been discussed at length in Chapter 4 under the label of 'heterogeneity within multinationals'. It has been argued that PCs are generally the main sources of proprietary advantages of multinational firms. Only part of these technological, managerial and organisational capabilities are transferred to FAs abroad in order to allow them to overcome the cost of doing business abroad, face competition with and absorb knowledge from, other local and multinational firms in host countries.[95] The dominant role of PCs in this respect is partially compensated by the fact that FAs can indeed accumulate further knowledge and capabilities through local R&D activities, learning and external linkages with host country counterparts. Nevertheless, parent companies can be expected to exhibit a persisting advantage as a locus of knowledge accumulation relative to both foreign and national affiliates, even in the presence of an increasing dispersion of innovative activities within multinationals. In fact, domestic PCs can also absorb external knowledge available locally, and it will eventually gain access to foreign knowledge through their foreign subsidiaries' reverse technology transfer (Criscuolo 2004). All things considered, one can thus expect a higher potential for spillovers in the case of domestic PCs relative to both national affiliates of the same company and to foreign affiliates of multinationals having their headquarters in another country. To simplify, our empirical analysis carried out below in this section will focus on the comparison between PCs of domestic multinationals and FAs in Italy.

How intense and effective will technology transfer be vis à vis local counterparts? This will largely depend on how the potential for spillovers we have just highlighted combines with competition effects of domestic multinationals. Conflicting forces are at play here. On one hand, domestic MNFs are usually considered by indigenous firms, and more generally by the local public opinion, as 'less dangerous' than foreign firms. By contrast, in many instances foreign multinationals are perceived as 'invaders' by other domestic firms and this could make cooperation and knowledge transfer more difficult. The perception that foreign firms are more 'footloose' than domestic ones, or in other words, that they can move their establishments abroad when it becomes less convenient to produce in a given host country, may nourish the fear that it is too risky to rely on these firms for long term plans. This sort of mistrust will generally decrease the likelihood that foreign and local parties adopt a cooperative behaviour, and might make competition fiercer in the market. To the extent that foreign firms have more market power relative to local firms, they will be more likely to win, to displace indigenous competitors and to force them below the efficient output level. In general this will reduce the actual externalities from foreign firms as compared to spillovers created by domestic multinationals.

On the other hand, domestic and foreign multinationals will have different competitive effects according to the local counterparts they deal with. Domestic multinationals fiercely compete in the international market with exporters originating from the same country. Think of two Italian shoemakers both selling in the US market, but one delocalises some stages of production abroad, and the other controls only national plants: the former is a multinational firm and the latter is an exporter. In the US market their products will be both perceived as made in Italy and the two firms will have to compete very hard to differentiate and gain international market shares, one at the expense of the other Italian competitor. In the presence of such tough competition we can expect that the two firms will place a considerable effort in preventing information leakages which could favour the competitor. FAs are less likely to consider local exporters as direct competitors outside the host country. Provided that they are both active in the same foreign markets, their product will be perceived as more different (and eventually trade barriers might have different intensity) if their country of origin is not the same.

In columns (2)–(4) of Table 6.2 we report the results from the estimation of a further modification of our basic equation where we split the externality from domestic firms in one component which captures externalities from domestic multinationals (M) and one which controls for any effect stemming from 'Other' non-PCs firms (O).

$$\log(A_{it}) = \delta_1 \log F_{jt} + \delta_2 \log M_{jt} + \phi \log O_{jt} + \eta_i + \varepsilon_{it} \qquad (20)$$

where

$$M_{jt} = \sum_{i \in j} PC_i * K_{ijt}$$

and

$$O_{jt} = \sum_{i \in j} (1 - PC_i) * (1 - FOR_i) * K_{ijt}.$$

Results in column (2) suggest that neither foreign nor domestic multinationals cause any spillover to domestic firms. However, a composition effect is at play here. In fact, if we allow heterogeneity of the domestic firms, by estimating different externality effects accruing to exporters, multinationals and non-internationalised firms (the baseline category), we obtain interesting insights. In particular, results in column (3) broadly confirm the finding presented in the previous section that FAs have a positive impact on exporters, although the estimated coefficient drops slightly and falls outside the confidence intervals at conventional levels. It also appears that domestic multinationals have a positive impact on non-internationalised domestic firms and a insignificant effect on exporters and other multinationals.[96] One way to interpret these results is to stress that exporters have the adequate absorptive capacity to benefit from FA, and the competition effect is not as strong as it is with domestic multinationals. Conversely, non-internationalised Italian firms may lack the adequate absorptive capacity to learn from the foreign firm, but they could benefit from the expansion of Italian multinationals, which are more rooted in the home economy and should be associated with relatively lower barriers to learning than foreign affiliates (such as the linguistic obstacles illustrated above).

In sum, foreign and domestic multinationals appear to have complementary effects on the Italian economy. An expansion of foreign firms' activity in Italy seems to benefit home exporters, while an increase in home activities of Italian multinationals would benefit other national firms. A word of caution is required in interpreting these results. When addressing the issue of the home effects Italian multinationals one should address the role of an increase in foreign activities on productivity in non-internationalised firms at home, rather than the effect of an increase in home activities of domestic multinationals. In fact, an increase in foreign activities may well deplete the home economy by moving production and employment abroad, causing a negative externality for the rest of the economy. However, other works along these lines of analysis provide some evidence that firms investing abroad increase their productivity and output at home and do not decrease employment (Barba Navaretti and Castellani, 2004). The main explanation for these findings is that firms expanding abroad increase their capacity to respond to negative shocks in the home market and become more efficient through access to cheaper inputs, exploitation of economies of scale and learning. This, however, opens up a different set of questions related to the fact that foreign affiliates may themselves benefit from spillovers from the host country.

6.5   A BROADER PERSPECTIVE: WHO LEARNS FROM WHOM?

As illustrated in Chapter 5 and in the preceding sections in this chapter, the literature on multinational firms and spillovers has traditionally focused on foreign multinationals as a source of externality for indigenous firms. This literature is rooted in the idea that multinationals invest abroad to exploit some sort of ownership advantage developed in their home country. Accordingly, foreign firms are expected to bring to the host country some superior technological or managerial competence which might be transferred to domestic firms through imitation, labour mobility and inter-firm linkages. In this chapter we have extended this view by introducing the hypothesis that domestic multinationals may also be a source of externality for indigenous firms, which could complement spillovers from foreign multinationals. However, our focus was on the effects that multinationals have on the local economy, while limited attention was given to the possibility that foreign affiliates may also benefit from their activities in the host countries. While emphasising the former direction of causality, we are perfectly aware of the growing importance of the latter, as well as the increasing interdependencies between the two flows of knowledge (from the MNF to host country firms and vice versa) (see Chapter 1, sections 3 and 4 for more on this issue).

To place the analysis of spillovers in a broader perspective, it is worth recalling that the view of FDIs as a source of spillovers for the MNF is clearly related to the literature on asset-seeking (Dunning and Narula 1995), technology sourcing (Driffield and Love 2003), or home-base augmenting, as opposed to the traditional home-base exploiting or asset exploiting FDIs (Kuemmerle 1999).[97] The importance of asset seeking FDI has been documented in Part I of this volume. It suffices here to recall that some of these studies are based on the comparison of the R&D intensity or patenting activity of given sectors in the home and in the host locations of foreign investments. This is the case of studies on Japanese FDI which found that FDI flows in the EU (Neven and Siotis 1996) and in the US (Kogut and Chang 1991) were higher in industries where Japan exhibited a lower R&D intensity than the host countries. The literature on the internationalisation of innovative activities also contains evidence that technology sourcing may be an important motive for FDI (Cantwell 1995; Zanfei 2000; Narula and Zanfei 2005).

The key issue to focus on here is not so much whether asset seeking FDI are increasing, but whether this is likely to impoverish the host economy's knowledge base (Serapio and Dalton 1999) or, vice versa, it induces a virtuous cycle of generation of new technologies, which would benefit both the MNFs and the local economy. In fact, affiliates of MNFs investing in a foreign country to access location-specific resources may have little technology to transfer to the local economy. This would be the case of a technological laggard firm choosing to invest in a knowledge intensive context in order to benefit from localised spillovers. However, this view neglects at least two important aspects. First, it does not recognise that learning requires the accumulation of absorptive capacity. Therefore, one should expect that asset seeking affiliates need to be endowed with a substantial amount of technology, which allows them to reap the benefits of localised spillovers, but at the same time, transforms them into an important source of potential spillovers to the local economy. Second, asset seeking FDIs can be driven by the need to access complementary resources. In this case, a MNF may well be a leader in some technological fields, but lagging behind in other fields. Then, it is plausible that this MNF is willing to accept some knowledge leakages or even actively transfer technology, provided that it can gain access to complementary assets to ameliorate its own technological profile (Cantwell and Piscitello 2005).

It remains, that multinationals may well take advantage of their 'foot-looseness' and behave as free riders: for instance, they could initially place high value added activities in the host location, and subsequently 'run away' with the local technology as soon as they gain access to it (Coombs et al. forthcoming). It thus appears that the existence of knowledge spillover from local firms towards the MNF does not automatically guarantee that local firms will also have some advantages from multinational presence. This opens the way to a wide, complex and largely unexplored area for future research, concerning the conditions enhancing mutual spillovers.

6.6   CONCLUDING REMARKS

In this chapter we have investigated the role of firms' heterogeneity in favouring horizontal spillovers from MNFs on domestic owned firms' productivity. With reference to a sample of Italian firms over the period 1994–2000, we have shown that foreign multinationals do not determine any significant intra-industry spillovers in the aggregate, but domestic firms seem to benefit from the activity of specific groups of foreign multinationals. Foreign firms creating a positive externality are those carrying out R&D locally, those established since longer periods of time, and those engaged in technological cooperation with Italian counterparts. Using the same dataset, we have extended the analysis by addressing the impact of heterogeneity across and within MNFs on productivity spillovers. In particular, we compared the impact of foreign affiliates (FAs) in host countries with the effect of the activities of parent companies (PCs) of domestic owned MNFs on their home countries. Building on the analysis presented in Chapter 4, where we found that PCs of Italian MNFs exhibit a higher propensity to carry out innovative activities and to establish cooperative linkages with local firms, we have submitted that PCs may provide higher opportunities for positive externalities, as compared with FAs. However, we have argued that this higher spillover potential combines with competition effects which may partially or

fully compensate the positive externality. We have argued that these competition effects are different according to the nature of local counterparts the
MNF deals with. To test this view we have estimated intra-industry productivity spillover from PCs and from FAs on Italian exporters and on non-
internationalised firms. We have found that the domestic MNFs have a
positive impact on purely national firms, while foreign affiliates positively
affect the productivity of exporters. The differential effect can be explained
by the different type of absorptive capacity required to benefit from domestic and foreign multinationals, and by the degree of competition between
Italian firms, domestic PCs and FAs.

From these results we derive two main implications. First, policies aimed
at attracting foreign investors should take the characteristics of the incoming multinationals into careful consideration, since not every MNF is a
good source of externality. From this perspective, the analysis we carried
out in this chapter connects to the view developed in Part I of this volume,
where we submitted that a transition towards a *double network structure* is
taking place in many MNFs. In fact, consistently with this view, we found
that the more foreign affiliates become involved in knowledge-intensive
activities and get embedded in the the host economy through networks of
external relationships, the greater will be the externalities accruing to local
firms. Second, there could be important complementarities between policies stimulating outward investors and policies aimed at attracting foreign
investors. In fact the two sets of policies would target firms which appear
to have effects on different categories of national firms. Domestic owned
multinationals seem to have a larger effect on non-internationalised firms,
while foreign MNFs determine a more significant externality on productivity of exporters.

Our results may, to some extent, be affected by some institutional and
economic characteristics of the country which we have used for our empirical analysis. In particular, it is worth mentioning that there are only a few
foreign and domestic multinationals in Italy,[98] while the propensity of FAs
to carry out R&D and other innovative activities is also rather low in this
country (see Chapter 4). This entails that the direct effect of such firms on
the country's productivity and innovation is likely to be relatively limited.
By contrast, negative competition effects might be lower than in other locations in the presence of such circumscribed number of MNFs, thus increasing the likelihood of positive spillovers. This calls for an extension of the
analysis of the effects of multinational firms on home and host economies,
which maintains a focus on the role of firms' heterogeneity, but places it in
a cross-country comparison.

A further extension of the analysis would concern the conditions enhancing the presence of both foreign and domestic owned multinationals in a

given location. In fact, while our results suggest that the two types of multinationals might generate complementary spillover effects, their coexistence in the same industry and within the same country might generate several problems which have been emphasised in the literature, like market stealing and human capital drain. Therefore, it is not enough to combine the attraction and selection of foreign investments with incentives for local firms to become themselves multinationals. A variety of other policies are also needed at the national and regional levels, ranging from antitrust to the creation of high quality infrastructures, from firm and plant level training to after care measures. Examining how these policies should be designed in order to favour a fruitful coexistence of foreign and domestic multinationals is a relevant and largely unexplored area for future research.

Appendix

DATA SOURCES

Together with data and illustrative information from different sources specified in the text in Parts II and III of this book we used a dataset which combines two main sources: Elios and CIS2.

THE ELIOS DATASET

The Elios dataset (acronym for *European Linkages and International Ownership Structure*) has been assembled at the University of Urbino and integrates information from two commercially available company directories: *Amadeus* (from Bureau Van Dijk) and *Who Owns Whom* (from Dun and Bradstreet). Using a common company ID we have been able to merge the two sources for five EU countries (France, Italy, Ireland, Portugal and Spain). Elisabetta Andreani, Elvio Ciccardini and Claudio Cozza contributed a remarkable amount of research assistantship in the construction of this dataset and in matching its data with complementary information as described below.

One of the most important features of the dataset is that for each firm included in the sample we can combine economic and financial information gathered from *Amadeus* with data on ownership structure derived from *Who Owns Whom*.

Amadeus

Amadeus is a company directory maintained by Bureau Van Dijk which provides economic and financial information for over 7 million firms operating in European countries. The current edition of the Elios dataset is based on the restricted version of *Amadeus*, which contains information on the Top 250,000 companies in Europe. Amadeus provides time-invariant information such as the sector of activity, the year of incorporation, the legal form and the address for each firm, as well as time-variant economic and financial data coming from balance sheet and profit/loss accounts for the latest years (up to eight years backward). For the purpose of this work, we have utilised the following information available in *Amadeus*: turnover, cost of materials, cost of staff, value added, cash flow, number of employees, total assets, tangible and intangible fixed assets, current assets, working capital, and total liabilities. For each of these variables we have information for up to eight years (from 1993 to 2000) with some missing values.

Who Owns Whom

Who Owns Whom is a directory maintained by Dun & Bradstreet which provides information on companies' ownership structures. In particular, for each firm *Who Owns Whom* identifies whether it is controlled by some other companies. With this information we were able to identify foreign-owned firms (i.e. affiliates of foreign multinationals FAs, which are companies whose ultimate owner is based in a different country. Unfortunately, this source does not provide any information on the share of ownership so we have to rely on Dun & Bradstreet's indication of the ultimate owner, and cannot apply the usual criteria based on the share of capital owned by the controlling company.

Who Owns Whom also facilitates tracking whether each firm controls any other company. This piece of information is used to identify domestic-owned firms that control affiliates abroad, which we have defined as domestic parent companies (PCs). In our terms, a parent company (PC) is a firm controlling ownership of at least one enterprise located in a different country (i.e. the host economy). We assume this participation to allow a majority or de facto control over this enterprise located abroad, and identify the latter as one of its foreign affiliates (FAs). A PC is assumed also to contribute to the assets of firms located in the same country (i.e. the home country), and identify these as national affiliates (NAs). In this perspective, PCs may not correspond to the 'holding company' nor to 'company headquarters' if within a diversified group more than one firm controls FAs. To illustrate, within the FIAT group, an Italian automotive multinational, one can identify at least three different PCs: Fiat Auto, which controls FAs in the car industry, Iveco, which is a PC in the truck business and Magneti Marelli, which controls FAs in parts and components.

By exploiting the information on the sector of activity available for each firm in *Who Owns Whom*, we were able to classify foreign affiliates according to the type of activity carried out abroad. It is worth mentioning that *Who Owns Whom* allows for diversified activities and provides more than one sector of activity for each firm (up to seven SIC codes are reported for each firm). We exploit this piece of information to classify as production affiliates those firms which, among the various sectors of activity, report at least one SIC code in a manufacturing industry. Conversely, we define as non-production affiliates those that report SIC codes only in non-manufacturing industries. This will allow us to distinguish PC controlling only non-production plants abroad (which, in Chapter 3, we define as MNF1s) from those controlling some foreign production activities (which we define as MNF2s). Domestic-owned firms which do not control foreign affiliates can be either part of a domestic MNF (we call them national affiliates (NAs), or be independent firms (which might eventually be involved in international operations through exporting). Figure A.1 illustrates the types of firms in *Who Owns Whom*. The empirical analyses carried out in Parts II and III of this book focused on firms located in Italy (which is our country H) and operating in one manufacturing industry (i.e. our sample firms carry out some production activity). Therefore, *Who Owns Whom* allows us to identify five types of Italian manufacturing firms: foreign-owned firms (i.e. Italian affiliates of foreign multinationals, FAs), parent companies controlling only non-production activities abroad (MNF1), parent companies controlling at least one production site abroad (MNF2), other firms which are part of a domestic MNC (NA) and firms which are not part of any multinational group. Merging *Who Owns Whom* with *Amadeus*, the Elios dataset allows us to track the economic performance of these five types of firms over the 1993–2000 period. In particular, we are able to compute measures of productivity (using the information on turnover, number of employees, tangible fixed assets and cost of materials), size (in terms of number of employees and turnover) and gross wages (obtained as cost of staff per employee).

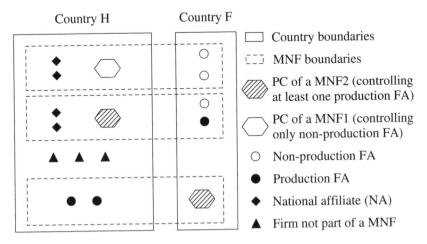

Figure A.1 Types of firms in Who Owns Whom

THE COMMUNITY INNOVATION SURVEY (CIS)

The *Community Innovation Survey* (CIS) is a key statistical instrument that
allows the monitoring of Europe's progress in the area of innovation by
creating a better understanding of the innovation process and analysing the
effects of innovation on the economy (in terms of, for example, competitiveness, employment, economic growth, trade patterns, etc.). It is based on
a common questionnaire administered to a large sample of firms in each
country by Eurostat through the statistical offices or competent research
institutes in the Member States. The CIS was carried out for the first time
in 1992, while CIS2 took place in 1996 and CIS3 in 2001. Thanks to a
confidentiality agreement with Italy's National Bureau of Statistics
(ISTAT), we had access to the Italian sample of CIS2, which consists of
about 5,256 firms and provides information on their innovative activity in
the 1994–96 period. The survey is organized into three sections. Section 1
provides general information on the firm, such as the total sales, the share
of export on total turnover, an indication of whether the firm is part of an
industrial group and, in this case, whether the headquarter is located
abroad. We used this latter information in order to double check details on
the ultimate parent company provided by *Who Owns Whom* and identify
FAs in Italy. Furthermore, firms reporting positive exports were identified
as exporters. This allowed us to introduce a further type of firm in our
sample, which we used in the empirical analysis of Chapter 3. In particular, among firms that do not belong to an MNF (denoted by a black trian-
gle in Figure A.1), we singled out those firms involved in exporting activity.
Section 2 of the CIS2 focuses on the characteristics of the innovative activity. Each of the sample firms is asked whether it has introduced new or
improved products and/or process over the 1994–96 period, what share in
its turnover was due to new products and processes, whether it has applied
for a patent and has carried out R&D. This latter piece of information has
been expanded by asking the amount of innovative expenditures in
different activities. In particular, the distinction between intra-muros R&D
and extra-muros R&D is made, and expenditures for the acquisition of
machinery and patents, as well as for marketing activities related to innovative products are considered. Finally, section 3 concentrates on the objectives, sources and employment effects of innovation, as well as the extent
to which the firm engages in cooperative innovation with other firms
belonging to the same group, competitors, clients, suppliers, universities
and other research institutions, located both in Italy and abroad.

THE CIS-ELIOS DATASET

Exploiting the fact that in the Italian samples of the CIS2 and the Elios dataset each firm can be identified by the VAT code, we could easily merge the two sources of information. This gives us a sample of 1,117 firms for which we gather information on multinationality and economic performance from Elios, while from the CIS2 we have an indicator of the export status, as well as a number of characteristics and sources of innovative activities. As shown in Table A.1, the sectoral distribution of the CIS-Elios sample is not significantly different from the initial distribution in the CIS2 (a Chi-square test does not reject the hypothesis on the equality of the two distributions) which is representative of the population of manufacturing firms in Italy. Nevertheless, it is worth mentioning that the CIS-Elios sample tends to over-represent large firms, reflected in the relatively larger share of firms in chemical and electrical machinery industries (where the average firm size is larger) and lower share of firms in textiles and apparel, leather and footwear, and wood industries (where firms are, on average, smaller).

The actual number of firms used in the empirical applications of Chapters 3, 4, 5 and 6 is lower than 1,117, due to occasional missing values in some economic and financial data. This is particularly the case of Chapters 5 and 6, where we require that our panel is balanced, in order to avoid that the dynamics of the measures of sectoral activities of foreign and domestic multinationals calculated within the sample, depend on the different number of firms used in different years. Finally, one needs to bear in mind that the size of the actual samples used in the various chapters differs from one analysis to another. In particular, for reasons that are specified in the text, in Chapters 3, 5 and 6 we do not consider FAs, while in Chapter 4 we exclude firms which are part of multinationals controlling only non-production plants abroad.

Table A.1   *Sectoral distribution of Italian firms in the CIS2 and in CIS-Elios*

Sector	No. of firms in the CIS2	%	No. of firms in the CIS-Elios dataset	%
Food products and beverages	359	6.8	62	5.6
Tobacco products	11	0.2	3	0.3
Textiles	431	8.2	77	6.9
Wearing apparel; dressing and dyeing of fur	277	5.3	37	3.3
Tanning and dressing of leather; footwear	230	4.4	18	1.6

Table A.1 (continued)

Sector	No. of firms in the CIS2	%	No. of firms in the CIS-Elios dataset	%
Wood and products of wood and cork, except furniture	169	3.2	6	0.5
Pulp, paper and paper products	133	2.5	35	3.1
Publishing, printing and reproduction of recorded media	173	3.3	42	3.8
Coke, refined petroleum products and nuclear fuel	38	0.7	15	1.3
Chemicals and chemical products	238	4.5	117	10.5
Rubber and plastic products	260	4.9	64	5.7
Other non-metallic mineral products	291	5.5	59	5.3
Basic metals	180	3.4	65	5.8
Fabricated metal products, except machinery and equipment	604	11.5	74	6.6
Machinery and equipment n.e.c.	658	12.5	179	16.0
Office machinery and computers	24	0.5	9	0.8
Electrical machinery and equipment n.e.c.	239	4.5	70	6.3
Radio, television and communication equipment and apparatus	88	1.7	26	2.3
Medical, precision and optical instruments, watches and clocks	122	2.3	34	3.0
Motor vehicles, trailers and semi-trailers	121	2.3	40	3.6
Other transport equipment	80	1.5	21	1.9
Furniture; manufacturing n.e.c.	530	10.1	64	5.7
Total	5.256	100.0	1.117	100.0

Endnotes

1. The share of high-tech products (including electrical and electronic equipment, aerospace products, precision instruments, fine chemicals and pharmaceuticals) in world exports rose from 8 per cent in 1976 to 23 per cent in 2000 (UNCTAD 2002, pp. 146–7). The average annual growth rate of patents obtained by national inventors in foreign countries rose from 0.9 per cent in 1970–1980 to 13.3 per cent in 1984–1994 (Archibugi and Iammarino 2002). Foreign-owned inventions, accounted for about 14.7 per cent of patents applied for in OECD countries over the 1999–2001 period (OECD 2005). The number of international technology collaborations recorded by the Merit-CATI database has almost doubled from 339 to 602 in the 1991–2001 period, with a growing dominance of non-equity partnerships, including supply agreements and strategic technical alliances, whose share has grown from 78 per cent to 91 per cent of total cooperative ventures (UNCTAD 2005; Hagedoorn 2002). MNFs steadily increased their R&D spending abroad from 15 per cent of their total R&D budget in 1995 to 22 per cent in 2001 (Roberts, 2001). More details and discussion on the evidence on the international dispersion of innovative activities and on international technology partnering in Chapter 2.
2. We are grateful to John Cantwell for calling our attention to this point.
3. The rest of this section draws heavily on Narula and Zanfei (2005).
4. Although the HBE-HBA terminology has become widely used in the literature, it is worth observing that this classification scheme is less accurate, and holds to a very traditional view of the MNF as centred in a dominant home base. In fact, by emphasising the role of home bases, the HBA-HBE jargon cannot be easily made consistent with the possibility that firms are evolving towards network structures. As internationalisation proceeds, the importance of a single home is reduced, and the number of countries wherein the firm ends up being based increases. We take the view that being accurate is more important than being fashionable, and avoid using the HBE-HBA terminology except where necessary to give precise account of existing literature.
5. Asset seeking (or asset augmenting) motives and technology sourcing have been partially incorporated in formal models of the FDI decision. In particular, Fosfuri and Motta (1999) and Siotis (1999) show that a technological laggard may choose to enter a foreign market by FDI because there are positive spillover effects associated with locational proximity to a technological leader in the foreign country. Where the beneficial knowledge spillover effect is sufficiently strong, Fosfuri and Motta show that it may even pay the laggard firm to run its foreign subsidiary at a loss to incorporate the benefits of advanced technology in all the markets in which it operates. In a dynamic framework, it has been shown that the presence of localised spillovers might not only affect the FDI decision, but also the amount of R&D carried out by multinational firms (Petit, Sanna-Randaccio and Sestini, 2005).
6. Denoting as Pij the number of patents granted in technological field j to firm (or country) i, the RTA index is calculated as follows: $RTAij = (Pij/\Sigma i\, Pij)/(\Sigma j\, Pij/\Sigma ij\, Pij)$. An $RTA > 1$ signals a relative advantage of the country (firm).
7. These results are by and large confirmed by an extensive interview-based survey carried out by Pearce (1999).
8. Le Bas and Sierra (2002) also consider a case wherein both the host location and the foreign investors reveal no technological advantage at all, and classify this as pure market seeking. They find that this case is the least frequent one (10 per cent of all recorded cases). This is not surprising, since their sample is clearly biased in favour of high technology firms.

9. Ietto-Gillies (2002) stresses that also other advantages may derive from multinational-isation, including a higher bargaining power vis a vis labour force and institutions at home and in other countries where the firm is active. However, we are interested here in host economies as key sources of complementary knowledge.

10. This is consistent with a view of institutions as interacting with both economic and technical change (Freeman and Perez 1988, North 1990). There is also some correspondence here between our line of argument and the one developed by other authors who emphasise that historically determined networks of personal and social relationships among economic agents influence the organisation of their transactions. Some scholars name these networks of personal and social relationships with the term *embeddedness*. Granovetter (1985, p. 503) suggests that, where such networks are stable and do not generate occasions for malfeasance and conflict, we should expect pressures towards vertical integration to be absent. This insight was developed and applied to the study of international business especially by scholars of the 'Swedish school' (Forsgren and Johanson, 1992; Andersson and Forsgren, 1996). Similarly, multinational growth is being analysed as an important case of internationalisation whose patterns are largely influenced by local institutional and social factors (Vaccà, 1996).

11. Examples of how the availability of cheap computational power may extend the application and the development of theoretical knowledge (and vice versa) can be drawn from the fields of biotechnology, new materials, airplane production and testing (Arora and Gambardella, 1994 pp. 525–527). For instance, a recently developed theorem using the principle of energy minimisation reduced the number of alternative molecular structures of a given protein chain in a way that information is processable by supercomputers. This made it possible to speed up the process of exploration of given molecular structures and of their interactions with other molecules.

12. Contextual knowledge adds economic value to generic, codified knowledge, and also fertilises it. But the reverse also holds. General and abstract knowledge increases the theoretical understanding of phenomena, and helps identify the proper way to solve specific application problems (David et al., 1992). By contrast, firms with a high contextual knowledge, but with no contact with general and abstract knowledge, will be easily locked into narrow learning paths, and will reduce their ability to exploit technological and market opportunities. Furthermore, being locked in circumscribed technological and market niches, firms will have limited outside options and will enjoy a low bargaining power. Altogether, these likely effects on learning and on bargaining power will diminish firms' ability to generate further knowledge in time.

13. We are not suggesting that all knowledge can (cost effectively) be generalised and codified. The argument is that the described changes are making it possible to *expand* the area of knowledge that can be, and actually is, generalised and codified.

14. The idea that internal networking interacts with external network development is consistent with part of the international business literature which has recognised that the MNF is not only an intra-organisational web of subsidiaries, but that each affiliate deals with its own local business units, which will eventually affect the firm's behaviour and performances (Nohria and Ghoshal, 1997, Andersson and Forsgren, 2000, Andersson et al., 2005).

15. A relationship is characterised by mutual trust when each of the parties involved in it chooses to refrain from opportunism (hence they are *trustworthy*), and believes that the others will do the same (hence they are *trusting*). See Lyons and Mehta (1997), Burchell and Wilkinson (1997) for extensive reviews of the literature on this concept.

16. By increasing the feasibility of retaliation in case of contractual breach, multinational experience increases the *trustworthiness* of foreign partners, i.e. their availability to refrain from defection given the credible threat of being sanctioned thereafter. This would be consistent with the notion of *calculative trust* (Dasgupta, 1988; Kreps, 1990; Williamson, 1993). However, multinational experience does not ensure that calculative trust is also *mutual*. In fact the described impact is unidirectional, and the local counterparts cannot be expected to become more *trusting* towards the MNF whenever this becomes more experienced.

17. One may incidentally observe that the lack of attention for these issues is admittedly a limit of approaches based on transaction cost economics. According to Williamson himself, transaction cost literature 'has been less responsive in dynamic, evolutionary respects' (Williamson, 1993 p. 337). See also Williamson (1988) for earlier considerations on the weaknesses of transaction cost approaches in dealing with these aspects of economic analysis.

18. Evidence on the complementarity between intra-firm networks and inter-firm collaborative ventures can be drawn from various studies on high technology industries. See Arora and Gambardella (1990) and Yamin and Otto (2004) for biotechnology, Malerba and Torrisi (1992) and Torrisi (1998) for software, Steinmueller (1992) and Ernst (2005) for semiconductor industry.

19. A weak manufacturing industry coupled with underdeveloped infrastructures and institutional setting in the host country, which is often the case of LDCs, may be detrimental even in the presence of innovative multinationals originating from highly developed economic and innovation systems: 'There will be little or no impact on developing countries that lack the basic production and adaptive capabilities needed for new product development' UNCTAD (2005 p. 180).

20. The reader should be advised that the reliability of international comparisons of R&D data has been questioned. As Warrant (1991, p. 42) has noted, quantitative measurement of R&D investments abroad is a problem because they represent relatively new modes of internationalisation, which are not often reported in official statistics on foreign direct investments. A number of studies have instead concentrated on patent data, examining the location of inventions registered by Patent Offices, and by USPTO in particular. As Archibugi and Michie (1995, p. 131) have noted, patents are a particularly appropriate measure to test the location of inventive activities, because they are attributed to the country of residence of the inventor rather than to that of the owner. More detailed data on innovative activities of multinationals can be derived from Eurostat's Community Innovation Surveys. See parts II and III of this volume for illustrative use of these data.

21. The high and rising share of foreign R&D in most developing countries (and in some new EU member countries) reflects not only the greater penetration by MNFs, but also the low level of domestic R&D efforts.

22. In order to extend their analysis to a sample of 66 US and European MNFs, Ghoshal and Bartlett (1989, p. 375) have asked managers at the headquarters to evaluate from 1 to 5 the subsidiaries' influence on decisions referring to 6 different types of decisions in such areas as innovation, organisation and human resource management.

23. See Castellani and Zanfei (2004) for a more detailed analysis of the characteristics of internal networks and of their impact on linkage creation. In this and in the following section we shall draw on this analysis and on Castellani and Zanfei (2001) for a synthetic overview on this issue.

24. As in Chapter 1, we shall use the terms internal network and multinational experience interchangeably. Although the two notions stem from different, often unrelated, streams of literature, there are clear affinities between the underlying concepts.

25. This juxtaposition recalls the one introduced by Arora and Gambardella (1994) in a different context. In their analysis of the evolution of pharmaceutical industry, the authors have suggested to distinguish what they define as 'ability to utilise' and 'ability to judge', each deriving from different knowledge assets of the firm and influencing behavioural patterns.

26. Thirty-two companies were European, 41 from North America (including 1 Canadian) and 21 were Japanese. Based on the Fortune list, firms were reclassified according to their core business using Dun & Bradstreet's *Who Owns Whom* data on the distribution of their affiliates and sales by SIC code. Forty of these companies had their core business in the chemical sector (of which 9 in industrial chemicals, 18 in petrochemicals, 9 in pharmaceuticals and 4 in other chemical activities) and 54 in the electronics sector (9 in telecommunications, 18 in computers, 4 in semiconductors, 9 in consumer electronics and 14 in other electronics sectors).

27. The database was initiated at Iefe-Università Bocconi, Milan, and has been reorganised and updated with the collaboration of a number of researchers at Cesit-Custom, Università di Urbino, and at LIUC Castellanza. The authors wish to mention Daniele D'Alba, Marco Giarratana, Sandro Sergiacomo and Claudia Siligeni for their useful research assistantship in the set up of, and elaboration on, this database. Claudia Beretta and Andrea Ferri helped in the construction of complementary datasets.

28. A total of 55 countries were considered, covering 23 industrialised countries and the 32 LDCs that scored highest in terms of per capita GDP in 1994, and for which we have data on control variables.

29. Several studies have utilised somewhat similar measures. Gomes-Casseres (1989) proposed an index of 'familiarity with host country' based on how often his sample's MNFs entered one country before another in a given period. Hennart and Larimo (1998) used the number of years of presence of affiliates in the host country as a regressor to explain ownership structure of foreign direct investments. Their effort was eased by the fact that they considered only one destination country, for which plenty of statistics are available (the US). Padmanabhan and Cho (1999) utilised the number of subsidiaries weighted by their age, thus assessing both the contribution of frequency and length of foreign operations. We prefer to keep the two effects distinct, as they capture two different aspects of multinational experience.

30. This index of multinationality was used by several authors, among which Kogut and Singh (1988) and Caves and Mehra (1986).

31. This is very similar to the indicator proposed by Ietto-Gillies (1998) and reproduced by UNCTAD (1998).

32. One should not conclude that innovation is associated only with geo-dispersed internal networking and/or to technical alliances. Knowledge of local contexts is a key asset in the application and adaptation of technology, while commercialisation and marketing agreements are fundamental mechanisms in its economic exploitation. It is well known that learning can occur through application and usage, especially when dealing with technology characterised by a high systemic complexity (Rosenberg 1982). What is being suggested here is that geo-dispersed networking produces a differential ability to enter alliances which have a prevailing technical content.

33. See Ietto-Gillies 2005, Chapter 6 for more details and for a recent discussion of Vernon's analysis of firms' strategies in international oligopolistic markets.

34. Buckley (1983, p. 45) acknowledges that 'it is a valid criticism of the internalisation rubric that market imperfections are taken as exogenous in the (internalising) firm'. A discussion of the theoretical consequences of the exogeneity of market imperfections can be found in Ietto-Gillies (2005).

35. This is for instance the case of Vernon (1966): the choice of exporting vs. investing abroad reflects demand, technological and market structure characteristics that are shared by all firms in a given country and sector. Vernon (1979) himself acknowledged the limits of his interpretive framework. In fact, the competitive environment has been changing since the early 1960s, when the original model was conceived: new high growth economies have emerged, the number and heterogeneity of actors involved in internationalisation processes have significantly augmented not only across countries and sectors, but also within industries.

36. Among many others, Bernard and Jensen (1999) for US firms, Castellani (2002a) for Italy and Clerides et al. (1998) for Columbia, Mexico and Morocco. Tybout (2003) provides an extensive review of such evidence.

37. A partial exception is the paper by Yeaple (2005). A general equilibrium model is presented in which the interaction between the characteristics of competing technologies, international trade costs, and the availability of workers of heterogeneous skills gives rise to firm heterogeneity. However, the model still waits for an extension to international investment strategies. Moreover, it assumes that heterogeneity is the *ex post* result of the choice of technology and skills made by firms which are homogeneous ex ante. Yeaple (2005, p. 18) admits that: 'While some of the stylised facts concerning within industry heterogeneity can be captured in a framework that considers heterogeneous firms and

representative workers, or representative firms and heterogeneous workers, many of the productivity dynamics observed in the data would be better explained by a model that allows for both dimensions of heterogeneity.'

38. We are grateful to John Cantwell for bringing this point to our attention.

39. Dunning (1980) enumerates at least 20 possible ownership advantages, at least 11 internalisation advantages, and at least 16 location specific advantages. Each of these groups of factors can be expanded if subcategories are considered.

40. This idea has been incorporated also in formal models wherein the existence of localised spillovers in foreign countries motivate investment abroad even by firms which do not exhibit any strong ex-ante advantage (Fosfuri and Motta, 1999; Petit et al. 2004).

41. Many thanks to Grazia Ietto-Gillies for calling our attention to this strand of literature.

42. Firms may grow large for a variety of reasons that have nothing to do with technical efficiency. As well, small firms in many sectors are more innovative than large ones. See Cohen and Levin (1989) for a review of the extensive and controversial literature on firm size and innovation.

43. A similar result is obtained by Delgado Gomez et al. (2004), who use Tobin's q as a measure of the level of intangible resources of Spanish firms in 1991–1997. They find that firms with a higher endowment of intangible resources increase their presence in their current markets, and that those with a multinational status also expand to new markets.

44. See Ietto-Gillies 2005 chapter 11 for a more extensive review of empirical studies carried out by scholars from the Scandinavian school.

45. We thank Giulio Perani from the Italian National Bureau of Statistics for allowing us access to the data.

46. Approximately one-third of all foreign subsidiaries controlled by the Italian multinationals in the CIS-ELIOS dataset are in the manufacturing industry. Among the affiliates carrying out non-production activities, 70 per cent are in the wholesale and retail trade industries, while 11 per cent are classified as holding companies. Only a very small number of these affiliates carries out engineering and R&D related activities (2.2 per cent) or business services (2.2 per cent). The proportion of affiliates carrying out commercial activities is even higher (82 per cent) when we concentrate on the category of multinationals carrying out only non-production activities abroad (MNF1).

47. We used three measures of productivity. First, we calculated labour productivity as value added per worker. Second, we obtained an 'approximate' TFP, calculated as value added per worker net of the contribution of capital (per worker), with an approximated elasticity of 0.3 (following Head and Ries (2003)). Third, we estimated TFP as the residual from a gross output production function, controlling for capital labour and materials, using a AR(1) random effect model, with sector-specific factor elasticities.

48. Here we rely on visual comparison of cumulative distributions, without a formal test of stochastic dominance, as in Girma et al. (2004) and Girma et al. (2003). Further on in the text we shall consider differences in means, controlling for various firms' exogenous characteristics in a regression framework.

49. Throughout this chapter we shall talk about different types of firms operating in a given country. A key distinction will be between domestic and foreign owned firms, according to whether they are part of a group whose parent company is located in the country (domestic) or outside (foreign). Foreign owned firms are, by definition, part of a multinational group (which we denote as MNF), while domestic-owned ones may or may not be part of an MNF. The former may either be parent companies or national affiliates (see section 4.3 for a more detailed discussion), while the latter are, by definition, uni-national firms.

50. Some contributions to the innovation systems literature adopts a sub- or supra-national level of analysis (Cooke 1992); as well as on the level of sectors (Breschi and Malerba 1997; Malerba 2005) or techno-economic aggregates (Carlsson and Stankievicz 1991; Carlsson 2003).

51. This is for instance the case of Japan's R&D programmes: while MITI usually allows foreign companies to join, 'the programmes continue to be set with national objectives in mind' (Fransman 1999).

52. This can be considered an extension of the 'focusing device' approach which was first introduced by Rosenberg (1976) in a different context to explain the rate and direction of technical innovation. The role of institutional bottlenecks in shaping technical change was implicitly acknowledged by Rosenberg himself (1976, pp. 117–121), who noted that the threat of worker unrest has acted as a powerful inducement to labour saving innovations in the 19th century. Today this mechanism can play a different role across countries according to such institutional characteristics as the unionisation of work force. More explicitly, Dosi (1982 pp. 153–155) suggests that institutional and social factors act as 'focusing devices' providing both negative and positive criteria in the selection of new technological paradigms. An extension of this approach to the globalisation of innovation was proposed by Zanfei (1993) with reference to international technological collaborations as a response to institutional change.

53. Molero (2002) provides evidence on different innovative strategies and performances of foreign affiliates active in Ireland and in Germany, with the latter being more innovative and more prone to resort to local technology. The author interprets this as evidence of the fact that Germany, being characterised by a higher level national system of innovation, 'induces a more important presence of subsidiaries with a "mandate" to augment their technological bases' (p. 310).

54. As Kogut (1989, p. 388) notes, 'what is distinctive in the international context . . . is the variance in country environments and the ability to profit through the system-wide management of this variance'.

55. Belderbos (2001) finds that medium-sized Japanese firms exhibit a higher propensity (in relative terms) to internationalise R&D than small or large-sized firms. A possible explanation is that medium sized firms are generally more capable than smaller firms of negotiating the risks of foreign R&D activities, while they take advantages of being able to follow larger customers in their internationalization processes (Florida 1997). A non-linear relationship can also be observed between firm size and external linkage creation. On one hand, SMEs have greater needs to rely on non-external resources (Zanfei 1994), on the other hand they suffer greater limitations in terms of resources and organisational capabilities needed to set up alliances (Narula 2003). However, small firms appear to be more prone to setting up cooperative agreements than is the case with new subsidiary creation, due to the lower sunk costs and higher flexibility associated to external network strategies (Powell and Grodal 2005).

56. In this perspective, PCs may not correspond to the 'holding company' nor to 'company headquarters' if within a diversified group more than one firm controls FAs. To illustrate, within the FIAT group, an Italian automotive multinational, one can identify various PCs: Fiat Auto, which controls FAs in the car industry, Iveco, which would be a PC in the truck business, Magneti Marelli, which controls FAs in parts and components, and so on. See the Appendix for more details.

57. These companies, positioned upstream in the control chain, do directly participate in foreign enterprises, they also will be considered as parent companies.

58. Le Bas and Sierra (2002) studied investment strategies of the 345 MNFs with the greatest patenting activity in Europe. They identify as technology seeking those investments occurring in countries with revealed technology advantages (RTAs) that are higher than the RTAs at home in a given technology; while asset augmenting strategies occur when both the home country and the host country have RTAs in that technology. The authors find that both investment categories have increased their frequency from 1988–1990 to 1994–1996.

59. See Birkinshaw et al. (1998) for a more general analysis of differences in business and competence mandates given to and obtained by foreign subsidiaries of multinational enterprises.

60. Le Bas and Sierra (2002) found that up to 40 per cent of FDIs in their sample take the form of asset exploiting and/or market seeking activities. These activities are not likely to be located in R&D intensive areas nor do they contribute to or take advantage of technological agglomeration economies.

61. Fors (1997), using evidence from a sample of 121 Swedish MNFs shows that knowledge transmission from affiliates to parent companies is not as effective and intense as the other way around. By contrast, using data from citations made on over half a million patents originating from 4,400 MNFs and domestic organizations in the US, Japan, Germany, France, UK, and Canada, Singh (2004) finds, *inter alia*, that MNFs are as good at transferring knowledge from their home base to the subsidiaries as from subsidiaries to the home base.

62. We thank Giulio Perani from the Italian National Statistical Office for allowing us access to these data.

63. In this chapter we do not consider the distinction, introduced in Chapter 3, between multinational firms controlling production activities abroad and those controlling only non-production affiliates. The latter group of firms has been excluded from the sample used in the following analysis. This choice is motivated by the fact that FAs are included in our sample only if they operate in the manufacturing industry. Therefore, the analogue to FAs are firms belonging to domestic multinational groups which control some production activities abroad.

64. As we illustrated in Chapter 4, a large fraction of Italian multinationals control only non-manufacturing subsidiaries abroad.

65. TFP has been obtained as the residual of a sector-specific Cobb-Douglas production function, with input elasticities estimated using the Levinsohon and Petrin (2003) semiparametric methodology. See Chapter 5 for a discussion of the methodological issues related to the estimate of TFP in the study of spillovers from multinationals.

66. Considering the taxonomy proposed by Pavitt (1984), one notices a relatively low weight of supplier dominated firms and specialised suppliers, in contrast with the key role of these activities in Italy's manufacturing industry. This probably reflects the fact that firms that control only non-manufacturing affiliates abroad are excluded from our sample. In fact, in these sectors, Italian firms disproportionately use this form of internationalisation.

67. For the sake of brevity, the estimates referred to in parentheses are not reported here, but are available from the authors upon request. The reader might also refer to Castellani and Zanfei (2005), where earlier evidence along these lines has been presented.

68. Criscuolo and Martin (2003) find that US owned firms active in the UK maintain a productivity advantage with respect to both domestic owned (uninational and multinational) companies, as well as relative to other foreign owned firms. Hagedoorn (2002) observes a relatively high involvement of US multinationals in international technological alliances in high-tech industries monitored by the Merit-Cati database. The propensity to pay higher salaries of US multinational companies in Europe has been highlighted *inter alia* by Basile, Castellani and Zanfei (2003).

69. Whether increasing competition ameliorates the effects of multinationals on the host economy is a controversial issue, as will be discussed in Chapters 5 and 6.

70. Suppliers can specialise in industry-specific intermediate inputs and services and workers can invest in the acquisition of specific skills, allowing the production of a larger variety of inputs at a lower price.

71. In these cases, one may think that the price of such goods falls from infinity (when the market does not exist) to a positive value.

72. One of the reasons is that multinational production tends to rise when firms face high firm-specific fixed cost, such as R&D and advertising (Barba Navaretti and Venables, 2004), which can act as structural barriers to entry. Furthermore, in these and other industries, large firms, such as multinationals, can raise strategic barriers.

73. Multinational firms can, in turn introduce further oligopolistic distortions (Hymer, 1960) and, in the medium-term, the exit of inefficient domestic firms can lead to an even higher concentration and inefficiency than before the entry of foreign multinationals. However, to the extent that other foreign or domestic multinationals can still enter the market, monopolistic power should be kept at a minimum.

74. This can be particularly relevant if we think of multinationals entering many utilities industries, such as telecom and energy: cheaper and more effective communication or

power supply can significantly raise the overall efficiency of local firms in downstream industries.

75. As illustrated by Altomonte and Resmini (2002), to the extent that multinationals enter both upstream and downstream industries, the outcome can be even more blurred, as there could be a situation where the benefits of pecuniary externalities accrue mainly to other MNFs rather than to local firms.

76. We thank Alberto Pozzolo and Carlo Altomonte for bringing this issue to our attention.

77. In other words, the marginal product of workers might be higher than its compensation.

78. While case studies and qualitative works provide important insights on how such mechanisms work, evidence from quantitative analyses of such mechanisms is still lacking. To the best of our knowledge, only Gorg and Strobl (2005a) have recently carried out an econometric study on the effect of workers' mobility on firms' productivity. In a sample of more than 200 Ghanaian firms, they find that those run by a manager with a previous experience in multinational firms have higher productivity growth than other domestic firms.

79. This measure is the product of the inputs sourced locally as a share of total external inputs used and the external inputs as a share of total employment.

80. Some recent research has investigated the effects of foreign multinationals on firms' entry and exit into the domestic market (Kosova 2004; Gorg and Strobl 2002 and 2005b; De Backer and Sleuwaegen 2003b; Altomonte and Resmini 2002), as well as domestic firms' exporting (among others, Aitken et al. 1996; Kneller and Pisu 2005) or patenting activities (Singh; 2004; Branstetter 2005), but still the vast majority of works carried out over the past decade has been looking at the effect of foreign presence on productivity of domestic firms.

81. The reader can refer to some recent reviews, such as Van Biesebroeck (2003) or Griliches and Mairesse (1995).

82. The reader is invited to refer to Olley and Pakes (1996), Levinsohon and Petrin (2003) or Smarzynska Javorcick (2004) for details on the estimation technique.

83. Lower case denote natural logarithm.

84. As we noted above, such a simple specification is used for illustrative purposes and is required to keep tractable the analytical derivation of the bias below (Greene, 1997 p. 402).

85. We thank Jack Lucchetti for an illuminating discussion on this point.

86. A balanced panel is required to ensure that variations in K_{jt}, which is obtained as the sum of capital in all firms in a given sector at time t, is determined by actual fluctuation in fixed assets, rather than by missing values.

87. To avoid log of zeros in sectors where we had no foreign firms in the sample, we took the log $(FP*100 + 1)$.

88. Consistent with the model, the overall externality is higher in column 2 since it is the sum of δ and θ.

89. Negative effects for domestic firms could arise also when multinationals tap into local knowledge and technology (imitation and demonstration channel), hire skilled workers previously employed in local firms (labour market channel), substitute local sourcing with imports (linkages channel) but empirical evidence seems to point to competition as the main source of negative externality.

90. A step in this direction has been taken by Girma and Gorg (2004), who disentangle the effect of foreign multinational firms on productivity growth of UK firms in a scale and a technological component.

91. These studies have a number of interesting features. In particular, by looking at firm entry end survival they address the role of competition and pecuniary externalities more directly, and go in the direction of disentangling the various channels through which external effects occur. Furthermore, their measure of external effect is not subject to the bias in productivity measurement which we have discussed above.

92. As Findlay (1978 pp. 2–3) notes: 'Stone age communities suddenly confronted with modern industrial civilisation can only disintegrate or produce irrational responses . . . Where the difference is less than some critical minimum, admittedly difficult to define

operationally, the hypothesis does seem attractive and worth consideration.' Findlay also observes that the educational level of the domestic labour force, which is a good proxy for what is currently named country's 'absorptive capacity', might also affect, *inter alia*, the rate at which the backward region improves its technological efficiency (Findlay 1978, pp. 5–6).

93. See Part I of this book and Chapter 4 for an extensive review of these empirical works.
94. Equation (15) is a slight modification of the specification proposed in Chapter 5. In fact, in the previous chapter we derived the specification of external effects from a model which included both the overall sectoral capital (K) and the one due to foreign owned firms (F). This could cause some multicollinearity problems between foreign (F_{jt}) and total activity (K_{jt}) (which includes F_{jt}), so here we substitute K, with a specific externality from domestic activities, captured by $D_{jt} = \Sigma_{i \in j} (1 - FOR_i)^* K_{ijt}$.
95. In Chapter 4 we also argued that NAs may benefit from lower technology transfer from PCs, relatively to FAs, although the former might still have easier and more direct access to knowledge bases at home.
96. In fact, the spillover on exporters and domestic multinationals is the sum of the parameter on the baseline category (domestic uninational firms) and the coefficient of appropriate interaction term. In both cases we cannot reject the hypothesis that the sum is different from zero.
97. As argued in Chapter 1, section 3, it is preferable to use the terms 'asset exploiting' and 'asset augmenting/asset seeking' rather than 'Home Base Exploiting' and 'Home base Augmenting'. In fact, the latter terminology holds to a very traditional view of the MNF as centred in a dominant home-base. This cannot be easily made consistent with the possibility that firms are evolving towards network structures, hence reducing the importance of a single home and, by the same token, expanding the number of countries wherein the firm ends up being based. See also Narula and Zanfei (2005) for some discussion on the use of these concepts in the literature.
98. See OECD (2005) and UNCTAD (2005) for recent data on inward FDIs and the activities of multinational firms across countries. In Table 5.3 (Chapter 5) we provide a comparison of the incidence of the activities of incoming multinationals in Italy as compared with France and Spain, using a sample of firms drawn from the Elios dataset.

References

Aftalion, F. (1989), *History of the International Chemical Industry*, Philadelphia, PA: University of Pennsylvania Press.

Aitken, B., G. Hanson and A. Harrison (1997), 'Spillovers, foreign investment and export behavior', *Journal of International Economics*, **43**, 103–32.

Aitken, B., Harrison A. (1999), 'Do domestic firms benefit from direct foreign investment? Evidence from Venezuela', *American Economic Review*, **89**(3), 605–18.

Alfaro, L. and A. Rodriguez-Clare (2004), 'Multinationals and linkages: an empirical investigation', *Economia* (Spring).

Almeida, P. (1996), 'Knowledge sourcing by foreign multinationals: patent citation analysis in the semiconductor industry', *Strategic Management Journal*, **17** (155–65).

Almeida, P. and B. Kogut (1999), 'The localisation of knowledge and the mobility of engineers in regional networks', *Management Science*, **45**, 905–917

Altomonte, C. and L. Resmini (2002), 'Multinational corporations as a catalyst for local development. The case of Poland', *Scienze Regionali*, **2**, 29–57.

Anderson, E. and H. Gatignon (1986), 'Modes of entry: a transaction cost analysis and propositions', *Journal of International Business Studies*, **3**, 1–26.

Andersson, U. and M. Forsgren (1996), 'Subsidiary embeddedness and control in the multinational corporation', *International Business Review*, **5**(5), 487–508.

Andersson, U. and M. Forsgren (2000), 'In search of centre of excellence: network embeddedness and subsidiary roles in multinational corporations', *Management International Review*, **40**, 329–350.

Andersson, U., I. Bjorkman and M. Forsgren (2005), 'Managing subsidiary knowledge creation: the effect of control mechanisms on subsidiary local embeddedness', *International Business Review*, **522**(14), 521–38.

Andersson, U., M. Forsgren and U. Holm (2003), 'The learning MNC – a case of knowledge transfer and/or knowledge creation', paper presented at the 29th European Academy of International Business Conference, December 11–13, Copenhagen, Denmark.

Archibugi, D. and S. Iammarino (2002), 'The globalisation of technological innovation: definition and evidence', *Review of International
Political Economy*, **9**(1), 98–122.

Archibugi, D. and J. Michie (1995), 'The globalisation of technology: a new
taxonomy', *Cambridge Journal of Economics*, **19**, 121–40.

Arellano, M. and S. Bond (1991), 'Some tests of specification of panel data:
Monte Carlo evidence and an application to employment equations',
Review of Economic Studies, **58**, 277–97.

Arora, A. and A. Fosfuri (2000), 'Wholly owned subsidiary versus technology licensing in the worldwide chemical industry', *Journal of
International Business Studies*, **31**(4), 555–72.

Arora, A., A. Fosfuri and A. Gambardella (2001), *Markets for Technology:
The Economics of Innovation and Corporate Strategy*, Cambridge MA:
The MIT Press.

Arora, A. and A. Gambardella (1990), 'Complementarity and external
linkages: the strategies of the large firms in biotechnology', *The Journal
of Industrial Economics*, **4**(38), 361–79.

Arora, A. and A. Gambardella (1994), 'Evaluating technological information and utilising it', *Journal of Economic Behavior and Organization*, **24**,
91–114.

Arora, A. and A. Gambardella (1998), 'Evolution of industry structure in
the chemical industry', in A. Arora, R. Landau and N. Rosenberg (eds),
*Chemicals and Long-term Economic Growth: Insights from the Chemical
Industry*, New York: John Wiley & Sons.

Arrow, K. (1962), 'The economic implications of learning by doing',
Review of Economic Studies, June, 155–173.

Arthur, B. (1988), 'Self-reinforcing mechanisms in economics', in
P.W. Anderson and K. Arrow (eds), *The Economy as an Evolving
Complex System*, Wokingham: Addison Wesley, pp. 9–31.

Arundel, A. and A. Geuna (2004), 'Proximity and the use of public science
by innovative European firms', *Economics of Innovation and New
Technology*, **13**(6), 559–80.

Audretsch, D. and M. Feldman (1996), 'R&D spillovers and the geography of innovation and production', *American Economic Review*, **86**,
253–73.

Aw, B., S. Chung and M. Roberts (1998), 'Productivity and the decision to
export: micro evidence from Taiwan and South Korea', NBER working
paper 6558.

Baily, M., C. Hulten and D. Campbell (1992), 'Productivity dynamics in
manufacturing plants', *Brookings Papers on Economic Activity, Microeconomics*, pp. 187–249.

Balcet, G. and R. Evangelista (2005), 'Global technology: innovative strategies of multinational affiliates in Italy, *Transnational Corporations*, **14**(2), August.

Barba Navaretti, G. and D. Castellani (2004), 'Does investing abroad affect performance at home? Comparing Italian multinational and national enterprises', CEPR discussion papers.

Barba Navaretti, G. and A. Venables (2004), *Multinational Firms in the World Economy*, Princeton NJ: Princeton University Press.

Barrios, S., H. Gorg and E. Strobl (2005), 'Foreign direct investment, competition and industrial development in the host country', *European Economic Review*, **49**(7), 1761–84.

Barrios, S. and E. Strobl (2002), 'Foreign direct investment and productivity spillovers: evidence from the Spanish experience', *Weltwirtschaftliches Archiv*, **138**, 459–81.

Barro, R. and J.W. Lee (1993), 'International comparisons of educational attainment', *Journal of Monetary Economics*, **32**(3), 363–94.

Bartlett, C.A. and S. Ghoshal (1989), *Managing Across Borders: The Transnational Solution*, Boston: Harvard Business School Press.

Basile, R. (2001), 'Export behaviour of Italian manufacturing firms over the nineties: the role of innovation', *Research Policy*, **30**(8), 1185–201.

Basile, R., D. Castellani and A. Zanfei (2003), 'Location choices of multinational firms in Europe: the role of national boundaries and EU policy', *Quaderni di Economia, Matematica e Statistica*, 78, Università di Urbino, available at http://papers.ssrn.com/sol3/papers.cfm?abstract_id=455040.

Basile, R., J. Nugent and A. Giunta (2003), 'Foreign expansion by Italian manufacturing firms in the nineties: an ordered probit analysis', *Review of Industrial Organization*, **23**, 1–24.

Basu, S. and J. Fernald (1995), 'Are apparent productive spillovers a figment of specification error', *Journal of Monetary Economics*, **36**, 165–88.

Becattini, G. and E. Rullani (1993), 'Sistema locale e mercato globale', *Economia e politica industriale*, **80**, 25–48.

Beckman, M. and J. Thisse (1986), 'The location of production activities', in P. Nijkamp (ed.), *Handbook of Regional and Urban Economics*, Amsterdam: Elsevier.

Belderbos, R. (2001), 'Overseas innovations by Japanese firms: an analysis of patent and subsidiary data', *Research Policy*, **30**, 313–32.

Benfratello, L. and A. Sembenelli (forthcoming), 'Foreign ownership and productivity: is the direction of causality so obvious?', International Journal of Industrial Organization.

Benito, G., B. Grogaard and R. Narula (2003), 'Environmental influences on MNE subsidiary roles: economic integration and the Nordic countries', *Journal of International Business Studies*, **34**, 443–56.

Bernard, A. and B. Jensen (1999), 'Exceptional exporter performance: cause, effect or both?', *Journal of International Economics*, **47**, 1–25.

Bernard, A., J. Eaton, J. Jensen and S. Kortum (2003), 'Plants and productivity in international trade', *American Economic Review*, **93**(4), 1268–90.

Birkinshaw, J. (1997), 'Entrepreneurship in multinational corporations: the characteristics of subsidiary initiatives', *Strategic Management Journal*, **18**, 207–29.

Birkinshaw, J. and N. Hood (1998), 'Multinational subsidiary development: capability, evolution and charterchange in foreign-owned subsidiary companies', *Academy of Management Review*, **23**(4), 773–795.

Birkinshaw, J., N. Hood and S. Jonsson (1998), 'Building firm specific advantages in multinational corporations: the role of subsidiary initiative', *Strategic Management Journal*, **19**, 221–41.

Birkinshaw, J., N. Hood and S. Young (2005), 'Subsidiary entrepreneurship, internal and external competitive forces, and subsidiary performance', *International Business Review*, **14**, 227–48.

Blalock, G. and P. Gertler (2004), 'How firm capabilities affect who benefits from foreign technology', mimeo, accessed at http://aem.cornell.edu/faulty_sites/g 678.

Blanc, H. and C. Sierra (1999), 'The internationalisation of R&D by multinationals: a trade-off between external and internal proximity', *Cambridge Journal of Economics*, **23**, 187–206.

Blomström, M. (1986), 'Foreign investment and productive efficiency: the case of Mexico', *Journal of Industrial Economics*, **15**, 97–110.

Blomström, M. and A. Kokko (1998), 'Multinational corporation and spillovers', *Journal of Economic Surveys*, **12**, 247–77.

Blomström, M. and E. Wolff (1994), 'Multinational corporations and productivity convergence in Mexico', in W. Baumol, R. Nelson and E. Wolff (eds), *Convergence of Productivity: Cross-National Studies and Historical Evidence*, Oxford: Oxford University Press.

Blundell, R. and S. Bond (1999), 'GMM estimation with persistent panel data: an application to production functions', IFS working papers W99/04.

Blundell, R.W. and S.R. Bond (1998), 'Initial conditions and moment restrictions in Dynamic panel data models', *Journal of Econometrics*, **87**, 115–43.

Boschma, R. and J. Lambooy (1999), 'Evolutionary economics and economic geography', *Journal of Evolutionary Economics*, **9**(4), 411–29.

Bottazzi, G., E. Cefis, G. Dosi and A. Secchi (2005), 'Crescita dell'impresa e struttura industriale: evidenze empiriche sull'industria manifatturiera italiana', in D. Delligatti and M. Gallegati (eds), *Eterogeneità degli agenti*

economici e interazione sociale: teorie verifiche empiriche, Bologna: Il
Mulino.

Brainard, L. (1993), 'A simple theory of multinational corporations and
trade with a trade-off between proximity and concentration', NBER
working paper no. 4269, February.

Brainard, L. (1997), 'An empirical assessment of the proximity-
concentration trade off between multinational sales and trade', *American
Economic Review*, **87**(4), 520–544.

Branstetter, L. (forthcoming), 'Is foreign direct investment a channel of
knowledge spillovers? Evidence from Japan's FDI in the United States',
Journal of International Economics.

Breschi, S. and F. Malerba (1997), 'Sectoral innovation systems: techno-
logical regimes, Schumpeterian dynamics, and spatial boundaries', in
C. Edquist (ed.), *Systems of Innovation: Technologies, Institutions and
Organizations*, London and Washington: Pinter, pp. 130–56.

Breschi, S., F. Lissoni and F. Montobbio (2005), 'The geography of know-
ledge spillovers: conceptual issues and measurement problems', in
S. Breschi and F. Malerba (eds), *Clusters, Networks and Innovation*,
Oxford: Oxford University Press.

Buckley, P.J. (1983), 'New theories of international business: some unre-
solved issues', in M.C. Casson (ed.), *The Growth of International
Business*, Boston: Allen and Unwin, pp. 34–50.

Buckley, P.J. and M. Carter (2004), 'A formal analysis of knowledge combination in multinational enterprises', *Journal of International Business
Studies*, **35**(5), 371–84.

Buckley, P.J. and M. Casson (1976), *The Future of the Multinational
Enterprise*, London: Macmillan.

Buckley, P. and M. Casson (1981), 'The optimal timing of a foreign direct
investment', *The Economic Journal*, **91**(361), 75–87.

Buckley, P., M. Carter and H. Tan (2003), 'The social component of collective knowledge: lessons from west-to-east technology transfer, paper
presented at the 29th EIBA Annual Conference, Copenhagen, 11–13
December.

Burchell, B. and F. Wilkinson (1997), 'Trust, business relationships and the
contractual environment', *Cambridge Journal of Economics*, **21**(2),
217–37.

Bureth, A., S. Wolff and A. Zanfei (1997), 'The two faces of learning by
cooperating: the evolution and stability of inter-firm agreements in the
European electronics industry', *Journal of Economic Behavior and
Organisation*, **32**, 519–37.

Caballero R. and R. Lyons (1991), 'Internal versus external economies in
European industry', *European Economic Review*, **34**, 805–30.

Caligiuri, P.M. and L.K. Stroh (1995), 'Multinational corporation management strategies and international human resource practices: bringing IHRM to the bottom line', *International Journal of Human Resource Management*, **6**, 494–507.

Cantwell, J. (1989), *Technological Innovation and Multinational Corporations*, London: Basil Blackwell.

Cantwell, J. (1995), 'The globalisation of technology: what remains of the product cycle model', *Cambridge Journal of Economics*, **19**, 155–74.

Cantwell, J. (2000), 'A survey of theories of international production', in C. Pitelis and R. Sugden (eds), *The Nature of the Transnational Firm*, 2nd edn, London: Routledge.

Cantwell, J. (2001), 'Innovation and information technology in MNE', in A.M. Rugman and T.L. Brewer (eds), *The Oxford Handbook of International Business*, Oxford: Oxford University Press, pp. 431–56.

Cantwell, J. and S. Iammarino (2003), *Multinational Corporations and European Regional Systems of Innovation*, London: Routledge.

Cantwell, J. and O. Janne (2000), 'The role of multinational corporations and national states in the globalisation of innovatory capacity: the European perspective', *Technology Analysis and Strategic Management*, **12**(2), 243–62.

Cantwell, J. and R. Mudambi (forthcoming), 'MNE competence-creating subsidiary mandates', *Strategic Management Journal*.

Cantwell, J. and R. Narula (2001), 'The eclectic paradigm in the global economy', *International Journal of the Economics of Business*, **8**(2), 155–72.

Cantwell, J and C.A. Noonan (2002), 'Technology sourcing by foreign-owned MNEs in Germany: an analysis using patent citations', EIBA Annual Conference, Athens, December.

Cantwell, J. and L. Piscitello (2000), 'Accumulating technological competence: its changing impact on corporate diversification and internationalization' *Industrial and Corporate Change*, **9**(1), 21–51.

Cantwell, J. and L. Piscitello (2005), 'Recent location of foreign-owned research and development activities by large multinational corporations in the European regions: the role of spillovers and externalities', *Regional Studies*, **39**(1), 1–16.

Cantwell, J.A. and F. Sanna Randaccio (1993), 'Multinationality and firm growth', *Weltwirtschaftliches Archiv*, **129**(2), 275–99.

Cantwell, J. and G.D. Santangelo (forthcoming), 'The boundaries of firms in the new economy: M&As as a strategic tool toward corporate technological diversification', *Structural Change and Economic Dynamics*.

Cantwell, J. and G.D. Santangelo (2002), 'The new geography of corporate research in information and communications technology (ICT)', *Journal of Evolutionary Economics*, **12**(1–2), 163–97.

Carlsson, B. (2003), 'Internationalization of innovation systems: a survey of the literature', Paper presented at the conference in Honour of Keith Pavitt, 'What do we know about innovation?', SPRU, University of Sussex, Brighton, 13–15.

Carlsson, B. and R. Stankiewicz (1991), 'On the nature, function, and composition of technological systems', *Journal of Evolutionary Economics*, **1**(2), 93–118.

Castellani, D. (2002a), 'Export behaviour and productivity growth: evidence from Italian manufacturing firms', *Welwirtschaftliches Archiv*, **138**(4).

Castellani, D. (2002b), 'Firms' technological trajectories and the creation of foreign subsidiaries', *International Review of Applied Economics*, **16**(3), 359–71.

Castellani, D. and A. Zanfei (2001), 'Multinational experience, absorptive capacity and knowledge exploitation. A comparative analysis of the electronics and chemical industries', with A. Zanfei, *Revue Économies et Sociétés*, **W**-(6), 613–42.

Castellani, D. and A. Zanfei (2002), 'Multinational experience and the creation of linkages with local firms. Evidence from the electronics industry', *Cambridge Journal of Economics*, **26**(1), 1–15.

Castellani D. and A. Zanfei (2003), 'Technology gaps, absorptive capacity and the impact of inward investments on productivity of European firms', *Economics of Innovation and New Technology*, **12**(6), 555–76.

Castellani, D. and A. Zanfei (2004), 'Choosing international linkages strategies in the electronics industry. The role of multinational experience', *Journal of Economic Behavior and Organization*, **53**(4).

Castellani, D. and A. Zanfei (2005), 'Multinationality and innovative behaviour in Italian manufacturing firms', in G. Santangelo (ed.), *Technological Change and Economic Catch-up*, Cheltenham, UK and Northampton, USA: Edward Elgar.

Caves, R. (1974), 'Multinational firms, competition and productivity convergence in host-country markets', *Economica* (May), 176–93.

Caves, R. (1996), *Multinational Enterprises and Economic Analysis*, 2nd edn, Cambridge, MA: Cambridge University Press.

Caves, R. and S. Mehra (1986), 'Entry of foreign multinationals into U.S. manufacturing industries', in M. Porter (ed.), *Competition in Global Industries*, Cambridge USA: Harvard Business School Press.

Clerides, S.K., S. Lach and J.R. Tybout (1998), 'Is learning by exporting important? micro-dynamic evidence from Colombia, Mexico, and Morocco', *Quarterly Journal of Economics* (August), 903–48.

Cohen, W.M. and R.C. Levin (1989), 'Empirical studies of innovation and market structure', in R. Schmalensee and R.D. Willig (eds), *Handbook of Industrial Organization*, New York: North-Holland.

Cohen, W.M. and D.A. Levinthal (1989). 'Innovation and learning: the two faces of R&D', *Economic Journal*, **99**, 569–96.

Cominotti, R. and S. Mariotti (2002), *Italia Multinazionale 2000*, Rome: Consiglio Nazionale per l'economia e il Lavoro.

Cooke, P. (1992). 'Regional Innovation systems: competitive regulation in the New Europe', *Geoforum*, **23**(3), 365–82.

Coombs, J., R. Mudambi and D. Deeds (forthcoming), 'An examination of the investments in US biotechnology firms by foreign and domestic corporate partners', *Journal of Business Venturing*.

Copithorne, L. (1971), 'International corporate transfer prices and government policy', *Canadian Journal of Economics*, **4**(3), 324–41.

Coriat, B. and G. Dosi (1998), 'Learning how to govern and learning how to solve problems: on the co-evolution of competencies, conflicts and organisational routines', in A.D. Chandler, P. Hagstrom and O. Solvell (eds), *The Dynamic Firm: The Role of Technology, Strategy, Organisation and Regions*, Oxford: Oxford University Press.

Cowling, K. and R. Sugden (1987), *Transnational Monopoly Capitalism*, Brighton: Wheatsheaf.

Creamer, D. (1976), *Overseas Research and Development by United States Multinationals 1966–1975*, New York: The Conference Board.

Criscuolo, P. (2004), 'R&D internationalisation and knowledge transfer. Impact on MNEs and their home countries', PhD thesis, UM Universiteit Maastricht.

Criscuolo, C. and R. Martin (2003), 'Multinationals, foreign ownership and US productivity leadership: evidence from the UK', paper presented at the Royal Economic Society Annual Conference.

Criscuolo, C., J. Haskel and M. Slaughter (2004), 'Why are some firms more innovative? Knowledge inputs, knowledge stocks and the role of global engagement', Tuck School of Business mimeo.

Criscuolo, P., R. Narula and B. Verspagen (2005), 'Role of home and host country innovation systems in R&D internationalisation: a patent citation analysis', *Economics of Innovation and New Technology*, **14**, 417–33.

Crone, M. and S. Roper (2001), 'Local learning from multinational plants: knowledge transfers in the supply chain', *Regional Studies*, **35**(6), 535–48.

Dacin, T., M. Ventresca and B. Beal (1999), 'The embeddedness of - organizations: dialogue and direction', *Journal of Management*, **25**, 317–56.

Damijan, J.P, M. Knell, B. Majcen and M. Rojec (2003), 'Technology transfer through FDI in top-10 transition countries: how important are direct effects, horizontal and vertical spillovers?', William Davidson working paper no. 549, February, Univeristy of Michigan.

Dasgupta, P. (1988), 'Trust as a commodity', in D. Gambetta (ed.), *Trust*, Oxford: Basil Blackwell, pp. 49–72.

David, P., D. Mowery and W.E. Steinmueller (1992), 'Analysing the economic payoffs from basic research', *Economics of Innovation and New Technology*, **2**, 73–90.

Davidson, W.H. (1980), 'The location of foreign direct investment activity: country characteristics and experience effects', *Journal of International Business Studies*, **11**, 9–22.

Davidson, W.H. and D.G. McFetridge (1984), 'International technology transactions and the theory of the firm', *Journal of Industrial Economics*, **32**, 353–64.

Davis, S. and J. Haltiwanger (1991), 'Wage dispersion between and within U.S. manufacturing plants, 1963–86', in *Brookings Papers on Economic Activity, Microeconomics*, pp. 115–80.

De Backer, K. and L. Sleuwaegen (2003a), 'Foreign ownership and productivity dynamics', *Economics Letters*, **79**(2), 177–83.

De Backer, K. and L. Sleuwaegen (2003b), 'Does foreign direct investment crowd out domestic entrepreneurship?', *Review of Industrial Organization*, **22**(1), 67–84.

Delgado-Gómez, J., M. Ramirez-Alesón and M. Espitia-Escuer (2004), 'Intangible resources as a key factor in the internationalisation of Spanish firms', *Journal of Economic Behavior and Organization*, **53**, 477–94.

Department of Trade and Industry (DTI) (2004), *The 2004 R&D Scoreboard: The Top 700 UK and 700 International Companies by R&D Investment*, London: DTI, accessed at www.innovation.gov.uk/projects/rd_scoreboard/home.asp.

Doms, M. and B. Jensen (1998), 'Comparing wages, skills, and productivity between domestically and foreign-owned manufacturing establishments in the United States', in R. Baldwin, R. Lipsey and J.D. Richardson (eds), *Geography and Ownership as Basis for Economic Accounting*, Chicago: University of Chicago Press.

Dosi, G. (1982), 'Technological paradigms and technological trajectories', *Research Policy*, **11**, 147–62.

Dosi, G., O. Marsili, L. Orsenigo, and F.L. Salvatore (1995), 'Learning, market selection, and the evolution of industrial structures', *Small Business Economics*, **7**, 411–36.

Driffield, N. and J. Love (2003), 'Foreign direct investment, technology sourcing and reverse spillovers', *The Manchester School*, **71**(6), 659–72.

Driffield, N. and J. Love (2004), 'Who learns from whom? Spillovers, competition effects and technology sourcing by foreign affiliates in the UK', Aston Business School working paper RP0215.

Driffield, N., M. Munday and A. Roberts (2002), 'Foreign direct investment, transactions linkages, and the performance of the domestic sector', *International Journal of the Economics of Business*, **9**(3), 335–51.

Dunning, J.H. (1958), *American Investment in British Manufacturing Industry*, London: Allen and Unwin.

Dunning, J.H. (1970), *Studies in International Investments*, London: Allen & Unwin.

Dunning, J.H. (1977), 'Trade, location of economic activity and the MNE: a search for an eclectic approach', in B. Ohlin, P. Hesselborn and P. Wijkman (eds), *The International Allocation of Economic Activity*, London: Macmillan.

Dunning, J.H. (1980), 'Explaining changing patterns of international production: in defense of the eclectic theory', *Oxford Bulletin of Economics and Statistics*, **41**(4), 269–95.

Dunning, J.H. (1988), *Multinationals, Technology and Competitiveness*, London: Unwin Hyman.

Dunning, J.H. (1993), *Multinational Enterprise and the Global Economy*, Wokingham: Addison Wesley.

Dunning, J.H. (1994), 'Multinational enterprises and the globalization of innovatory capacity', *Research Policy*, **23**, 67–88.

Dunning, J.H. (1995) 'Re-appraising the eclectic paradigm in an age of alliance capitalism', *Journal of International Business Studies*, Third Quarter, 461–91.

Dunning, J.H. (1996), 'The geographical sources of the competitiveness of firms: some results of a new survey', *Transnational Corporations*, **5**(3), 1–29.

Dunning, J.H. (1998), 'Location and the multinational enterprise: a neglected factor?' *Journal of International Business Studies*, **29**(1), 45–66.

Dunning, J.H. and R. Narula (1995), 'The R&D activities of foreign firms in the US', *International Studies in Management & Organisation*, **25**(1–2), 39–73.

Dunning, J.H. and C. Wymbs (1999), 'The geographical sourcing of technology based assets by multinational enterprises', in D. Archibugi, J. Howells and J. Michie (eds), *Innovation Policy in a Global Economy*, Cambridge: Cambridge University Press.

Edler, J., F. Meyer-Krahmer and G. Reger (2002), 'Changes in the strategic management of technology: results of a global benchmark survey', *R&D Management*, **32**(2), 149–64.

Edquist, C. (2005), 'Systems of Innovation', in J. Fagerberg, D. Mowery and R. Nelson (eds), *The Oxford Handbook of Innovation*, Oxford: Oxford University Press.

Edwards, R., A. Ahmad and S. Moss (2002), 'Subsidiary autonomy: the case of multinational subsidiaries in Malaysia', *Journal of International Business Studies*, **33**(1), 183–91.

Egelhoff, W.G. (1984), 'Patterns of control in US, UK, and European multinationals, *Journal of International Business Studies*', **3**, 73–83.

Egelhoff, W., L. Gorman and S. McCormick (2003), 'Causes of knowledge flow in MNCs', paper presented at the 29th EIBA annual conference, Copenhagen, 11–13 December.

EIU (2005), *CEO Briefing: Corporate Priorities for 2005*, London: EIU.

Ernst, D. (1997) 'From partial to systemic globalisation: international production networks in the electronics industry', Berkeley Roundtable on the International Economy working paper no. 98, University of California at Berkeley.

Ernst, D. (2005), 'Complexity and internationalisation of innovation: why is chip design moving to Asia?', *International Journal of Innovation Management*, **9**(1), 47–73.

Erramilli, M. (1991), 'The experience factor in foreign market entry behavior of service firms', *Journal of International Business Studies*, **3**, 479–501.

Evans, P.A. (1992) 'Management development as glue technology', *Human Resource Planning*, **15**(1), 85–105.

Findlay, R. (1978), 'Relative backwardness, direct foreign investment and the transfer of technology: a simple dynamic model', *Quarterly Journal of Economics*, **92**, 1–16.

Florida, R. (1997), 'The globalisation of R&D: results and a survey of foreign-affiliated R&D laboratories in the USA', *Research Policy*, **26**, 85–103.

Foray, D. (1995), 'The economics of intellectual property rights and systems of innovation: the persistence of national practices versus the new global model of innovation', in J. Hagedoorn (ed.), *Technical Change and the World Economy: Convergence and Divergence in Technology Strategies*, Aldershot, UK and Brookfield, US: Edward Elgar, pp. 109–33.

Fors, G. (1997), 'Utilization of R&D results in the home and foreign plants of multinationals', *Journal of Industrial Economics*, **XLV**(2), 341–58.

Fors, G., and R. Svensson (2002), 'R&D and foreign sales in Swedish multinationals: a simultaneous relationship?' *Research Policy*, 95–107.

Forsgren, M. and J. Johanson (1992), 'Managing in international multicentre firms', in M. Forsgren, J. Johanson (eds), *Managing Networks in International Business*, Philadelphia: Gordon & Breach.

Fosfuri, A. and M. Motta (1999), 'Multinationals without Advantages', *Scandinavian Journal of Economics*, **101**(4), 617–30.

Fosfuri, A., M. Motta and T. Ronde (2001), 'Foreign direct investment and spillovers through workers' mobility', *Journal of International Economics*, **53**, 205–22.

Foss, N. and T. Pedersen (2002), 'Transferring knowledge in MNCs: the role of sources of subsidiary knowledge and organizational context', *Journal of International Management*, **8**, 1–19.

Foss, N. and T. Pedersen (2004), 'Organizing knowledge processes in the multinational corporation: an introduction', *Journal of International Business Studies*, **35**(5), 340–49.

Franko, L. (1976) *The European Multinationals*, New York: Harper.

Fransman, M. (1999), *Visions of Innovation: The Firm and Japan*, Oxford: Oxford University Press.

Freeman, C. and C. Perez (1988), 'Structural crises of adjustment, business cycles and investment behaviour', in G. Dosi et al. (eds), *Technical Change and Economic Theory*, London: Francis Pinter, pp. 38–66.

Frenz, M. and G. Ietto-Gillies (2005), 'The impact of multinationality on the propensity to innovate: an analysis of the UK Community Innovation Survey 3', mimeo.

Frost, T. (2001), 'The geographic sources of foreign subsidiaries' innovation', *Strategic Management Journal*, **22**, 101–23.

Fujita, M., P. Krugman and A.J. Venables (1999), *The Spatial Economy: Cities, Regions, and International Trade*, Cambridge, MA: MIT Press.

Gatignon, H. and E. Anderson (1988), 'The multinational corporation's degree of control over foreign subsidiaries: an empirical test of transaction cost explanation', *Journal of Law, Economics, and Organization*, **IV**(2), 305–36.

Geroski, P. (2000), 'The growth of firms in theory and practice', in N. Foss and V. Malinke (eds), *New Directions in Economic Strategy Research*, Oxford: Oxford University Press.

Ghoshal, S. and C.A. Bartlett (1989), 'Creation, adoption and diffusion of innovations by subsidiaries of multinational corporations', *Journal of International Business Strategy*, **3**, 365–88.

Ghoshal, S. and C.A. Bartlett (1995), 'Building the entrepreneurial corporation: new organisational processes, new managerial tasks', *European Management Journal*, **13**(2), 139–55.

Giarratana, M., A. Pagano and S. Torrisi (2004), 'The role of multinational firms in the evolution of the software industry in India, Ireland and Israel', in A. Arora and A. Gambardella (eds), *From Underdogs to Tigers: The Rise and Growth of the Software Industry in Brazil, China, India, Ireland, and Israel*, New York: Oxford University Press, pp. 207–35.

Gilbert, R. (1989), 'Mobility barriers and the value of incumbency', in

R. Schmalensee and R. Willig (eds), *Handbook of Industrial Organization*, North Holland.

Girma, S. (forthcoming) 'Absorptive capacity and productivity spillovers from FDI: a threshold regression analysis', *Oxford Bulletin of Economics and Statistics*.

Girma, S. and H. Görg (2004), 'Multinationals' productivity advantage: scale or technology?', CEPR discussion papers.

Girma, S., H. Görg and E. Strobl (2004), 'Exports, international investment, and plant performance: evidence from a non-parametric test', *Economics Letters*, **83**(3), 317–24.

Girma, S., R. Kneller and M. Pisu (2005), 'Exports versus FDI: an empirical test', *Review of World Economics*, **141**(2), 193–218.

Godoe, H. (2000), 'Innovation regimes, R&D and radical innovations in telecommunications', *Research Policy*, **29**(9), 1033–46.

Gomes, L. and K. Ramaswamy (1999), 'An empirical examination of the form of the relationship between multinationality and performance', *Journal of International Business Studies*, **30**(1), 173–87.

Gomes-Casseres, B. (1989), 'Ownership structures of foreign subsidiaries', *Journal of Economic Behavior and Organization*, **2**, 1–25.

Görg, H. and D. Greenaway (2004), 'Much ado about nothing? Do domestic firms really benefit from foreign direct investment?', *World Bank Research Observer*, **19**(2), 171–97.

Görg, H. and E. Strobl (2001), 'Multinational companies and productivity spillovers: a meta-analysis', *The Economic Journal*, **11** (November), F723–39.

Görg, H. and E. Strobl (forthcoming), 'Spillovers from foreign firms through worker mobility: an empirical investigation', *Scandinavian Journal of Economics*.

Görg, H. and E. Strobl (2002), 'Multinational companies and indigenous development: An empirical analysis', *European Economic Review*, **46**, 1305–22.

Görg, H and E. Strobl (forthcoming), Spillovers from foreign firms through worker mobility: an empirical investigation', *Scandinavian Journal of Economics*.

Görg, H. and E. Strobl (2005b), 'Foreign direct investment and local economic development: beyond productivity spillovers', in T.H. Moran, E.M. Graham and M. Blomström (eds), *Does Foreign Direct Investment Promote Development?* Washington DC: Institute for International Economics, pp. 137–57.

Graham, E. (1990), 'Exchange of threat between multinational firms as an infinitely repeated non-cooperative game', *The International Trade Journal*, **4**, 259–78.

Grandinetti, R. and E. Rullani (1996), *Impresa transnazionale ed economia globale*, Firenze: Nuova Italia Scientifica.

Granovetter, M. (1985), 'Economic action and social structure: the problem of embeddedness', *American Journal of Sociology*, **91**(3), 481–510.

Granstrand, O., L. Hakanson and S. Sjolander (1993), 'Internationalization of R&D – a survey of some recent research', *Research Policy*, **22**, 413–30.

Greene, W.H. (1997), *Econometric Analysis*, 3rd edn, Upper Saddle River NJ: Prentice Hall.

Gregersen, B. and B. Johnson (1997), 'Learning economies, innovation systems and European Integration', *Regional Studies*, **31**(5), 479–90.

Griffith, R. (1999), 'Using the ARD establishment level data to look at foreign ownership and productivity in the UK', *The Economic Journal*, **109** (June), F416–42.

Griffith, R., R. Harrison and J. Van Reenen (2004), 'How special is the special relationship? Using the impact of US R&D spillovers on UK firms as a test of technology sourcing', IFS working papers W04/32.

Griffith, R., S. Redding and H. Simpson (2003), 'Productivity convergence and foreign ownership at the establishment level', IFS working papers W02/22.

Griliches, Z. and J. Mairesse (1995), 'Production functions: the search for identification', NBER working paper 5067, March.

Gupta, A. and V. Govindarajan (2000), 'Knowledge flows within multinational corporations' *Strategic Management Journal*, **21**(4), 473–96.

Hagedoorn, J. (2002), 'Inter-firm R&D partnerships: an overview of patterns and trends since 1960', *Research Policy*, **31**, 477–92.

Hakanson, L. and R. Nobel (2001), 'Organizational characteristics and reverse technology transfer', *Management International Review*, **41**(4), 395–420.

Hanson, G.H. (2001), 'Should countries promote foreign direct investment?', G-24 discussion paper 9, UNCTAD, New York and Geneva.

Harris, R. (1988) 'Market structure and external control in the regional economies of Great Britain', *Scottish Journal of Political Economy*, **35**, 334–60.

Harris, R. (1991), 'External control and government policy: some further results for Northern Ireland', *Regional Studies*, **25**, 45–62.

Harris, R. and C. Robinson (2002), 'The effects of foreign acquisitions on total factor productivity: plant-level evidence from U.K. manufacturing, 1987–1992', *The Review of Economic and Statistics*, **84**(3), 562–68.

Haskel, J., S. Pereira and M. Slaughter (2002), 'Does inward foreign direct investment boost the productivity of domestic firms?', NBER working paper 8724.

Head, K., J. Ries and D. Swenson (1999), 'Attracting foreign manufacturing: investment promotion and agglomeration', *Regional Science and Urban Economics*, **29**, 197–218.

Head, K. and J. Ries (2003), 'Heterogeneity and the FDI versus export decision of Japanese manufacturers', *Journal of the Japanese and International Economies*, **17**, 448–67.

Hedlund, G. (1986), 'The hypermodern MNC – A heterarchy?', *Human Resource Management*, (Spring).

Hedlund, G. and D. Rolander (1990), 'Action in heterarchies: new approaches to managing the MNC', in C.S. Bartlett, Y. Doz, and G. Hedlund (eds), *Managing the Global Firm*, London and New York: Routledge.

Helpman, E., M. Meliz and S. Yeaple (2004), 'Export versus FDI with Heterogenous Firms', *American Economic Review*, **94**(1), 300–316.

Hennart, J.F. and J. Larimo (1998), 'The impact of culture on strategy of multinational enterprises: does national origin affect ownership decisions?', *Journal of International Business Studies*, **29**(3), 515–38.

Hirschman, A.O. (1958), *The Strategy of Economic Development*, New Haven: Yale University.

Hirsch, S. (1976), 'An international trade and investment theory of the firm', *Oxford Economic Papers*, **28**, 258–70.

Holm, U., A. Malberg and O. Solvell (2003), 'Subsidiary impact on host-country economies – the case of foreign-owned subsidiaries attracting investment into Sweden', *Journal of Economic Geography*, **3**, 389–408.

Horst, T. (1971) 'The theory of the multinational firm: optimal behaviour under different tariff and tax rates', *Journal of Political Economy*, **79**, 1959–72.

Hymer, S.H. (1960), 'The international operations of national firms: a study of direct foreign investment', doctoral dissertation published in 1974 by MIT Press, Cambridge, MA.

Ietto-Gillies, G. (1998), 'Different conceptual frameworks for the assessment of the degree of internationalisation: an empirical analysis of various indices for the top 100 transnational corporations', *Transnational Corporations*, **7**(1), 17–39.

Ietto-Gillies, G. (2002), *Transnational Corporations. Fragmentation Amidst Integration*, London: Routledge.

Ietto-Gillies, G. (2005), *Transnational Corporations and International Production. Concepts, Theories and Effects*, Cheltenham UK and Northampton MA, USA: Edward Elgar.

International Labour Organization (ILO) (1981), *Multinationals' Training Practices and Developments*, Geneva: ILO.

Jaffe, A. and J. Adams (1996), 'Bounding the effects of R&D: an investigation using linked establishment and firm data', *Rand Journal of Economics*, (Winter).

Jaffe, A., R. Henderson and M. Trajtenberg (1993), 'Geographic localization of knowledge spillovers as evidenced by patent citations', *Quarterly Journal of Economics*, **108**(3), 577–98.

Jenkins, R. (2005), 'Comparing foreign subsidiaries and local firms in LDCs: theoretical issues and empirical evidence', *Journal of Development Studies*, January 1990, **26**(2), 205–28.

Johanson, J. and J.E. Vahlne (1977), 'The internationalisation process of a firm – a model of knowledge development and increasing market commitment', *Journal of International Business Studies*, **8**, 23–32.

Johanson, J. and J.E. Vahlne (1990), 'The mechanism of internationalisation', *International Marketing Review*, **7** (4), 11–24.

Johanson, J. and F. Wiederheim-Paul (1975), 'The internationalization of the firm: four Swedish cases', *Journal of Management Studies*, (October), 305–22.

Jovanovic, B. (1982), 'Selection and the evolution of industry', *Econometrica*, **50**(3), 649–70.

Kaldor M., H. Anheier and M. Glasius (2003), 'Global civil society in an era of regressive globalisation', in London School of Economics (ed.), *Global Civil Society, 2003*, Oxford: Oxford University Press.

Kindleberger, C.P. (1969), *American Business Abroad,* Cambridge, MA: MIT Press.

Kneller, R. and M. Pisu (2005), 'Industrial linkages and export spillovers from FDI', paper presented at the Workshop on Foreign Direct Investment, International Trade and Competitiveness, *Urbino*, 27–28 May.

Knickerboker, F.T. (1973), *Oligopolistic Reaction and the Multinational Enterprise*, Cambridge, MA: Harvard University Press.

Kogut, B. (1983) 'Foreign direct investment as a sequential process', in C.P. Kindleberger, D.B. Audretsch (eds), *The Multinational Corporation in the '80s*. Cambridge, MA: MIT Press.

Kogut, B. (1989a), 'A note on global strategies', *Strategic Management Journal*, **10**, 383–89.

Kogut, B. (1989b), 'The stability of joint ventures: reciprocity and competitive rivalry', *The Journal of Industrial Economics*, **38**(2), 183–98.

Kogut, B. and S. Chang (1991), 'Technological capabilities and Japanese foreign direct investment in the United States', *The Review of Economics and Statistics*, **73**(3), 401–13.

Kogut, B. and H. Singh (1988), 'The effect of national culture on the choice of entry mode', *Journal of International Business Studies*, **19**, 411–32.

Kogut, B. and U. Zander (1993), 'Knowledge of the firm and the evolutionary theory of the multinational corporation', *Journal of International Business Studies*, **24**, 625–45.

Kokko, A. (1994), 'Technology, Market characteristics and spillovers', *Journal of Development Economics*, **43**(2), 279–93.

Kokko, A., R. Tansini and M. Zejan (1996), 'Local technological capability and productivity spillovers from FDI in the Uruguayan manufacturing sector', *Journal of Development Studies*, **32**(4), 602–11.

Kosova, R. (2004), *Do foreign firms crowd out domestic firms? Evidence from the Czech Republic*, PhD thesis, University of Michigan.

Kraay, A. (1999), 'Export and economic performance: evidence from a panel of Chinese enterprises', *Revue d'Economie du Developpement*, 1–2, 183–207.

Kreps, D., (1990), 'Corporate culture and economic theory', in J. Alt and K. Shepsle (eds), *Perspectives on Positive Political Economy*, Cambridge: Cambridge University Press, pp. 90–143.

Krugman, P. (1991), *Geography and Trade*, Cambridge, MA: The MIT Press.

Kuemmerle, W. (1999), 'The drivers of foreign direct investments into research and development – an empirical investigation', *Journal of International Business Studies*, **30**, 1–24.

Lall, S. (1978), 'Transnational, domestic enterprises and industrial structure in host LDCs. A survey', *Oxford Economic Papers*, **30**(2), 217–48.

Lall, S. (1979), 'The international allocation of research activity by US multinationals', *Oxford Bulletin of Economica and Statistics*, **41**, 313–31.

Lall, S. (1980), 'Vertical inter-firm linkages in LDCs: an empirical study', *Oxford Bulletin of Economics and Statistics*, **42**, 203–26.

Lam, A. (1997), 'Embedded Firms, Embedded Knowledge: Problems of Collaboration and knowledge transfer in global cooperative ventures', *Organization Studies*, **18**(6), 973–96.

Lane, S. (1993), 'Corporate restructuring in the chemical industry', in M. Blair (ed.), *The Deal Decade*, Washington, DC: The Brookings Institution.

Lane, P.J. and M.A. Lubatkin (1998), 'Relative absorptive capacity and interorganizational learning', *Strategic Management Journal*, **19**, 461–77.

Le Bas, C. and C. Sierra (2002), 'Location versus country advantages' in R&D activities: some further results on multinationals' locational strategies', *Research Policy*, **31**, 589–609.

Levinsohon, J. and A. Petrin (2003), 'Estimating production functions using inputs to control for unobservables', *Review of Economic Studies*, **70**, 317–42.

Levitt, T. (1983), 'The globalization of markets', *Harvard Business Review*, May–June, 92–110.

Linder, S.B. (1961), *An Essay on Trade and Transformation*, New York: Wiley.

Lipsey, R.E. and F. Sjoholm (2004a), 'Foreign firms and Indonesian manufacturing wages: an analysis with panel data', EIJS working paper, no. 166, Stockholm School of Economics.

Lipsey, R.E. and F. Sjoholm (2004b), 'Host country impacts of inward FDI: why such different answers?', in T.H. Moran, E.M. Graham and M. Blomström (eds), *Does Foreign Direct Investment Promote Development?*, Washington, DC: Institute for International Economics.

Lundvall, B.A. (1993), *National Systems of Innovation: Towards a Theory of Innovation and Interactive Learning*, London: Pinter.

Lyons, B. and J. Mehta (1997), 'Contracts, opportunism and trust: self-interest and social orientation', *Cambridge Journal of Economics*, **21**, 239–57.

Malerba, F. (2005), 'Sectoral systems: how and why innovation differs across sectors', in J. Fagerberg, D. Mowery and R. Nelson (eds), *The Oxford Handbook of Innovation*, Oxford: Oxford University Press.

Malerba, F. and S. Torrisi (1992), 'Internal capabilities and external networks in innovative activities. Evidence from the software industry', *Economics of Innovation and New Technology*, **2**, 49–71.

Manolopoulosa, D., M. Marina Papanastassiou and R. Pearce (2005), 'Technology sourcing in multinational enterprises and the roles of subsidiaries: an empirical investigation', *International Business Review*, **14**, 249–67.

Mansfield, E. and A. Romeo (1980), 'Technology transfer to overseas subsidiaries by US based firms', *Quarterly Journal of Economics*, **95**(4), 737–50.

Mansfield, E., A. Romeo and Wagner (1997), 'Foreign trade, and US research and development', *Review of Economics and Statistics*, **61**, 49–57.

Mansfield, E., D. Teece and A. Romeo (1979), 'Overseas research and development by US-based firms', *Economica*, **46** (May), 187–96.

Mariani, M. (2002), 'Next to production or to technological clusters? The economics and management of R&D location', *Journal of Management and Governance*, **6**(2), 131–52.

Marin, A. and M. Bell (2004), 'Technology spillovers from foreign direct investments (FDI): an exploration of the active role of MNC subsidiaries in the case of Argentina in the 1990s', SPRU working paper SEWP 118.

Markusen, J. (2002), *Multinational Firms and the Theory of International Trade*, Cambridge, MA: MIT Press.

Markusen, J. and A.J. Venables (1999), 'Foreign direct investment as a catalyst for industrial development', *European Economic Review*, **43**, 335–56.

Martin, R. (1999), 'The new "geographical turn" in economics: some critical reflections', *Cambridge Journal of Economics*, **23**, 65–91.

Martinez, J.I. and J.C. Jarrillo (1989), 'The evolution of research on coordination mechanism in multinational corporations', *Journal of International Business Studies*, (Fall).

Martinez, J.I. and J.C. Jarrillo (1991), 'Co-ordination demands of international strategies', *Journal of International Business Strategies*, **3**, 429–44.

McAlesee, D. and D. McDonald (1978), 'Employment growth and the development of linkages in foreign owned and domestic manufacturing enterprises', *Oxford Bulletin of Economics and Statistics*, **40**, 321–39.

McEvily, B. and A. Zaheer (1999), 'Bridging ties: a source of firm heterogeneity in competitive capabilities', *Strategic Management Journal*, **20**, 1133–56.

Meade, J. (1952), 'External economies and diseconomies in a competitive situation', *Economic Journal*, **62**(245), 54–67.

Melitz, M. (2004), 'The impact of trade on aggregate industry productivity and intra-industry reallocation', *Econometrica*, **71**(6), 1695–725.

Miller, R. (1994), 'Global R&D networks and large scale innovations: the case of automobile industry', *Research Policy*, **23**(1), 27–46.

Molero, J. (2002), 'The innovative behaviour of MNC subsidiaries in uneven European systems of integration: a comparative analysis of the German and Irish cases', *Journal of Interdisciplinary Economics*, **13**, (1–2–3), 305–41.

Moris, F. (2005), 'Foreign direct investment, R&D, and innovation: concepts and data', background note prepared for UNCTAD US by the National Science Foundation, Arlington, VA.

Mowery, D.C. (ed.) (1988), *International Collaborative Ventures in US Manufacturing*, Cambridge, MA: Ballinger.

Mudambi, R. and P. Navarra (2004), 'Is knowledge power? Knowledge flows, subsidiary power and rent-seeking within MNCs', *Journal of International Business Studies*, **35**(5), 385–406.

Mueller, D. and B. Raunig (1999), 'Heterogeneities within industries and structure-performance models', *Review of Industrial Organization*, **15**(4), 303–20.

Mutinelli, M. and L. Piscitello (1998), 'The entry mode choice of MNEs: an evolutionary approach', *Research Policy*, **27**, 491–506.

Narula, R. (2003), *Globalisation and Technology*, Cambridge: Polity Press.

Narula, R. and A. Zanfei (2005), 'Globalization of innovation: the role of multinational enterprises', in J. Fagerberg, D. Mowery and R. Nelson (eds), *The Oxford Handbook of Innovation*, Oxford: Oxford University Press.

Nelson, R. (1991), 'Why do firms differ and how does it matter?', *Strategic Management Journal*, **12**, 61–74.

Nelson, R. (1993) *National Innovation Systems: A Comparative Analysis*, Oxford: Oxford University Press.

Nelson, R. and S. Winter (1982), *An Evolutionary Theory of Economic Change*, Cambridge, MA: Harvard University Press.

Neven, D. and G. Siotis (1996), 'Technology sourcing and FDI in the EC: an empirical evaluation', *International Journal of Industrial Organization*, **14**, 543–60.

Niosi, J. and B. Bellon (1996), 'The globalization of national innovation systems', in J. de la Mothe and G. Paquet (eds), *Evolutionary Economics and the New International Political Economy*, London: Pinter.

Nisbet, P., W. Thomas and S. Barrett (2003), 'UK direct investment in the United States: a mode of entry analysis', *International Journal of the Economics of Business*, **10**(3), 245–59.

Nohria, N. and S. Ghoshal (1997), The Differentiated Network: Organizing Multinational Corporations for Value Creation, San Francisco: Jossey-Bass Publishers.

North, D.C. (1990), *Institutions, Institutional Change and Economic Performance*, Cambridge: Cambridge University Press.

O'Donnell, S.W. (2000), 'Managing foreign subsidiaries: agents of headquarters, or an interdependent network?', *Strategic Management Journal*, **21**, 525–48.

Odagiri, H. and H. Yasuda. (1996), 'The determinants of overseas R&D by Japanese firms: an empirical study at the industry and company levels', *Research Policy*, **25**(7), 1059–79.

Olley, S. and A. Pakes (1996), 'The dynamics of productivity in the telecommunications equipment industry', *Econometrica*, **64**(6), 1263–98.

Organisation for Economic Co-operation and Development (OECD) (2002), *Measuring Globalisation. The Role of Multinationals in OECD Economies*, CD-ROM edition, Paris: OECD.

Organisation for Economic Co-operation and Development (OECD) (2005), *Science, Technology and Industry Scoreboard 2005*, Paris: OECD.

Oulton, N. (1996), 'Increasing returns and externalities in UK manufacturing: myth or reality?', *The Journal of Industrial Economics*, **XLIV** (1), 99–113.

Ozawa, T. (1979), *Multinationalism, Japanese Style: The Political Economy of Outward Dependency*. Princeton, NJ: Princeton University Press.

Padmanabhan, P. and K.R. Cho (1999), 'Decision specific experience in foreign ownership and establishment strategies: evidence from Japanese firms', *Journal of International Business Studies*, **30**(1), 25–44.

Pakes, A. and R. Ericson (1998), 'Empirical implications of alternative models of firm dynamics', *Journal of Economic Theory*, **79**(1), 1–46.

Papanastassiou, M. and R. Pearce (1997), 'Technology sourcing and the strategic roles of manufacturing subsidiaries in the UK: local competences and global competitiveness', *Management International Review*, **37**(1), 2–25.

Patel, P. (1996), 'Are large firms internationalising the generation of technology? Some new evidence', *IEEE Transactions on Engineering Management*, **43**, 41–7.

Patel, P. and K. Pavitt (1991), 'Large firms in the production of the world's technology: an important case of "non-globalisation"', *Journal of International Business Studies*, **22**(1), 1–21.

Patel, P. and K. Pavitt (2000), 'National systems of innovation under strain: the internationalisation of corporate R&D', in R. Barrell, G. Mason and M. O'Mahoney (eds), *Productivity, Innovation and Economic Performance*, Cambridge: Cambridge University Press.

Patel, P. and M. Vega (1999), 'Patterns of internationalisation of corporate technology: location vs. home country advantages', *Research Policy*, **28**, 145–55.

Pavitt, K. (1984), 'Sectoral patterns of technical change: towards a taxonomy and a theory', *Research Policy*, **13**, 33–45.

Pearce, D. (1999), 'Decentralised R&D and strategic competitiveness: globalized approaches to generation and use of technology in multinational enterprises (MNEs)', *Research Policy*, **28**(2–3), 157–78.

Pearce, R. (1990), *The Internationalisation of Research and Development*, London: Macmillan.

Peoples, J. and R. Sugden (2000), 'Divide and rule by transnational corporations', in C.N. Pitelis and R. Sugden (eds), *The Nature of the Transnational Firm*, 2nd edn, London: Routledge, pp. 174–92.

Petit, M.L. and F. Sanna-Randaccio (2000), 'Endogenous R&D and foreign direct investment in international oligopolies', *International Journal of Industrial Organization*, **18**, 339–67.

Petit, M.L., F. Sanna-Randaccio and R. Sestini (2004), 'Localized spillovers and foreign direct investment: a dynamic analysis', mimeo, University of Rome, La Sapienza.

Pfaffermayer, M. and C. Bellak (2002), 'Why foreign-owned are different: a conceptual framework and empirical evidence for Austria', in R. Jungnickel (ed.), Foreign-owned Firms: Are They Different?, Houndsmill: Palgrave-Macmillan.

Porter, M. (ed.) (1986), *Competition in Global Industries*, Cambridge, MA: Harvard Business School Press.

Potter, B., B. Moore and R. Spires (2003), 'Foreign manufacturing investment in the United Kingdom and the upgrading of supplier practices', *Regional Studies*, **37**(1), 41–60.

Powell, W. and S. Grodal (2005), 'Network of innovators', in J. Fagerberg, D. Mowery and R. Nelson (eds), *The Oxford Handbook of Innovation*, Oxford: Oxford University Press.

Powell, W., K. Koput, L. Smith-Doerr and J. Owen-Smith (1999), 'Network position and firm performance', in S. Andrews and D. Knoke (eds), *Research in the Sociology of Organizations*, Greenwich, CT: JAI Press, **16**, 129–59.

Reinganum, J. (1989), 'The timing of innovation: research, development and diffusion', in R. Schmalensee and R. Willig (eds), *Handbook of Industrial Organization*, North Holland.

Richardson, G.B. (1972), 'The organisation of industry', *Economic Journal*, **82**(327), 883–96.

Roberts, Edward B. (2001), 'Benchmarking global strategic management of technology', *Research Technology Management*, **44**(2), 25–36.

Robertson, T. and H. Gatignon (1998), 'Technology development mode: a transaction cost conceptualization', *Strategic Management Journal*, **19**(6), 515–31.

Rodriguez-Clare, A. (1996), 'Multinationals, linkages, and economic development', *American Economic Review*, **86**(4), 852–73.

Romer, P. (1986), 'Increasing returns and long run growth', *Journal of Political Economy*, (October), 1002–37.

Ronen, S. and O. Shenkar (1985), 'Clustering countries on attitudinal dimensions: a review and synthesis', *Academy of Management Review*, **10**(3), 435–54.

Ronstadt, R.C. (1978), 'International R&D: the establishment and evolution of research and development abroad by seven US multinationals', *Journal of International Business Studies*, **9**(1), 7–24.

Rosenberg, N. (1969), 'The direction of technical change. Inducement mechanisms and focusing devices', *Economic Development and Cultural Change*, **18**, 1–24.

Rosenberg, N. (1976), *Perspectives on Technology*, Cambridge: Cambridge University Press.

Rosenberg, N. (1982), *Inside the Black Box: Technology and Economics*, Cambridge: Cambridge University Press.

Rosenberg, N. (1990), 'Why do firms do basic research (with their own money)?', *Research Policy*, **19**(2), 165–74.

Rosenkopf, L. and M. Tushman (1998), 'The coevolution of community networks and technology: lessons from the flight simulation industry', *Industrial and Corporate Change*, **7**(2), 311–46.

Rosenzweig, P. and N. Nohria (1994), 'Influences of human resource management in multinational corporations', *Journal of International Business Studies*, **2**, 229–51.

Ruane, F., A. Ugur (2002), 'Foreign direct investment and productivity spillovers in Irish manufacturing industry: evidence from firm level panel data', Trinity economic papers 02/06, Trinity College Dublin.

Ruef, M. (2002), 'Strong ties, weak ties and islands: structural and cultural predictors of organizational innovation', *Industrial and Corporate Change*, **11**(3), 427–49.

Sachwald, F. (1998) 'Cooperative agreements and the theory of the firm: focussing on barriers to change', *Journal of Economic Behavior and Organization*, **35**, 203–25.

Safarian, A.E. (1966), *Foreign Ownership of Canadian Industry*, Toronto: McGraw Hill.

Sands, A. (2004), 'The Irish software industry', in A. Arora and A. Gambardella (eds), *From Underdogs to Tigers: The Rise and Growth of the Software Industry in Brazil, China, India, Ireland, and Israel*. New York: Oxford University Press.

Sanna-Randaccio, F. (2002), 'The impact of foreign direct investment on home and host countries with endogenous R&D', *Review of International Economics*, **10**, 278–98.

Santangelo, G.D. (2001), 'The Impact of the information technology and communications technology revolution on the internationalisation of corporate technology', *International Business Review*, **10**(6), 701–26.

Santangelo, G.D. (2004), 'FDI and local capabilities in peripheral regions: the Etna Valley case', *Transnational Corporations*, **13**(1), 73–107.

Saxenian, A.L. (1994), *Regional Advantage: Culture and Competition in Silicon Valley and Route 128*, Cambridge, MA: Harvard University Press.

Schoors, K. and B. van der Tol (2002), 'Foreign direct investment spillovers within and between sectors: evidence from Hungarian data', Faculty of Economics and Business Administration working paper 10/2002, Ghent University.

Scitovsky, T. (1956), 'Two concepts of external economies', *Journal of Political Economy*, **62**(2), 143–51.

Sembenelli, A. and G. Siotis (2002), 'Foreign direct investment, competitive pressure and spillovers. An empirical analysis on Spanish firm level data', Centro Studi Luca d'Agliano development studies working paper no. 169, accessed at www.ssrn.com/abstract=348360.

Serapio, M. and D. Dalton (1999), 'Globalization of industrial R&D: an examination of foreign direct investments in R&D in the United States, *Research Policy*, **28**(2–3), 303–16.

Shaver, J.M. and F. Flyer. (2000), 'Agglomeration economies, firm heterogeneity, and foreign direct investment in the United States', *Strategic Management Journal*, **21**, 1175–93.

Siler, P., C. Wang and X. Liu (2003), 'Technology transfer within multinational firms and its impact on the productivity of Scottish subsidiaries', *Regional Studies*, **37** (1), 15–25.

Singh, J. (2004), 'Multinational firms and knowledge diffusion: evidence using patent citation data', Academy of Management best papers proceedings.

Siotis, G. (1999), 'Foreign direct investment strategies and firms' capabilities', *Journal of Economics and Management Strategy*, **8**(2), 251–70.

Smarzynska, Javorcik B. (2004), 'Does foreign direct investment increase the productivity of domestic firms? In search of spillovers through backward linkages', *American Economic Review*, **94**(3), 605–27.

Smith, A. (1987), 'Strategic investment, multinational corporations and trade policy', *European Economic Review*, **31**, 89–96.

Steinmueller, W. (1992), 'The economics of flexible integrated circuit manufacturing technology', *Review of Industrial Organization*, 1992, **7**(3–4), 327–49.

Sterlacchini, A. (2002), 'The determinants of export performance: a firm level study in Italian manufacturing', *Welwirtschaftliches Archiv*, **137**(3).

Stoker, T. (1993), 'Empirical approaches to the problem of aggregation over individuals', *Journal of Economic Literature*, **31**(4), 1827–74.

Stopford, J.M. and L.T. Wells (1972), *Managing the Multinational Enterprise: Organisation of the Firm and Ownership of Subsidiaries*, New York: Basic Books.

Sugden, R. (1991), 'The importance of distributional considerations', in C.N. Pitelis and R. Sugden (eds), *The Nature of the Transnational Firm*, 1st edn, London: Routledge, 168–93.

Sutton, J. (1997), 'Gibrat's legacy', *Journal of Economic Literature*, **35**(1), 40–59.

Swanson, R.A. (1986), 'Entrepreneurship and innovation: biotechnology', in R. Landau and N. Rosenberg, (eds), *The Positive Sum Strategy. Harnessing Technology for Economic Growth*, Washington, DC: National Academy Press.

Szulanski, G. (1996), 'Exploring internal stickiness: impediments to the transfer of best practice within the firm', *Strategic Management Journal*, **17**, 27–43.

Taggart, J.H. and N. Hood (1999), 'Determinants of autonomy in multinational corporation subsidiaries', *European Management Journal*, **17**(2), 226–36.

Tallman, S. and K. Fladmoe-Lindquist (2002), 'Internationalization, globalization, and capability-based strategy', *California Management Review*, **45**(1), 116–35.

Teece, D.J. (1977), 'Technology transfer by multinational firms: the resource cost of transferring technological know-how', *Economic Journal*, **87**(346), 242–61.

Teece, D.J. (1986), 'Profiting from technological innovation: implication for integration, collaboration, licensing and public policy', *Research Policy*, **15**, 285–305.

Teece, D.J. (1992), 'Competition, cooperation and innovation. Organizational arrangements for regimes of rapid technological progress', *Journal of Economic Behaviour and Organization*, **18**(1), 1–26.

Todo, Y. and K. Miyamoto (2002), 'Knowledge diffusion from multinational enterprises: the role of domestic and foreign knowledge-enhancing activities', OECD Development Centre technical paper no. 196, August 2002.

Torrisi, S. (1998), *Industrial Organisation and Innovation: An International Study of the Software Industry*, Cheltenham, UK and Lyme, USA: Edward Elgar.

Tsai, W. and S. Ghoshal (1998), 'Social capital and value creation: the role of intra-firm networks', *Academy of Management Journal*, **41**, 464–476.

Tsurumi, Y. (1976), *The Japanese are Coming: A Multinational Spread of Japanese Firms*, Cambridge, MA: Ballinger.

Tunisini, A. and A. Zanfei (1998), 'Exploiting and creating knowledge through customer-supplier relationships. Lessons from a case-study', *R&D Management*, **2**, 111–18.

Tybout, J.R. (2003), 'Plant and firm-level evidence on "new" trade theories', in Choi E. Kwan and J. Harrigan (eds), *Handbook of International Trade*, Oxford: Basil Blackwell.

UNCTAD (1998), *World Investment Report 1998: Trends and Determinants*, New York: United Nations.

UNCTAD (1999), *World Investment Report: The Challenge of Development*, Geneva and New York: United Nations.

UNCTAD (2001), *World Investment Report: Promoting Linkages*, Geneva and New York: United Nations.

UNCTAD (2002), *World Investment Report 2002: Transnational Corporations and Export Competitiveness*, New York and Geneva: United Nations.

UNCTAD (2005), *World Investment Report 2005. Transnational Corporations and the Internationalization of R&D*, New York and Geneva: United Nations.

Vaccà, S. (1996), 'Imprese transnazionali e contesto ambientale, socio-culturale ed istituzionale', *Economia e politica industriale*, **90**, 37–82.

Vaccà, S. and A. Zanfei (1995), 'Capturing value from local contexts: the decentralization of decisions within transnational corporations', in R. Schiattarella (ed.), *New Challenges for European and International Business*, proceedings of the 21st EIBA Conference, Urbino, December 10–12.

Van Biesebroeck, J. (2003), 'Revisiting some productivity debates', NBER working paper no. 10065.

Van den Bulcke, D. and E. Halsberghe (1984), *Employment Decision-Making in Multinational Enterprises: Survey Results from Belgium*, Geneva: International Labour Office.

van Pottelsberghe de la Potterie, B. and F. Lichtenberg (2001), 'Does foreign direct investment transfer technology across borders?', *Review of Economics and Statistics*, **83**, 490–97.

Vernon, R. (1966), 'International investment and international trade in the product cycle', *Quarterly Journal of Economics*, **80**.

Vernon, R. (1971), *Sovereignty at Bay: The Multinational Spread of US Enterprises*, New York: Basic Books.

Vernon, R. (1974), 'The location of economic activity', in Dunning J.H. (ed.), *Economic Analysis and the Multinational Enterprise*, London: Allen and Unwin, 89–113.

Vernon, R. (1979), 'The product cycle hypothesis in a new international environment', *Oxford Bulletin of Economics and Statistics*, **41**, 255–67.

Verspagen, B. and W. Schoenmakers (2004), 'The spatial dimension of patenting by multinational firms in Europe', *Journal of Economic Geography*, **4**(1), 23–42.

Veugelers, R. and B. Cassiman (2004), 'Importance of International linkages for local know-how flows: some econometric evidence from Belgium', *European Economic Review*, **48**(2), 455–476.

Vinding, A. (2002), 'Interorganizational diffusion and transformation of knowledge in the process of product innovation', PhD thesis, Aalborg University.

von Zedtwitz, M. and O. Gassmann (2002), 'Market versus technology drive in R&D internationalization: four different patterns of managing research and development', *Research Policy*, **31**(4), 569–88.

Wakelin, K. (1998), 'Innovation and export behaviour at firm level', *Research Policy*, **26**, 829–41.

Wakusagi, R. (1994), 'On the determinants of overseas production: an empirical study of Japanese FDI', Center for International Trade Studies working paper 94-2, Yokohama National University.

Warrant, F. (1991), Le deploiement mondial de la R&D industrielle', Bruxelles, Commission des Communautes Europeennes, Fast, Decembre.

References

Wheeler, D. and A. Mody (1992), 'International investment location decisions: the case of US firms, *Journal of International Economics*, **33**, 57–76.

Williamson, O.E. (1988). 'Technology and transaction cost economics. A reply', *Journal of Economic Behavior and Organization*, **10**, 355–64.

Williamson, O.E. (1993), 'Calculativeness, trust and economic organisation', *Journal of Law and Economics*, **36**, 453–86.

Winter, S. (1971), 'Satisficing, selection, and the innovating remnant', *The Quarterly Journal of Economics*, **85**(2), 237–61.

Yamin, M. and J. Otto (2004), 'Patterns of knowledge flows and MNE innovative performance', *Journal of International Management*, **10**: 239–58.

Yeaple, S.R. (2005), 'A simple model of firm heterogeneity, international trade, and wages' *Journal of International Economics*, **65**, 1–20.

Yoshihara, K. (1978), *Japanese Investment in Southeast Asia*, Honolulu: The University Press of Hawaii.

Yoshimo, M.Y. (1975), 'Emerging Japanese multinational enterprises', in F. Vogel (ed.), *Modern Japanese Organisation and Decision Making*, Cambridge, MA: Harvard University Press.

Young, S. and A.T. Tavares (2004), 'Centralization and autonomy: back to the future', *International Business Review*, **13**(2), 215–37.

Young, S., N. Hood and J. Hamill (1985), *Decision-Making in Foreign-Owned Multinational Subsidiaries in the United Kingdom*, Geneva: International Labour Office.

Zander, I. (1999), 'How do you mean "global"? An empirical investigation of innovation networks in the multinational corporation', *Research Policy*, **28**, 195–213.

Zanfei, A. (1993), 'Patterns of collaborative innovation in the US telecommunications industry after divestiture', *Research Policy*, **22**, 309–25.

Zanfei, A. (1994), 'Technological alliances between weak and strong firms: cooperative ventures with asymmetric competences', *Revue d'Economie Industrielle*, **67**, 255–79.

Zanfei, A. (2000), 'Transnational firms and the changing organisation of innovative activities', *Cambridge Journal of Economics*, **24**, 515–42.

Zanfei, A. (2004), 'Globalisation at bay? Multinational growth and technology spillover', *Critical Perspectives on International Business*, **1**, 7–19.

Zucker, L. (1986), 'Production of trust: institutional sources of economic structure 1840–1920', *Research In Organisational Behaviour*, **8**, 53–111.

Index

absorptive capacity 3, 11, 12, 30, 50,
  54, 66, 67, 98, 115, 145, 146, 165,
  167, 175, 185, 192
  France, Spain and Italy 170–73
  and internationalisation 186–7
  of local companies 140
  and R&D investments 166
Adams, J. 118
adaptation to local practices 45–6
affiliates *see* foreign affiliates; national
  affiliates
Aftalion, F. 65
agglomeration forces 70–71
agglomeration economies 14, 50, 107,
  115, 116
Aitken, B. 143, 153, 160, 162
Alfaro, L. 145, 151, 164, 179
Almeida, P. 17, 47, 110
Amadeus 5, 91, 122, 197–8
Anderson, E. 25, 56, 84
Andersson, U. 23, 25, 29, 45, 46, 47,
  49, 57, 110, 115
appropriability regimes 53
Archibugi, D. 10
Arellano, M. 156
ARGO (Agreements, Restructuring
  and Growth Operations) 58, 62
Arora, A. 20, 21, 26, 65, 66, 89, 120, 146
Arrow, K. 159
Arthur, B. 30
Arundel, A. 104
asset exploiting 9, 16, 22, 24, 37, 40, 67,
  114, 193
  distinguished from asset seeking
  12–15
asset seeking 2, 3, 9, 22, 23, 24, 27, 36,
  37, 44, 66, 82, 114, 118, 193–4
  distinguished from asset exploiting
  12–15
  and double network structure 39
  importance of 15–18
  and technical change 18–20

asset seeking FDIs 12, 18–20, 22, 27, 194
Audretsch, D. 15
automotive industry
  car makers 150
  R&D 42
Automotive News Europe 150
autonomy 28–9, 31, 32, 39–40, 67
  of decentralised innovative units
  47–50
Aw, B. 86

backward linkages *see* linkages
backward vertical integration 103
Baily, M. 69
Balcet, G. 121, 122
Barba Navaretti, G. 76, 77, 87, 107,
  141, 142, 185, 192
bargaining power 119, 120
Barrios, S. 156, 164, 166, 186
Bartlett, C.A. 23, 29, 31, 49, 50
Basile, R. 88
Basu, S. 158
Becattini, G. 21, 66, 120
Beckman, M. 112
Bellak, C. 77, 189
Bell, M. 178
Bellon, B. 33, 104
Benfratello, L. 156
Benito, G. 40
Bernard, A. 77, 86
biotechnology 42
biotechnology firms, network
  centrality 110
Birkinshaw, J. 29, 49
Blalock, G. 157, 163, 173
Blanc, H. 14, 28
Blomström, M. 141, 153, 166
Blundell, R.W. 156
Bond, S.R. 156
Boschma, R. 107
Bottazzi, G. 69
Brainard, L. 78, 87, 102

firm growth, differences in patterns of 69
fixed-effect 156, 184, 188
Fladmoe-Lindquist, K. 117
Florida, R. 17, 29, 48, 110
Flyer, F. 117
Foray, D. 33, 104
foreign affiliates 14, 25, 27–8, 31, 83, 87, 101, 111, 114, 115, 122, 152, 174, 189–90, 195
  age of 179–81
  collaborative activities of 179
  comparing performance with national affiliates 118–21
  comparing performance with parent company 116–18
  competition with domestic firms 164, 188
  constraints on adoption of new technology by 30
  costs of operating 78
  heterogeneity of 176, 177
    evidence from Italy 181–5
  innovation 127
  investment in R&D 5, 42, 43, 51, 140
  in Italy 124, 134, 135
  knowledge flow among 150
  local linkage and age of 151
  Northern Ireland 149
  obstacles to transfer of knowledge from 30–31, 192
  patents 42
  performance 108, 113
  R&D activities of 177–9
  sectoral distribution 124
  spillovers from 175, 176
foreignness 71, 80
foreign subsidiaries *see* foreign affiliates
foreign systems 106–9
Fors, G. 51, 88, 113
Forsgren, M. 23, 28, 46, 47, 49, 57, 110
Fortune 500 58
forward linkages *see* linkages
Fosfuri, A. 89, 144, 146
Foss, N. 23, 118
France 41, 150, 167, 170, 171, 174
  employment in foreign owned firms 168–9

Franko, L. 34, 103
free riding 12, 180, 194
Frenz, M. 88, 122, 189
Frost, T. 11, 17
Fujita, M. 107

Gambardella, A. 20, 26, 65, 66, 89, 120, 146
Gassmann, O. 42
Gatignon, H. 25, 55, 56, 84, 180
Germany 17–18
Geroski, P. 69
Gertler, P. 157, 163, 173
Geuna, A. 104
Ghoshal, S. 23, 29, 31, 49, 50, 110
Giarratana, M. 146, 147
Gilbert, R. 78
Girma, S. 87, 165, 186, 187
Glaxo 49
globalisation 1, 20, 80
  Italy 124
  of markets 18, 19, 46
  of NIS 104
  of R&D 10, 208
  social consequences 19
globalisation of technology 10–11, 36, 43, 67, 105, 112
global knowledge creation and exchange 7
Godoe, H. 110
Gomes-Casseres, B. 54, 55, 84, 115, 180
Gomes, L. 116
Görg, H. 154, 161, 164
Govidarajan, V. 30, 50, 115
Graham, E. 187
Grandinetti, R. 32
Granstrand, O. 23
Greenaway, D. 154, 161
Greene, W.H. 159
Gregersen, B. 33, 104
Griffith, R. 156, 166
Grodal, S. 110
Gupta, A. 30, 50, 115

Hagedoorn, J. 23, 46, 47
Hakanson, L. 31, 50
Halsberghe, E. 48
Haltiwanger, J. 69
Hanson, G.H. 139, 141